CONFESSIONS
of a
TEST DRIVER

From a Pedal Car to Formula One
The Story Behind the Stories
By Roberto Giordanelli

TO WOS. I HOPE YOU ENJOY READING THIS BOOK
ALL THE BEST Roberto

Roberto Giordanelli

WWW. ROBERTO - GIORDANELLI. COM/BOOK/

A catalogue record for this book is available from the British Library.

ISBN 978 1 3999 3344 5

Published by Auto Italia Magazine, Building 52, Enterprise House, Wrest Park, Silsoe, MK45 4HS, United Kingdom
Web: www.auto-italia.co.uk

Printed in the UK by Short Run Press, Bittern Road, Sowton Industrial Estate, Exeter, EX2 7LW
Tel: 01392 211909
www.shortrunpress.co.uk

DEDICATION

This book is dedicated to my family and friends, with special thanks to Jane, without whom this book would not exist.

Contents

Confessions of a Test Driver
Introduction

Countless earlier experiences steered me into the role of a test driver. In chronological order, I recall thoughts and publishable antics that occurred behind the scenes. I submitted freelance work to about a dozen performance car magazines, with Chief Test Driver for *Auto Italia* magazine being my main outlet. The book also mentions my lifetime in motor racing, as racing is responsible for my becoming a test driver and a motoring journalist. While I have driven six Formula One cars, I have yet to race one. This book is not a re-run of decades of magazine articles. Be aware that I steer away from the technical, and regularly go *off-piste* describing related events, and some of the people I met along the way.

Test-driving involves risk, both physical and financial should litigation raise its ugly head. My test-driving has two divisions: Firstly, down-to-earth appraisals for magazine articles. This type of testing simply requires the stories to be entertaining and informative. The second type of testing is for racing, which is far more complicated. This is because race testing includes evaluations, adjustments, modifications, data analysis, engineering knowledge, analysing at race speeds, and re-testing *ad infinitum*. Race testing can also be confrontational. Think about it. The engineers present a car that is race-ready, and then a test driver suggests that it needs work. It is often better to give the engineers feedback, so that they can decide on adjustments, rather than tell them what to change. I like to know every detail of the race car in question, which can also appear meddling. This requires diplomacy and psychology.

Journalistic work is more upbeat, and also included travel stories and columns. Re-reading my words from 25 years ago I am horrified when I spot grammatical errors. Worse than horrifying were my political references and generalisations. Some of my early comments would be censored to suit today's readers. While in some ways the world is trying to increase our choice, it is also more censorial. Being outspoken gains supporters and opponents; better to appear thought-provoking. Quoting Tom Stoppard, "Age is a very high price to pay for maturity." That said, the job is fun and can be a steppingstone to open other doors.

My motorsport career began in 1966 and continues into 2023 and beyond. Due to my age, I am often asked when I shall stop racing. My reply is, "You are only as old as your lap times." It was via motor racing in the 1980s that I met the Auto Italia co-founder and editor, Phil Ward. Phil is ex-RAF, ex-BBC and ex-editor of the magazines: World Sports Cars, Italian Cars and Ferrari World. In the early 1990s, Phil needed a freelance test driver and writer for these titles, and I got the job. After a while, all three titles crashed because the publishers folded. Good can come from bad. Phil gained publishing experience and useful contacts. Meanwhile I had test-driven some amazing cars and gained some journalistic skills. This was when Phil and the motoring historian and photographer Peter Collins came up with the daring idea to launch Auto Italia magazine. They were looking for investors and asked if I would be interested. As I was running my own specialist car business and had several other commitments, I declined.

Trips to Italy became frequent. The size of the team varied from just me, to four or five people. My Italian-ness helped. Part of my job was to interact with Italians, which speeded up the opening of doors. The real Italy varies enormously depending on region and is more complicated than that perceived by non-Italians.

Roberto Giordanelli
About Me

I began my test-driving career in a pedal car when I was four years old. The big boys on bicycles would tow me at speed around dirt tracks. This is where I learnt to consider understeer and oversteer. In Calabria, Southern Italy, aged five, I became addicted to powered propulsion when standing on the footboard of a Vespa. In the UK in my teens, twenties, and thirties, I was a nuisance on public roads. That said, when I started being an automotive pest, there were only five million cars on the UK's roads, compared with 31 million in 2022. In my youth, if there was a weather report of ice and snow somewhere, I would drive there to slide about. Aged 18, my first competitive event was in 1966, at Wimbledon Stadium. It was a sprint competition and I landed a lucky entry into the Production Car Finals. Driving a self-prepared road-going Ford Anglia, I came second by 0.002 seconds to a Jaguar E-Type driven by the World Hot Rod champion. This 'measurement' was worthwhile and – despite parental disapproval – provided me with a sport to pursue. In 1967, I went to Brands Hatch Motor Racing Stables for a course in a Formula Ford where my abilities were again measured and confirmed. At this point, I should have sought funds to race in Formula Ford and climb the single seater ladder targeting F1. An opportunity missed. Unfortunately, life's crossroads do not have signposts. Instead, I went my own way with self-built cars in the knowledge that I could always race. The addiction never goes away.

In 1970, I became a qualified mechanical engineer and worked at BOAC/BEA, now British Airways. I left after one year to fool around with cars. At the time, the

1: My first test car and the family Buick.
2: Calabria 1951. Going fishing. Sometimes with ex-WW2 explosives - allegedly.
3: British Airways staff Mary Giordanelli with Dino and the family car in 1970.
4: West London 1959, school uniform complete with cap and short trousers.
5: 1967 Brands Hatch Motor Racing Stables Lotus Formula Ford.
6: Test drive with my wife Jane as co-driver.

airline career was considered a job for life, so the company subjected me to a lengthy interrogation as to why I was leaving. In the 1970/80s, I was racing, running my own specialist car business Rossi Engineering, a bi-product of which included test-driving. I also wrote a few car stories that were published. I became registered with the Law Society to write legal reports concerning court cases relating to classic cars and racing cars. I won a few cases and even had a world-famous client, although client confidentiality prevents me disclosing the identity. I became a member of the Guild of Motoring Writers, a qualified ARDS race instructor and an Ofqual qualified sports coach for motorsport.

I was born in Kensington to Italian parents and reared unconventionally by an extended Italian family, with nannies in Italy and the UK. As a child I was bilingual. I was educated in a Dickensian English private school in West London where I learnt to cope with regular beatings from the staff and the prefects. I shall not describe the depravity that the boys endured, because you would not believe me. I learnt the apparent importance of being able to recite long passages from Chaucer and Shakespeare. Language lessons included French, Latin and Russian. My private school prepared the boys for Oxford or Cambridge universities, and then a career in the City, MI6 or the KGB. A by-product of the school's sadistic regime was that I had a basic understanding of manners and literacy. Most important of all, it was first-rate preparation should I ever be imprisoned or tortured.

I was at the school from 1953 to 1965. As a schoolboy, I spent long periods in Italy. My English school reports said that I would have done well, had I attended. I left at the earliest opportunity gaining five GCE O-Levels (which are harder than today's GCSEs). I wanted to be an aircraft pilot or a weatherman. My father steered me away from those ambitions, fearing that they would take me away from the family. The fact that I could dismantle, tune and reassemble my Lambretta saw me sent on a five-year apprenticeship to Fluidrive Engineering Company and Twickenham Technical College. I have dual nationality, two passports and love both countries equally, although for different reasons.

I have two sons with my ex-wife Mary. We divorced in the 1980s and keep in touch. In 1999, I met my wife-to-be Jane Watson who has transformed my life.

1992 – 1995
A Posh Do in Mayfair

Let us begin with an activity that did not include risk, pain, illegal acts, madness, sickness, car crashes, death threats, injury, drowning, plane crashes, sex, drugs, rock 'n' roll, court cases, bankruptcy, or the police. However, this posh do in Mayfair did include a disturbance. First some history: Ettore Bugatti was born in Milan in 1881 and died young in 1947 aged 66, from lung disease and a stroke. In 1909, aged 28, the Italian went to the German city of Molsheim to create Bugatti Automobiles. In 1919, at the post-World War One Versailles Treaty, the German city of Molsheim became part of France. Owners of Bugatti cars prefer to call their cars French rather than German or Italian. That the company's first ten years of making cars were by an Italian in Germany was – for some reason – forgotten. Enter the modern world. In 1987, another Italian, the entrepreneur Romani Artioli, bought the rights to the Bugatti brand. Artioli built a new factory near Modena where – in 1991 – he produced the amazing Bugatti EB110 supercar. It was named after the founder's initials and the years of the company's anniversary.

There were several sumptuous black-tie launch parties, one of which Phil Ward and I attended at London's Grosvenor House Hotel on Park Lane with our other halves, Josie Ward and Judy Coop. There must have been a thousand glittering guests. Bugatti brought along a fleet of EB110s to circulate the area, whizzing down Park Lane and around Hyde Park Corner and wriggling through Mayfair to create a London test circuit. I was one of the fortunate few who had already test-driven the car for *World Sports Cars* magazine. It was outstanding by being fast, stable, and luxurious. With a top speed of 213mph, a 0–60mph in 3.5 seconds, four-wheel-drive and a sumptuous interior, it was a supercar game-changer. Artioli invited VIPs, the press and a who's who in the supercar business. He also invited a prominent figure in the Bugatti Owners Club. My partner Judy was attractive and self-confident. She marched me up to Artioli and persuaded him to fly me out to the massive Nardò test track in Puglia, so that I could test an EB110 with the development engineers. Artioli agreed. Judy gave him no choice, and Artioli confirmed the request to one of his staff.

There was a brief presentation and then the shouting started. In front of a thousand guests – and after a five-course dinner with limitless Champagne – the prominent man from the Bugatti Club was introduced and took the microphone. We were all expecting some thanks and congratulatory words. Instead, this speaker launched into a tirade of insults. He loudly and embarrassingly rubbished the new cars, his host, and the relaunched Bugatti Company as Johnny-come-lately who were soiling the brand. There was a deathly hush, followed by the speaker storming off and leaving the Bugatti ball. However, one thing is certain, Artioli stuck his neck out by reviving the brand. Valiantly, he entered the Le Mans 24-hour race and other races. Had it not been for Artioli, today's bedroom – poster – cars, the Bugatti Veyron or Chiron may never have existed. While everyone was thinking about the shouting match, an unlikely guest swooped to the rescue. This was the boxing champion Chris Eubank. While every woman was in evening dress and every man in black-tie dinner suits, Eubank upstaged us all by wearing immaculate designer horse-

1: 1994 RG and Judy at the Grosvenor House Hotel Bugatti EB110 GT launch.
2: Displayed on the dance floor.
3: 1994 Phil and Josie at the Grosvenor House Hotel reception.
4: Bugatti EB 110SS used for 'demonstrations' around Hyde Park.

riding gear, perfect tweeds, camel jodhpurs and shiny knee-high boots. He carried a leather riding crop and briefcase, presumably full of cash with which to buy an EB110. Eubank's public address to Artioli to buy a car that evening was rightly applauded. Also well received was Eubank's clipped, lisping, eloquent and unplaceable accent that lifted the mood, so we could all forget Mr Grumpy from the owner's club. The chic party went on until late.

GOODWOOD AND LEGENDS

Imagine the winter of 1993, the first Goodwood Revival was merely a twinkle in the inspired eye of Lord March (now the Duke of Richmond). The Goodwood track was just that: a strip of tarmac used for testing, not the magical place of today. It is almost unique in maintaining its original layout, unspoilt by modern-day efforts to slow the speeds. Goodwood and Indianapolis are the only circuits where period lap times may be compared with today's times. I was at Goodwood with the legend that was European Touring Car Champion Carlo Facetti, complete with a 1992 Maserati Barchetta Corsa fresh from the Italian one-make racing series. Facetti's racing credentials are extraordinary. Our plan was for Facetti and me to test drive the Barchetta. Then, like buses, up popped the legend that is F1 Italian GP winner Peter Gethin (1940–2011). This is the man who – in 1971 – held the lap record at Monza for decades, at an amazing average of over 150mph. Gethin ran the race school at Goodwood and offered to take Facetti around the circuit in a saloon car to point out the booby traps. All racetracks have booby traps, and a racer's first task is to learn their intricacies before trying to defuse them. Facetti spoke no English, not that he needed tips from a passenger seat. However, any advice from a local specialist speeds up the learning process. Pro-drivers learn circuits quickly, at 60 years of age, Facetti was still quick. I was volunteered to ride in the back of the saloon car and act as interpreter. Off we go, no one wearing seat belts as these were different times. I squatted on the centre back seat, leaning forward in the middle of a

legend sandwich, describing the obvious.

It was a culture shock to exit my workshop sheds, where my job was solving other people's problems, to spend a day with two racing celebrities. Instead of the stress involved with running a business, I was mucking about at a race circuit with cheerful people. On the Goodwood track, we noted other people's tell-tale rubber marks disappearing into the scenery at the exit of Fordwater. Fordwater is very fast and has a grip-diminishing, descending exit. Goodwood has subtle gradients that significantly affect grip. I kept my commentary short. Facetti raced in the real Mille Miglia and real Targa Florio, as well as in all the world's major races. Pointing out three or four Goodwood booby traps was enough. Having recently navigated Sir Drummond Bone's Ferrari in the Mille Miglia and on two Targa Florio retrospective events, I raise my hat to Facetti and to all those who did the real thing.

Back to 1993 at Goodwood and Facetti's Maserati Barchetta Corsa was in a truculent mood and refused to run cleanly enough to be driven. So, there we were, suited and booted with game over but for a couple of Alfas on hand for a twin test and oh yes…, a 'works' Lancia Delta integrale rally car. With Phil acting as navigator, we hurled the low-geared rally car around the high-speed circuit where – of course – it was totally unsuited, as it ran out of gearing before we reached turn–1 (Madgwick). We needed a plan. The transporter that delivered the integrale had gone, and the car was not road legal. This will be my first use of the useful

5: 1994 track test at Goodwood with Carlo Facetti and the Maserati Barchetta.
6: Stationary red Alfa, with moving green Alfa. Phil using a slow shutter speed for effect.
7 and 8: 1994. Works Lancia Delta integrale and a press car on Goodwood's fields.

word 'allegedly'. Allegedly, I drove the integrale out of the circuit, for some road-testing, and then up onto Lord March's estate to find muddy tracks as an apt photo location for skidding about. A few days later, a brand-new road-going integrale from Lancia's press fleet was delivered to my Surrey home. The higher up the food-chain of motoring journalism, the more press cars you are given. A week was the norm. Writing gods are given cars long-term. Having a new car on the drive was unusual, and my two teenage sons Dino and Niki were most impressed. Editor Phil rapidly worked out that I could understand a car quickly. For me, this was an own goal. No long-term cars for me then. There were times when I was presented with several cars on the same day. I think the record was a dozen cars in one day at our Surrey test track, and a similar number at the Kyalami GP Circuit in South Africa.

VARANO AND GREENS

A trip to the Varano Circuit near Parma was a real treat. For me, any trip to Italy is a delight. Despite the country's limitless and infuriating problems, I and many others find the place irresistible. Ex-F1 driver and ex-Alfa Romeo Autodelta works driver Andrea de Adamich ran, and still runs, a race school at the circuit. Alfa Romeo supplied him with an array of Alfas. At the time, this race school was more advanced than anything I had ever seen and came complete with a moving ground-level platform (called a kick plate) that flicked your moving car out of control. Your job then was to gather up the chaos on a smooth wetted surface. Cars were fitted with video recorders that showed the instructor and journalist in action. After each discipline, you took your personal video cassette with you and plugged it into the next car. On one occasion, some

12

13

9 and 10: 1995. Varano Circuit, Italy. When Alfa Romeo SZs were driving school cars.

11: 1995. Varano Circuit, Italy. RG with the legendary Andrea de Adamich and Fleet Street's Andrew English.

12: 1960/70. Works Alfa Romeo driver Andrea De Adamich making comeback in my lightweight 715kg Alfa? I offered but sadly not.

13: 1990. Building this Group A Maserati Biturbo race car achieved official recognition with Maserati.

cassettes got mixed up. Part of a female journalist's footage ended up on my cassette. Naturally, the Italian instructors were all good-looking, and the female journalist was very friendly, so I best not describe what accidentally ended up on my cassette.

De Adamich called the race school *Centro Internazionale Guida Sicura* or International Safe Driving Centre. De Adamich was under constant attack from the local Green Party who would sneak about taking photos and constantly issue expensive legal challenges. De Adamich's playing of the 'safety card' in his school's title helped to keep him in business; the God of Safety being big enough to slug it out with the Green God. De Adamich told me what the Greens get up to. If he moved a shed or tried to make any improvements, the Greens would issue legal challenges. If he moved a small tree or bush but planted many more to compensate, this would anger the Greens. The circuit has a river running alongside. If de Adamich did anything to prevent his track from flooding, another legal challenge would be thrown at him. The Greens demanded that the river be able to meander wherever it wanted, especially if it swallowed up a race circuit. At the end of the three-day course, and knowing de Adamich's prowess with works GTAs, I offered him a race drive in my own 715kg/180bhp super-lightweight GTA replica. He knew about the car but declined, as he had retired from racing. They say never meet your heroes, but I had recently met three: Gethin, de Adamich and Facetti. All were modest and agreeable people. I was the new boy and had much to learn.

GOODWOOD AGAIN

Back to Goodwood to drive some Alfa Romeos, Fiats, Maseratis, a Chevy Corvette, a Dodge Viper, a Lamborghini LM002 and a Nissan Skyline GT-R. The magazine's photo choice and captions are chosen and composed not by the writer, but by the editorial staff. It was a standing joke that occasionally I might complement the staff if the captions or images they selected related to the words that I had written. It was a

battle over which a freelancer has no control. Also, an irrelevant pin-sharp picture always had priority over an imperfect relevant or dramatic image. Many of the images in this book are my unprofessional snaps taken over decades. I hope the publishers and I have presented a balance of real-life images and hopefully relevant chocolate box pictures. It is the combination of photos and words on these pages that tell the tale. The challenge is for today's speed-readers to step back in time and read a whole book.

The UK Maserati Club is a fine organisation filled with delightful people. This was their day at the Sussex circuit. Club members knew that I have much 'previous' with the marque both via racing a Group A Maserati Biturbo in the 1980s, and with engineering. This was enough for me to be handed the keys of precious possessions to speed around the track. When faced with anyone who didn't know of me, rather than approaching an owner and asking, "May I test-drive your car?", it is better if an editor asks if his test driver may try the car? There is a subtle difference and it works.

As for insurance, I had my own specialist engineering company insurance that covered me for any of my customers' cars but no doubt it would have excluded journalist work or tracks. "The large print giveth, and the small print taketh away." Rightly or wrongly, I assumed that *Auto Italia's* insurers covered me. There was no risk when driving new cars from manufacturers as they were fully insured by the manufacturer for any type of claim. In later years, I learned that *Auto Italia* insurance existed. It covered accident damage but not mechanical issues; the latter being the most likely with old cars. Fortunately for me, the insurance was not tested, as I never did anything that required a claim. I scraped a wheel rim of an Alfa Romeo SZ on a high kerb once, but it was not enough to justify an insurance claim. A fortunate – or perhaps lucky – record for decades of testing countless cars. Kindly, the publisher paid for the scraped wheel repair. However, much later, another freelancer was not so fortunate. All racing cars are time-bombs. It is not 'if' they break, but 'when' they break. A car he was testing jumped out of gear and damaged the top-end of the engine. There was a five-figure bill for mechanical damage and massive six-figure court case that bankrupted the impecunious freelancer who was abandoned by his publishers. After the trial, the judge told the freelancer (who could not afford a good lawyer) that if the car's owner had signed a waiver, the freelancer would have won the case. Learning from other people's mistakes, I now insist on a signed waiver from a car owner, be it for journalism testing, instructing or racing.

Goodwood is very fast and has few appreciable run-off areas. To the driver's left, there is a narrow strip of slippery grass ending with hard barriers embedded in solid earth. There is, however, an uncanny feeling of space. The historic airfield on the driver's right is wide open. However, the laws of physics regarding centrifugal forces generally send wayward cars to the driver's left, and into the nearby barriers. One good thing about Goodwood's indestructible barriers is that the 'walls' are at 90 degrees to the ground level. This means damaged cars tend to stay upright after the impact. Race circuits with soft tyre walls absorb forces better and limit the damage. Deformable tyre walls can sometimes act as ramps when they distort. This can send an errant car into an upward spiral and consequential roll-over. No Maseratis were injured in this test.

We also had two Ferraris at Goodwood: a gentlemanly 456GT and some thunder in the form of an unsilenced road-going racing car, namely the ex-Maranello Concessionaires Ferrari Daytona. The 456GT was a simple road test, so let's forget that one. What no one present at the time can ever forget is Sally Mason-Styrron and her Maranello Concessionaires racing Daytona, especially when it is driven at the Goodwood Motor Circuit. I can still hear the deafening V12 howl as she blasted around the Goodwood Motor Circuit. Sally and her uber-butch Daytona. What a sight, and while southern England reverberated to the sound waves, no one complained; different times…

LEONARDO DA VINCI AND ICE CREAM

Being new boys, we had yet to build our reputation for returning priceless cars to their owners in the same condition as we received them. This was not easy, as mainstream motoring journalists have a poor reputation for care, or for track driving. Being multi-skilled has always been my ethos. I blame my schoolboy hero, who was not a racing driver, but one Leonardo da Vinci (1452–1519). He was an accomplished artist, mathematician, engineer, architect, botanist, sculptor, geologist, anatomist and inventor. He was renowned in the fields of human anatomy, hydrodynamics, geology, geometry, optics, physics, chemistry and more… He designed things like flying machines, armoured tanks, bicycles, the parachute, diving suits and much more 400 years before their time. If Leonardo had not existed, I might have spent my whole life at British Airways, retired in 2003 on a final salary pension at 55 years of age and died three years later. Instead, in 1971, I left British Airways Engineering at Heathrow to manage my mother's family business G. Rossi and Sons, which was established in West London in the 1930s. It consisted of a two-storey four-bed apartment, a garage business, a café/restaurant, an ice cream factory, and 15 ice-cream vans. All departments were losing money and the company was in debt. I revolutionised each department into profit and paid off the banks. Unsurprisingly, the garage department was my main interest. It was useful for my early motorsport in 1966, and where in 1973, Steve Minton and I built a giant killing Ford Anglia twin cam special saloon. In 1977, the business was forced to close, receiving no compensation. This was due to a town-centre redevelopment. I consulted a City of London property lawyer, and there was nothing we could do. The company had been renting the premises and was instantly wiped out. Three people in the apartment were made homeless and 30 people made unemployed. Where Nazi bombers failed, the local council succeeded. With zero funds, I created Rossi Engineering, which after 24 years, I closed in 2000. So why am I telling you all this? It is because this is where

14: Sally Mason-Styrron's ex-Maranello Concessionaires Le Mans Ferrari Daytona.
15: Leonardo da Vinci's Vitruvian Man.
16 and 19: Unique Bob Wallace Lamborghini Jarama. The test track, the hotel and Talacrest showroom all very close.
17: Early 1970s. Lotus Anglia & Lotus Cortina at Rossi Garage, West London.
18: 1974. Brands Hatch Dealer Team Firenza, RG in the Lotus-Anglia, ex-works Cologne Escort.
20: Rossi opened in West London during the 1930s.

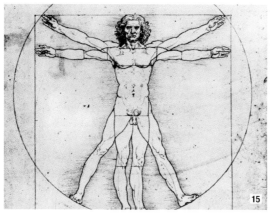

necessity confirmed that I needed to be multi-skilled for my survival. The ghost of Leonardo is currently telling me to be a better writer.

TICKET TO THE TOP

In 1995, journalistic things were looking up when high-end dealer Talacrest gave *Auto Italia* the famous Bob Wallace Lamborghini Jarama hotrod to play with at our Chobham test track. Having Talacrest on-side was a great help and worked both ways. Talacrest was our ticket to the top. American Bob Wallace (1949–2002) was the Lamborghini factory development engineer. He wanted the company to go racing but CEO Ferruccio Lamborghini was having none of it. Perhaps his indifference to racing stemmed partly from his crash whilst racing in the 1948 Mille Miglia. To appease Wallace, Lamborghini allowed him to create a more powerful and lightweight Jarama. Tipping the scales at 1,170kg and with 380hp, it equated to 325hp per tonne. When you look at the car, you see into the mind of Bob Wallace. Simple, fabulous road/racer engineering from an era when just about anyone, could fix any car.

BROOKLANDS AND TAZIO NUVOLARI

The next car – a 1929 Alfa Romeo 6C 1500 Supercharged – was driven by my second favourite hero, Tazio Nuvolari (1882–1953) although a conjuring trick with number plates has muddied the waters. Whilst racing a motorcycle, Nuvolari crashed and was badly injured breaking some bones. At the hospital, he asked the medics to set the plaster casts on his body in the 'riding position' as he had another motorcycle race the following weekend at Monza. That tells me everything I need to know about the man. Enzo Ferrari said of

21: Giulio Ramponi's Double Twelve race-winning Alfa Romeo at the Brooklands Museum in Surrey, UK.
22: The 1500SS on the famous banked track where it raced in 1929.
23: Judy Coop in her two storey penthouse apartment overlooking Hampstead Heath.
24: Lamborghini Miura SV found in a Hertfordshire farm yard by Judy.

Nuvolari, "He spent his life trying to kill himself racing and failed." Great men received great quotes. This one from Ferdinand Porsche (1875–1951), "Tazio Nuvolari is the greatest driver of the past, the present and the future." Nuvolari died in bed aged 60 from heart and lung problems. I suspect that a combination of cigarettes and cars did kill him via constant exposures to automotive toxins.

Back to 'Nuvolari's' supercharged Alfa 6C. We tested it at the most fitting place in the UK, namely at Brooklands. With no safety features like roll-over protection or seat belts, period race drivers relied on the tried-and-tested strategy of being thrown out of crashing cars to land unhurt on haystacks. For our test, some of the famous banking was used for short runs, although quite bumpy and devoid of haystacks. The Alfa 6C was my first drive in a car where the brake and accelerator pedal positions are reversed. This is no problem when you are thinking about it with your conscious mind. However, most driving actions are performed with your subconscious mind. A race car driver uses his/her subconscious mind most of the time. Your subconscious brain functions are vastly faster than your conscious reactions. Studies show four billion bits per second (BPS) subconscious, compared with 2,000 BPS conscious.

Today, Brooklands is well worth a visit for adults and children. It is now divided into two separate worlds: firstly, Brooklands Car and Aircraft Museum, complete with various sections of historic track, secondly, since 2006, the location for Mercedes Benz World (MBW). Their facility houses a museum-type showroom, café, several race car simulators and a test track for customers. Pre-MBW, i.e. pre-2006, Auto Italia staged track action on the huge old concrete runway. With help, I laid out the 1.25-mile Circuito Giordanelli using an open trailer continually replenished with hundreds of old tyres to delineate the track. We ran countless amazing cars, including unsilenced Formula One cars at high speed inside London's orbital M25 motorway. More on this later…

JUDY AND THE MIURA

Auto Italia magazine can be as much about the people as the cars. Let us finish 1995 on a personal note. My partner at the time – the late Judy Coop – lived in Hampstead, which meant that for 14 years I had a daily commute to and from my home in Sunbury on Thames. Judy enjoyed long country walks. It was on one such walk, accompanied by a girlfriend, that in a farmyard in Hertfordshire, she stumbled upon a wrecked Lamborghini Miura. When she phoned me to describe the car, I could hardly believe it. She told me that the badges read Lamborghini Miura, with Bertone on the interior sill plates. I thought that it could have been a prank or a kit car. I asked her to describe the engine,

she said that it was in the back of the car, sideways (transverse), and had the word 'Lamborghini' written on it in braille (raised cast lettering). "Do the headlights have eye-brows," I asked. "No" she replied. With that description, I knew it could be a Miura SV. Whatever I was doing was put on hold. The car world is small, and it turned out that – via the farmer's information – we both knew the owner of the wreck. I contacted him but he categorically did not want to sell the car. Judy took over and changed his mind. Just as she did with Artioli at the Bugatti ball, Judy gave the Miura owner no choice; something I could not have done. A short while later, one of my Sunbury sheds was occupied by a dream car. The Miura was original, low-mileage, complete, crashed at both ends and rusty in the middle. Restoring such a car would require enormous funds. Eurospares offered a substantial amount for them to break the car for spare parts. I declined, telling Eurospares two things: Firstly, profit was not the reason for acquiring the wreck. Secondly, breaking a restorable piece of automotive history for spare parts would be sacrilege of the highest order. The Miura's future life would have to wait for a complete change in my circumstances. Restoring the car would need time and money; two things I have never possessed.

I covered it with a sheet and tried to forget about it.

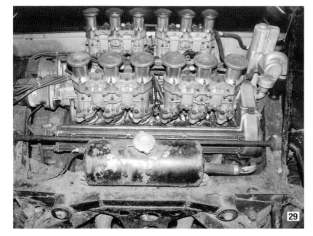

25 and 26: Initial dismantling and restoration preparation.

27: New front and rear bodywork made by Mabert Srl in Turin.

28: The Miura shell fresh from the paintshop in the UK.

29 and 30: The beating heart, restored by RG with help from specialists.

31 and 32: The finished car at Goodwood and in Italy. If you must have a supercar, this is it. Easy to maintain.

1996

Maserati Biturbo. What Could Go Wrong?

The year started with testing a used unloved Maserati Biturbo. By now secondhand values had plummeted, bringing the bargain Biturbo into the territory of diy-man, or find a local-hero-to-look-after-it man. For an average spanner-man, the Biturbo bridged the gap between old cars that are easy to maintain and modern cars that are not. In the 1980s, Maserati was bankrupt and saved by Alejandro de Tomaso and the Italian government. This Italo-Argentinian was not a man born with a silver spoon in his mouth. He was intelligent and hard-working, and I suspect – like Colin Chapman – ruthless. At this level, a car maker can be nothing else. He fled Argentina for Italy in 1955 as he was on a death list. Nothing serious, he was simply plotting to overthrow the President Juan Perón. In Modena, he married an American heiress, Isabelle Haskell whom he bumped into at the parts counter of the Maserati factory. The De Tomaso badge looks like it has a 'T', but it is a fancy 'I' for Isabelle. de Tomaso was a race driver including in Formula One, an engineer and an entrepreneur who gradually bought up various companies including the ailing Maserati. Previous Maserati models were big bangers and expensive. With the Biturbo, De Tomaso made a medium-sized mass-produced car that was affordable. Whether the Biturbo is any good or not is secondary to the fact that Maserati was saved until a future date when it could flourish in the hands of a forthcoming buyer. Today, the Biturbo is

still unloved, although for the few survivors, their day will come. And survivors there will be. During the 1980s and early '90s, a total of 37,966 Biturbos in 46 different models were made. McGrath Maserati in the UK knows them all and looks after countless cars for clients.

In the late 1980s, I was drawn into the world of Biturbos when I built and raced a Group A version. Then in 1998 I also raced a Ghibli Cup for Natty Racing in the British GT Championship, although purely as a driver with no technical input. More on that sex-drugs-and-rock-n-roll adventure later…

In the late 1980s, Maserati's own Pro Team entered a Biturbo in the World Touring Car Championship (WTCC), while in the British Touring Car Championship (BTCC), Nick May lacking any factory backing did at least find some sponsorship from drinks company Campari. Nick's car was unsuccessful, scoring no points. Nick visited the De Tomaso factory in Modena, to seek some backing but was unsuccessful. It seems that it would have been easier to gain an audience with the Pope than with Sig. de Tomaso. As I was also building a car for the BTCC, Nick May's experience saved me much time by not going on a similar trip. Instead, I was backed independently by renowned furniture designer Peter Crutch who owned the BTCC project. Peter's Biturbo was an immaculate road car that he wanted me to transform into a BTCC 2.5-litre racer. I mentioned that it felt like vandalism to tear a perfect car to pieces. Peter

1: 1988. RG at Brands Hatch with the Group A Biturbo.
2: Donington Park 1987. The late Peter Crutch with his Group A Biturbo, built and raced by RG.
3: The Biturbo's interior.
4: 1988. Druid's Bend, Brands Hatch. Maserati Biturbo on three wheels.

put me at ease saying, "It will be like transforming a normal person into an athlete." The transformation was complete, and then came a slight hitch. Peter's Biturbo was race-ready just in time to coincide with a BTCC rule change – no more turbos – and a two-litre capacity. In the end, none of the Group A Biturbos were successful in international races. As for our now obsolete Group A Biturbo, I raced the Peter Crutch car in the UK in the *Auto Italia* Championship with success. Failing to get the car into the BTCC, the only consolation was that the lap times of the Peter Crutch car were slightly quicker than those of the Campari BTCC car.

The swansong for our car came at Brands Hatch where I qualified on the front row. It was to be a standing start, which is a cruel thing for a heavy car with sticky slicks. At the start, I held the engine at about 5,000rpm, let the racing clutch out, and bang, the diff broke and locked solid. In a split second – and fearing 30 cars slamming into the rear of the jammed Biturbo – I grabbed second gear, instinctively thinking the initial bang might have been a stripped first gear. Another bang, and now the gearbox also disintegrated. I was waiting for the explosion as a fast-moving, blind-sided backmarker slammed into my full fuel tank at 100mph. No one hit the car, which was craned off the front row. With the transmission repaired, I'd had enough and the car was sold. End of that Biturbo racing story. Tragically, in 2002 Peter Crutch died from cancer.

SAVED BY CHRIS REA

Phil and I hastened to a Goodwood Ferrari UK day to see if I could drive the latest model – the F355. Arriving at the circuit, we were faced with a disappointment: Ferrari UK gave us the cold shoulder and declined to give us new boys a car to test. However, all was not lost. I got into conversation with Chris Rea who was there with his brand-new F355. On hearing the news that Ferrari UK refused us a car, Chris chauffeured me around the track for a couple of laps and then handed me the keys to his F355. "Take it for as long as you like," were his words. Bingo, we had a new Ferrari F355

track test story in the bag. Ferrari's UK top brass looked on in surprise or perhaps embarrassment. After this episode at Goodwood, Ferrari UK never hesitated to supply *Auto Italia* with cars. I rounded off the day with Chris recalling our common Italian heritage. "Your family history is astonishing, write a book." he exclaimed. That history book, relating exceptional events from 1911 to 1948, is in the pipeline.

5: 1988. Donington Park track day with my son Dino as passenger in the Maserati Biturbo.
6: Auto Italia feature with Chris Rea and a Ferrari F355 at Goodwood.

Jan / Feb 1996 £2.95

Auto Italia

FORZA 355 FERRARI
Chris Rea plays a different kind of music

THE ONES THAT GOT AWAY
Lancia Gamma and Fiat 130
MONSTERS
Lambo LM002 v Dodge Viper
DEREK AND THE DINOS
Derek Bell - a Ferrari reunion
ROAD TESTS :
Fiat Barchetta
Alfa Romeo Spider

BITURBO-THE £6K MASERATI

SPY IN THE CAMP

Time for some motorsport in the form of a summary of the Alfa Romeo racing championship (AROC). The organiser, Michael Lindsay, deserves a knighthood for his incomparable work keeping Alfa Romeos on track. Michael wrote a feature that culminated with me track-testing my rival's car: Chris Snowdon's 3-litre GTV6 racer. Battles between us were always close and often went his way, with some wins for my 2-litre naturally aspirated car. Chris is another of motor racing's lifers. Like me he will be in motorsport until he drops. Free from BTCC rules, Chris's GTV6 had been lightened and upgraded to be much quicker than a BTCC version. It was good to be a spy in the camp and learn just how very quick Chris's car was. It is also weird that after so many close battles, we never crashed into each other. *Autosport* magazine gave us the 'Race of the Year' award for our battle at the 1994 Castle Combe Easter Monday meeting, while I was awarded 'Driver of the Day' for crossing the finish line side-by-side, and later 'Driver of the Year' by AROC. The clock gave the win to Chris's GTV6, it being 0.01 seconds ahead. Series coordinator Michael Lindsay was watching from race control, overlooking Camp Corner. He said that as Chris and I took Camp Corner side by side, neither of us giving an inch, officials in the tower were preparing to duck. Chris tells me that nearly 30 years later, Castle Combe officials still talk about that race.

RALLY MADNESS AND THE PLAGUE

Time for another rally car. In this case Dermot O'Brien's Lancia Delta S4 Stradale. The venue was the track at Enstone airfield. It was snowing, correction, it was trying to snow but it was too cold for that. Everyone was frozen, as an arctic blast assaulted the open airfield. To add to the fun, I was as weak as a kitten and about to die with the world's worst ever case of man flu. I soldiered on. The 940kg S4 is a crazy car built around the loose Group B rally rules. Group B was eventually banned because the cars were killing too many people. The S4's 1800cc 4-cylinder engine with double overhead cams, 16 valves, intercoolers, oil coolers, a supercharger and a turbocharger take up a lot of space. It is a mass of engineering that – in certain fleeting conditions – could run to 1500bhp. The Stradale at Enstone is quoted at 250bhp in a car weighing 1,200kg. The car is a gorgeously, hideously mad conglomeration of mechanical components. The designer had a great mind. Based on a roomy five-seater with ample luggage space, the S4 version of the five-seater Lancia Delta has only just enough room for two people. "No great mind has ever existed without a touch of madness." Aristotle.

SUPERCARS AT GOODWOOD

Looking back through old magazines, I can't believe how many times I had been to the Goodwood Motor Circuit in the 1990s. This time with car collector, architect and fine fellow John Braithwaite. He brought along a wild De Tomaso Mangusta, an elegant Ferrari 250 Lusso and a Lamborghini Miura S. My order of preference would be Miura (for beauty, if upgraded to SV), De Tomaso (for left-field brilliance), Ferrari (too sensible).

I once had an enquiry from a Lamborghini Countach owner who was a trackday virgin. He asked me to teach

7: 1994. Donington Park. Michael Lindsay interviews RG after a race win.
8: RG and Chris Snowdon. Very diferent cars and a constant battle.

9

him to drift sideways at high speed in his car around a race circuit, "Like they do on the telly," he said.
I declined the job. It got me thinking about the purpose of a supercar. Who buys them, and why? Then another circuit virgin – a Diablo owner – asked me to spend a trackday with him at Croft Circuit, so that he could enjoy his car at speed. After two laps of being dive-bombed by trackday junkies in hot hatches, the Diablo owner was a bundle of nerves and had enough. Game over.

Let's look at the Ferrari F40 and F50. They are named after the anniversary years of Ferrari's founding. The F40 is always trying to kill you, while the F50 is not. When the F40's boost arrives, the sudden rush of torque can spin the fat tyres in the dry, requiring much car control and the ability to foresee things. A white line, cat's eye, or discarded cigarette packet, can cause the F40 to snap sideways and ram whatever is alongside. The interior is devoid of trim. There are no driver aids, and welders giggle when they look under the bonnet.

Now the F50, which is much more stable and refined. Similar speed and similar lap times at the Nürburgring Nordschleife. The naturally aspirated F50 is a conventional screamer with a linear power delivery. I tested one at Silverstone and the only complaint was that the dashboard wanted to remove my kneecaps and

the steering was too low-geared. How can a company like Ferrari make such a mistake? Anyway, which would you have? No contest for me, it would be the F40. Why? The F40 looks better and has more character. It is more hardcore and less showy, if you can say that about an F40.

STRATOS: TO BE OR NOT TO BE?

How about some replicas? Shock horror. In this case a bunch of Lancia Stratos replicas pitched against an original. There is a place for replicas despite efforts by major manufacturers and lawyers to exterminate them and bankrupt those involved. If a person cannot afford the real thing, why not have access to replicas? Banning them is yet another assault on freedom. Imitation is the highest form of flattery. No one buying a replica Stratos or replica Jaguar D-Type, etc. is ever going to buy the real thing, so zero financial loss to original manufacturers. Indeed, the opposite is true, as the replicas add publicity to originals, and we all know that there is no such thing as bad publicity.

The Stratos has weird handling. A heavy transverse rear/mid-engine can overload the outside rear wheel when cornering hard. The front end is feather-light, and under acceleration, the front is hardly in contact with the

9: 1996. An early Auto Italia test at Goodwood with the Lamborghini Miura and De Tomaso Mangusta from the John Braithwaite collection.
10: Sandro Munari in action.
11: Sandro Munari talking Stratos with RG.
12 and 13: The unique GT1 De Tomaso Pantera at Silverstone – broken by the team but the test driver gets the blame.

ground. The short wheelbase demands reaction times and predictions possessed only by aliens, which makes Lancia works driver Sandro Munari an alien. I shall ask him that when I meet him later in the book. Once mastered, the Stratos can be quick, as shown by its World Rally Championship wins. It also looks the business, so that is enough to add one to my 'acceptable supercar' list.

THE ONLY GOOD PANTERA IS A RE-ENGINEERED ONE

Off to Snetterton Circuit, to test a freshly built GT1 De Tomaso Pantera race car. I do like Panteras and despite being anti supercar, a Pantera is on my personal weird wish list of supercars. Warning: unless a Pantera has been sorted by a clever engineer, it will be hell on earth. They were no good even when they were new. However, I repeat; a sorted Pantera is a thing of joy. This racing GT1 Pantera was as far from an original car as it is possible to get. Effectively, it was a Group C racing car wearing Pantera clothing. This was early days for this car. Much later, after it was battle-hardened, I tested it again at Silverstone where the team orders were not to use reverse gear as it would break the gearbox. After a few laps, I trundled back down the pit lane and parked in front of the pit garage. Job done, no problems. Editor Phil Ward and I retreated to the pit wall to soak up the Silverstone scene. We then saw a team member using reverse on the Pantera and heard a clonk and saw a piece shrapnel exit from under the car. This was followed immediately by their team's race driver going on track. He returned a lap later trailing oil. The gearbox had a big hole in the casing caused by one of the crew using reverse. Some weeks later, the rumour went round that I had broken the gearbox. The team needed someone to blame. That is the thing with letting a journalist into racing cars, or even road cars. Even if a car breaks six months after a journalist has driven it, "It must have been that journalist that initiated the problem."

10

11

12

13

1997
Big Names

1997 began at Castle Combe Circuit with a track test of a 1970s Maserati Bora. This was a trackday run by the eminent 96 Club. Started in 1975 by Michael Scott, the 96 Club was the first to offer such a service. This was an exclusive club and many of its members went on to race cars. My friend and car collector Peter Crutch was a great fan of motorsport and of the 96 Club. Peter was purely a collector, who was not interested in driving or being driven in his amazing assemblage of rare cars. At Castle Combe, we had his Ferrari Dino 246 GT and one of his three Alfa Romeo SZs. This was the old 101 series egg-shaped SZs, not the 1990s version, which he also had in his collection. He also had two TZs and much more… Peter's friends and colleagues included Sir Basil Spence (1907–1976) for Peter's first job, Sir Terence Conran (1931–2020) Rodney Fitch (1938–2014), the designer Alan Zoeftig, and eminent artist David Hockney, who had a crush on Peter.

In the early 1980s, before I knew Peter, he was a spectator at Brands Hatch. He spotted me racing an Alfa Romeo, and liking what he saw, he took me under his wing. We went racing with his Alfa Romeo Junior Zagato that I rebuilt in one of my sheds in Sunbury-on-Thames. It arrived as a race car from Portugal whereupon I changed everything. The 2-litre Junior Zagato was a flyer because it could be driven beyond-the-limit with impunity. We won the big-engined modified class of the Alfa Romeo Championship in 1985 and 1986. We also won most of the *Auto Italia* Championship races that we entered. We were a two-man team: Peter watched, while I did everything else.

Preparation for a race would start with me checking and loading the car on the trailer the day before a race meeting. Peter preferred not to stay in a hotel, no matter how far away the circuit was located. If we were racing at Oulton Park, this would mean picking Peter up at 4am hours from his home in West London. I would drive the tow-car and trailer for four hours to reach the circuit in time to sign on at 8am I would unload the car, take it for scrutineering, drive it in qualifying, fix any issues, race the car, load it up, and eventually drive the rig for five hours back to London on a Sunday night 'return traffic jam'. I would drop Peter off and get home after 1am. Peter, bless him, was the tall quiet guy who stood and oversaw. Love him as I did, I didn't mind at all. Think: Enzo Ferrari when he went to the races.

When interviewed at a race circuit for a radio show, Peter was asked why he went motor racing and never got in any of the cars. He replied, "My wife only feeds me with healthy food. I go racing so that I can eat nice food at the circuits' greasy spoon restaurants." From 1984 to his death from cancer in 2002, Peter financed the racing. He enjoyed every second of being at the races. He would have made a good poker player, as his facial expression and body language never gave anything away.

ROWAN ATKINSON AND AN EGG-SHAPED CAR

I was lapping Castle Combe's lovely fast old chicane-free circuit on a 96 Club day in Peter's 1950s Alfa Romeo Sprint Zagato and found myself in a race with a well-driven Renault 5 Turbo. I kept the Renault behind

1: The late Peter Crutch who supported my racing for nearly 20 years.
2: 1985. First race in the Junior Zagato and an outright win at Snetterton.
3: Peter Crutch's Junior Zagato. Built and raced by RG.
4: Alfa Romeo Junior Zagato. Championship winner in modified class 1985 and 1986.
5: The Alfa SZ befriended by Rowan Atkinson at Castle Combe. Here it is at Mallory Park.
6: Keen car enthusiast Rowan Atkinson the Mille Miglia.
7: One of three SZs restored at Rossi Engineering.

me. Afterwards, in the paddock, the owner of the Renault joined us to examine the rapid old SZ. This was Rowan Atkinson. A great car enthusiast and soon to be racing driver. Despite being an introvert, he wanted to know all about the SZ. "Why is it so fast?" he asked. Shrugging my shoulders, I omitted to tell him that the 1300 engine had been replaced with a 2-litre motor, or that it only weighed 750kg. I offered him a passenger ride, which he eagerly accepted. The SZ's suspension was original so the body-roll angles were somewhat dramatic. The Alfa's pace left an impression with Atkinson. He later bought himself a Zagato but with Aston Martin underpinnings.

SURREY AND THE BEST FERRARI

Off to our test track at Chobham in leafy Surrey. This ex-military establishment has an extremely fast two-mile-long track with no barriers and is lined with trees. It is also a favourite for the film industry and TV shows. Talacrest trusted me with their priceless cars. Being multi-skilled is good and bad. Good for obvious reasons, and bad when the mono-skilled call me a 'Jack of all trades, master of none' to which I reply that I am a "Jack of all trades and master of eight," (obviously without mentioning what they are). At this point I raise my hat to the best motoring journalists. I know that I shall never be half as good as them.

Out of the Talacrest showroom rolled a Ferrari 250 GTO and a racing Ferrari Daytona. The older the Ferrari, the more I like it. Two or three years in, and now we had a back catalogue of crown jewels that would give us access to anything we wanted.

Now, for one of the best things I ever did, a track-test of the famous 1970 Mark Donohue/Sunoco Le Mans Ferrari 512M. The transporter dropped the unsilenced 5-litre V12 screamer at the Chobham test track, where there is a noise limit. Back then, there were no houses nearby, but there was a golf course on the infield, and the golfers didn't like noise. We had a plan. Do everything else first: take photos both static and car-to-car at slow quiet stuttering near-zero-rpm speeds. Then

after the photo shoot: drive the car like I stole it, in the knowledge that we would be stopped and chucked out. The noise from the unsilenced 5-litre high-revving V12 was epic. Decades later, and I am still energised when I think about it. At 630bhp and 785kg (803hp per tonne), it didn't hang about. In Le Mans spec it could reach 220mph. It was also beautifully sorted and easy to drive. The thing that amazes me about Ferraris of the 1990s is the ergonomics: rubbish on the road cars, perfect on the race cars. At the factory, the two departments obviously never communicated.

Back at our test track, I was flat-out, hurtling past the golfers and making ear-bleeding noise, and discombobulating half of Surrey. After a few laps, the trackside red lights illuminated, ordering us to desist. Rolling back into the paddock, it was job done. The track controller was out of his tower and waiting for me, arms folded and stern. Wearing my innocent and inquisitive face, he said we had to stop driving immediately. To which I gave the usual answer, "I shall have you know that I have been chucked out of better circuits than this." Having also tested this car's predecessor, Talacrest's Le Mans Ferrari 512S, useful comparisons were made. This was also the ticket the magazine needed to get me into some Formula One cars. When the 512M story was published and reached the USA, don't quote me, but I believe – allegedly – it opened a can of worms regarding its ownership. Its history and provenance were never in question. The car is now in the USA. When I am asked, what was my favourite racing car test? this is it.

SPA AND A DEVILISH PLAN

Next stop Spa-Francorchamps circuit in Belgium for a controversial track test in a Lamborghini Diablo SVR race car. Here is a background of how this came about. Ferruccio Lamborghini was born in 1916 and died in 1993. He retired in 1974 to his farming roots. 'La Fiorita' farm was next to Lake Trasimeno near Perugia. He oversaw some business interests and spent much of his retirement hunting and producing wine from his

8 to 11: 1970 Ferrari 512M track-tested at the fast Chobham test track. This USA-based car was re-engineered in the states in 1970 and was claimed to be the fastest and most powerful 512M ever. RG was entrusted with the car by John Collins, owner of Talacrest and the world's leading dealer in exotic Ferraris.

vineyards. During his time making cars at Sant' Agata, he was always against involvement with motor racing. His rivalry with Ferrari had been easily satisfied. The Miura saw to that. However, perhaps Lamborghini knew that to challenge Ferrari on the racetrack would have ended in failure and/or bankruptcy. With Ferruccio Lamborghini gone, the new owners of the company felt the need for a supercar company to be involved in motorsport. Lamborghini supplied engines to some Formula One teams, and even a complete F1 car, the 291. In the 1990s, the company launched the Supertrofeo one-make race series, which was to run for four years.

Back in 1997 at Spa Francorchamps, this was a race weekend that included the new Diablo Supertrofeo series. Editor Phil and I needed a cunning plan to get me into one of the race cars. Anyone familiar with how race meetings are run will know that to turn up unannounced and get a drive on the same day is an impossible task. My apologies, but how the impossible was achieved is too illegal to publish. Please assume the word 'allegedly' for this entire piece. After a chat with an infamous competitor and a relaxed official, we had a plan. It was raining heavily as I ventured out on track on a race weekend. The spray removed visibility. There were some incidents in the lethal conditions. For obvious reasons, it was imperative that I brought the car home without violations and undamaged, which I

12 to 14: The Pullicino Classics-entered Lamborghini Diablo Supertrofeo.
15: Alfa Romeo 159 and Maserati 8CL being 'raced' at Brooklands.

16: RG poses for an Auto Italia feature with the Maserati 8CL on the Brooklands banking. Another car generously provided by Talacrest.

did. I even overtook a few cars and presented the driver who was to race the next day with a good qualifying time, allegedly. My first drive at Spa was another big box ticked. We put mayonnaise on our fries and headed home.

BROOKLANDS: TO ACT, OR NOT TO ACT?

We had two big-banger pre-war/post-war legends: an Alfa Romeo 159 and a Maserati 8CL, both courtesy of Talacrest, with words written by historian Ed McDonough. My job was to sit in the cars on the Brooklands banking, pretending that we were tearing around the historic concrete. The ancient banking is far too damaged for any serious speeds.

Acting can be useful in action photography. If the snapper is using a slow shutter speed, typical for car-to-car photography, this keeps the subject in focus and the background speedily blurred. If this is happening whilst cornering at low speed, it is necessary for the driver to tip his/her head slightly to replicate real-world action. However, such fake shots are easily spotted by the cognoscenti because the suspension is not in roll, and the tyres are not distorted. Such deception is purely to help the photographer achieve what looks like an action shot on a car that – for whatever reason – is impossible to drive fast. It was an exceptional occurrence but it did happen.

TECHNOLOGY

There were times when I had many cars to test on the same day. I mentioned previously that a dozen cars at the test track all at once was the record. However, a solution was on its way that would make multiple tests on the same day much easier. Track hire is expensive. Economies of scale were *de rigueur*. As I also had my own specialist car business, and racing activities to run, I was always time and money poor. I used to scribble words onto paper as an *aide-memoir* for when – days or weeks later – I came to write the stories. I also used to panic at much time being lost during the test days as cars were being shunted about and photographed. A bit like the film industry, where there is a lot of hanging about. I needed to use this downtime. Enter the Psion Series 5 palmtop and a Canon SLR camera. These revolutionised my work. Once the photos were developed (pre-digital), this enabled me to recall and study countless details on the cars. A Psion palmtop would fit into a pocket. I know that today a smartphone can take notes, but it is not as convenient as the old Psion palmtop, which was like a mini folding laptop. I could now write words while photographers did their thing, or write in the cars whilst moving, or trackside, roadside, or in the field. I could also write words – whilst waiting for my next customer – when I was working part-time at race schools; just don't tell anyone. The Psions (I had several) had a high attrition rate. Some froze or broke, one got crushed at the Lamborghini factory when a mechanic motored a driver's seat over it, and one fell off a yacht into the Solent, sending 12,000 unsavable words to the seabed.

AUTO ITALIA GOES RACING, AND A MINISTER OF TRANSPORT

During the 1990s, the *Auto Italia* Racing Championship was extremely popular both with spectators and competitors with full grids of diverse machines. Cars from the Ferrari Championship and the Alfa Romeo Championship joined the party. There were also entries from the Irish Fiat Championship with their fearless drivers. Cars from Lancia, Maserati, De Tomaso, etc, now

17: Southern Italy and working with a Psion 5 palmtop, a mini laptop that fitted in a pocket.

18: Passing the time writing at the airport.

19: Howling Laud Hope of the Monster Raving Loony Party offered me Minister of Transport.

20: One of many battles with John Day in the Auto Italia Championship at Castle Combe.

21: Oh no, not another £50 million Ferrari 250GTO to test.

had somewhere to race competitively. As one of those competitors, I enjoyed much success in the races. Towards the end of my time in that series, I proposed two rule changes: 'Reverse grids' and 'Passengers in Cars'. Reverse grids was a serious suggestion, and it was adopted. The fastest cars started at the back of the grid. Passengers in cars? I knew this would be rejected, even though in pre-war years, riding mechanics (i.e. passengers) were common in long races. The main reason for my suggestion was that unless you have been in a motor race, you can have no idea of the violence and madness. Video or onboard footage conveys little; perhaps 5% of the sensory assaults. Just as the drivers must sign their lives away, so too would the passengers. A driver could also sell the rides to boost finances. Passenger rides could also be offered as prizes to the unwary. To make things fair, a time penalty, or pit-stop drive-through, would be added to cars without a passenger. This would also bring huge publicity to the series. Mad idea? Maybe, but – for certain categories – I still like the concept.

For many years, I attended the annual Multiple Hosts Ball in Bath. It was a riotous three-day party with 1,000 guests. It was best attended by single people as divorces are expensive. I was approached by Howling Laud Hope, who had just become the leader of the Monster Raving Loony Party. The previous leader, Screaming Lord Sutch, had committed suicide. Howling Laud Hope had a cat called Kathmandu. I suggested that the cat should now

lead the party, or at least be a joint leader, like Cameron and Clegg. The new leader, Howling Laud (Alan) Hope loved the proposal of passengers in racing cars, and then popped the question, "Would you like to be the Minister of Transport for the Monster Raving Loony Party?" I declined but now wish I had accepted.

The Auto Italia Championship saw great battles and great cars. Noteworthy were Giovanni Di Gennaro with his jewel of a Fiat 128, John Day a natural talent and hard charger with his Lancia Beta Coupe, plus many others, too numerous to mention. Club racing is often derided by pro drivers. However, club racing encompasses all skill levels from 'hopeless' to 'professional standard'.

MILLIONS OF POUNDS ON A TEST TRACK

Between 1962 and 1964, Ferrari made thirty-six 250 GTOs and on this sunny day, I find myself sitting in one of the most famous 250 GTOs of all time: the ex-Innes Ireland 250 GTO, valued back then at only £10 million, and today at £50 million. The lightweight 3-litre GTO ended all racing hopes for Jaguar with their Lightweight 3.8-litre E-Types. As few people get to thrash a £50 million car, I am often asked what they are like to drive. At the time I said that they are like a cross between a Lightweight E-Type and a Ford Escort rally car. I still think that. A GTO has the speed of the E-Type with the chuckability of the Escort. Another year gone, and I wonder what awaits...

Launch Party in Spain

A press launch for the new Alfa Romeo 156 saw me jetted out first class to Southern Spain. Usual thing, a bunch of impoverished motoring writers handed five-star treatment for two or three days, before returning home to their humble existence. Upon arrival at Malaga Airport, a hostess escorted us to limousines that whisked us away to a luxurious hotel. In your room you find a press pack on the new car, an itinerary for your stay and a goody bag with a gift or two. Dinners are sometimes in the hotel but usually somewhere special. There is a presentation by the manufacturer that covers all relevant points, followed by a Q and A session. This is where a journalist who likes the sound of his/her own voice asks questions. There are two types of questions: those regarding the future, which are never answered, and some daft questions. Thankfully, most of the press are clever professionals who know their stuff. Ample alcohol is consumed late into the night, making some of the hacks over the drink-drive limit for the following morning's test drives. Different times…

The journos are given a route map. Rally chaps call it a tulip map. This is when races take place. Not official races, just forceful driving as this is some writers' opportunity to prove themselves to their peers. These words are a generalisation, indeed they only refer to a minority, so apologies to the sensible motoring writers who read this. There are morning coffee stops to dilute the alcohol and lunch stops to top it up again. Same thing in the afternoon, another big dinner somewhere posh, then some hit the bar until they are just about capable of returning to their hotel rooms. Eventually, at some point during the next day, it is time for limos to

make the return trip to the airport for the homecoming first class or club class flight. After some complimentary on-board drinks and jovial banter, some write their copy, others fall asleep. The launch described above was typical of the frequent launches that I attended.

TWIGGY'S MIURA

Back in the UK, and waiting for me at our Surrey test track, was a Lamborghini Miura S. This bright green car is the famous 'Twiggy' car in which the 1960s skinny cultural icon, whose real name is Lesley Lawson, was often seen. In the 1960s, I remember seeing her in Twickenham in this very car.

Lamborghini launched the Miura in 1966 after displaying a chassis and engine at the 1965 Turin Motor Show where buyers lined up with their cheque books, even before a body had been styled. A clever marketing coup happened when one of the very first Miuras was parked outside the Casino in Monte Carlo in the build-up to the 1966 Grand Prix. Even today, the front of the Casino is the place for exotic cars. The Miura at the 1966 Monaco GP was then used as a course car for the event. Orders flooded in. The car was improved with the 'S' model and then perfected with the 'SV', which had many important upgrades. It was a beauty. At our test track and knowing what a 1960s icon I was about to test, I dressed up for the occasion with my old 1960s mod suit. All that was missing was Twiggy.

Track tests were getting ever more serious. How about a Ferrari 288 GTO vs a Porsche 959? Both rare manufacturer specials, both reassuringly expensive, both extremely fast. Acceleration is fun. We like the

push in the back as we increase speed. However, pleasure turns to pain when it gets too much, a bit like tickling someone. Funny at first, but if exaggerated, it becomes an assault. Acceleration is the same. Once you get down to sub-three seconds for a 0–60mph time, acceleration enters the world of discomfort.

A DRIVE TO THE SOUTHERN TIP OF EUROPE AND THE MAFIA

The Alfa Romeo 146 is a forgotten Alfa. I had a new 1.6-litre version on a long-term loan and used the opportunity for two stories: a long-term road test and a travel story. The southern tip of Europe was the target destination, right down to deepest Calabria, located at the toe of the Italian boot. My navigator was my then 15-year-old son Niki. At one point, we were on an empty motorway – for legal reasons, let us say it was in Germany – and noticed that we had a very strong tail wind. The car's top speed was officially 112mph. I also noticed that the road ahead was descending for miles. I knew the car was highly geared for quietness and economy. Allegedly, I wondered if the car could reach the rev limiter in its high top gear. It could: the 112mph car reached about 150mph. As for the drive story, I was ruthlessly frank about Southern Italy's problems, for which I received much criticism, as well as a death threat.

My son and I visited the Giordanelli family home in Cetraro before heading back to Blighty. It was about this time that the Mafia kidnapped our family's heirlooms. Twice! My favourite uncle Ciccio, (*Dottore* Francesco Giordanelli) negotiated two ransom deals, but unsurprisingly most of the heirlooms were lost. The family home was in the narrow, densely populated part of the town centre. The huge pieces of furniture, large paintings and sculptures would not have looked out of place in a palace. Naturally no one saw or heard anything. This behaviour is called *omertà* (the code of silence). This was a petty crime for the mob as they are usually concerned with more lucrative targets like drugs, arms, construction rackets, blackmail, bribery,

prostitution, money laundering and extortion. The Calabrian Mafia is called the *'Ndrangheta*. They are ruthless but they leave tourists alone, as tourists bring money to the area, which the *'Ndrangheta* then collects from local businesses. The same thing happens in Naples with the *Camorra* and in Sicily with the Sicilian Mafia, the *Cosa Nostra*. It is ok though, as I said, if you are a tourist you will not be targeted enjoy the place at your leisure. Driving a new UK-registered 146 made me look like a tourist.

An attempt by the Italian government to improve the economy of Southern Italy, included building an Alfa Romeo factory in Pomigliano d'Arco, which is in a suburb of Naples. Over a million Alfasuds were made there. Alfasuds today are much sought after by the cognoscenti and have rising asking prices for the few that survived. I tested several and had two Alfasuds as family cars and remember them with affection. They had their weaknesses, as did most cars of the period. Nevertheless, I travelled internationally with a Ti version and personally crash-tested another one. I was in the UK, stationary at some red traffic lights with three more stationary cars ahead. A chap in a Volvo estate who was travelling at dual-carriageway speed whilst using his phone, slammed into the rear of the Alfasud, which then piled into the three cars ahead. The backrest of the Alfa's front seat broke, and I found myself relatively unharmed and momentarily comatose on the back seat. The Alfasud's front and rear crumple zones (whether by design or chance) worked perfectly. As for the old factory, it is having a one-billion euro investment for the next generation of cars from Fiat.

BRITISH GT CHAMPIONSHIP WITH SEX, DRUGS AND ROCK 'N' ROLL

1998 was the year that I was asked by Natty Racing to drive in the British GT Championship. Philip Jones-Lloyd acquired a Maserati Ghibli Cup car from the Italian one-make race series. *Auto Italia's* Charis Whitcombe was the team manager. A host of helpers, including Lee Penn, Dermot McGivern, Russ Yates and

1: Cetraro, Southern Italy. A childhood hometown.
2: Cetraro town square in 2004.
3: Producer and director Helen Ostler who made the film 'Phil's Fantasy' about the Natty Racing team.
4: Team manager Charis Whitcombe, Tony Soper and RG at Silverstone.
5 and 7: The sponsor's friendly girls.
6: Russ Yates and Linsey Dawn Mckenzie

many more, swooped into Mario Grech-Xerri's workshop to help modify the car from its reliable one-make-series state of tune to the significantly wilder GT2 specification. Much midnight oil was burnt, and much partying took place.

A film crew led by director/producer Helen Ostler was there to make a film called 'Phil's Fantasy'. Helen's film title of 'Phil's Fantasy' derives from the car owner's desire to enter the world of a professional racing championship with an impossibly low budget. The film had no script. We made it up as we went along, documentary style. Being a driver, I was lucky enough to land one of the prominent roles. This in turn led me to Elstree Studios where I enrolled in a TV presenters' course where I learnt much. The camera sees all. You must be natural. If natural is not good enough, find another job. Helen was also an assistant director on BBC's Grange Hill, EastEnders and a legal documentary series called Rough Justice, where I was tasked with an acting role as an extra: a ruffian in a Birmingham pub, to be precise. As for the race team's budget, some sponsorship came from the publishers of adult magazines and adult websites. I say 'adult', but you know what I mean… The sponsor's friendly girls would also be present at some of the races, which gave the team much publicity.

The second driver was Tony Soper, who had plenty of racing experience. With a low budget and an unlikely car, the team struggled, and although inhabiting the rear section of the starting grids, surprisingly we were not the slowest car in the series, although the over-boosted Maserati broke regularly. The last race of the 1998 British GT Championship was at Silverstone, but the Maserati could not be fixed in time. With the race being televised by the BBC, our adult media sponsors demanded that we compete and paid for the team to hire an ex-Le Mans Harrier-Cosworth GT1. On a previous occasion, at RAF Wittering, I compared a Harrier car with the Harrier jump-jet. But that is another story… Back to Silverstone and our sponsor's condition for renting the ex-Le Mans car, was that if for any

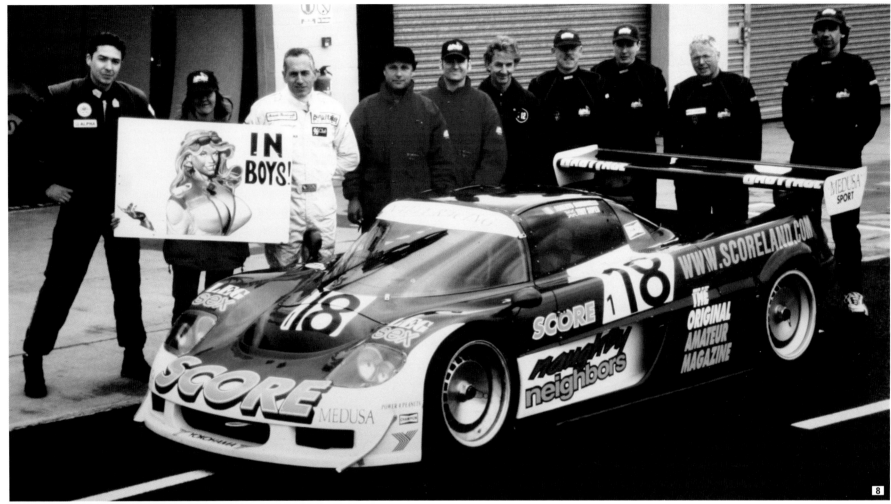

8: With the Maserati broken, Natty Racing hired the Harrier-Cosworth. A better car but not without issues. It was later purchased and raced by co-driver Tony Soper.

reason we did not race at Silverstone, the sponsor's money – which the team had spent – would have to be returned to the sponsor on pain of death or worse. No excuses.

Silverstone race weekend arrived. In qualifying, the rear coil-overs were gently machining themselves through the soft aluminium rear wheel rims. This was because the original suspension had been sold and inappropriate units were fitted. After some panic, the clearance problem was solved, although the overly stiff suspension units remained. The car was unsorted and not race-ready, but we had to proceed. My co-driver's qualifying session was in the dry. Then the rain arrived. My session was in the wet, and I knew immediately that we were in trouble as the set-up was too stiff.

Race day arrived and the rain evolved into a constant deluge. The organisers said that it was too wet to race as there was 'standing water' everywhere; meaning drivers could not tell if the mirror-like water was 1mm deep or 100mm deep; not that they would have been able to see anything in such impossible conditions. The final decision from race control would be made later. Fears of reprisals from the sponsors proliferated. If the race were cancelled, the team would be in serious trouble. Then more bad news arrived. The police were coming to seize the hired Harrier-Cosworth as it related, allegedly, to a drug dealing gang. Before the boys in blue arrived, race control gave the go-ahead for the race to begin despite the permanent monsoon. Tony Soper was to start the race, a rolling start. I had warned

9: Bizzarrini drifting onto the main straight at Brooklands.
10: Talacrest-loaned Ferrari 250 GT Cabriolet cornering hard.
11: F1 Alfa Romeo circulating the 1.25 mile circuit.

may have come nowhere in the championship, but we had the best parties in the pit garages and the best après-race parties at various venues. Helen Ostler's film *'Phil's Fantasy'* came to a close with a customary 'wrap' party; an acronym for Wind, Roll And Print. The film is still available on Amazon. It was 25-year-old Helen Ostler's first film and was remarkable considering she made it on a zero budget. As for the legal problems with the Le Mans Harrier-Cosworth, they were eventually sorted and today it is now in private hands and restored.

EVENTS TIME AND NOBODY DIED

When *Auto Italia* opened the door to 'events', it added income, boosted magazine sales and helped with more advertising revenue. These meetings took off in a big way when we gained access to the aircraft runway at Brooklands. The Vickers runway was an expanse of concrete and tarmac, almost a mile long and very wide. It was my job to lay out a circuit on the site using hundreds of car tyres to mark out the track. I took several factors into consideration: avoidance of potholes, location of spectators, a slow chicane on the approach to the crowd-line, an opening radius curve on the exit for power-slides onto the main straight, a fast turn at the deserted far end for the returning straight. Fast cars were able to exceed 100mph, especially F1 cars. Spectators were offered hot rides in priceless cars. There were no crowd safety barriers, even though the spectators were close to the action. Safety was in the layout.

Come the busy weekend, my job was easy. My reward this year was to have charge of Jeremy Agace's ground-shaking Bizzarrini A3/C racer. I loved this car: beautiful, front/mid engined, and all the torque in the world. Fabulous. The car had recently won the Spa 3-Hour Sports Car Race. As for its value, who knows? Talking to car collector Peter Crutch, he remarked, "Back in the good old days I would have bought that Bizzarrini – whatever the cost." He meant it.

Two beautiful Hollywood *dolce vita* 1960s spyders were also waiting for me to give hot rides: a Ferrari 250

Tony – who had not driven the car in the wet – that it was undriveable. Unable to keep up with the pace car, Tony had a spin on the formation lap behind the pace car and several high-speed spins during his half of the race. I very much doubt that the Harrier was insured, so I have no idea what would have happened if the car got wrecked. Thankfully, being Silverstone with its wide-open spaces, Tony didn't hit anything. Many other cars did, and there was much carnage in biblical rain on the flooded track. At half distance, there was a pit stop for a driver change, and it was my turn. Finishing this race would be the gallant team's greatest moment. I felt the weight of the team on my shoulders and in the end brought the undrivable car home 20th out of 30 entrants. Threats from the sponsors disappeared. We

California Spyder from Talacrest, and Roger Lucas' Maserati Mistral Spyder. Nobody died. No one was injured. There were no crashes. Thousands of spectators attended. This annual event lasted until 2006 when Mercedes took over the site for Mercedes Benz World.

VALENTINO BALBONI AND ME
It was at the Lamborghini factory that I first met the legend that was their test driver Valentino Balboni. We shook hands, and like Masons, we instantly understood each other because neither of us had soft hands, but the hands of toil. On this visit, my job was to test-drive a new Murciélago. Balboni knew that I was a racer/engineer and that for some time, I had a Miura lurking in a shed at home, so he knew that we were on the same side – aided no doubt by Italian-ness. This being the case, he led me away from the Murciélago to show me their 'development' Diablo. This was a bit like the factory's original 1970s Miura Jota. It had more

12 to 15: Ferrari 275GTB/C NART, power-sliding onto one of the straights of the Circuito Giordanelli. (Brooklands, Vickers runway).
14: Unique Ferrari 268SP.
13: RG hands-on laying out a 1.25-mile circuit using hundreds of old tyres.

went ballistic. His high speeds on the public roads were inconceivable. In those days the local police took no notice of speedy factory cars.

Warning: the following words may cause offence. In the days when Ferruccio Lamborghini was running the company, a journalist noted that all the office girls were beautiful. He asked Mr Lamborghini why that was. Ferruccio Lamborghini replied, "They cost the same as the ugly ones." This was a quote from long ago when it was considered humorous. I understand that today it could cause shock and offence, and for some, the need for counselling. Please forgive those words because as the American astrophysicist Neil deGrasse Tyson said, "The past is on another planet." I presented the words to provoke readers. If you don't push the envelope, your writing will be dull. Knowing where to draw the line is difficult because the line moves, and the readers' offence thresholds vary. Current thinking and current sensitivities are that such statements should be blocked. However, the above observation did happen. Those words were said. Therefore, it is history. Real history may be overlooked but not censored, although it is already happening. Old films on TV have certain footage removed. It beggars the question, "At what point do we burn the books?"

SILVERSTONE AND COMEDY TYRES

A sunny day at Silverstone and waiting for me is a highly successful red racing car. The Ferrari 330LMB – courtesy of race engineer Tim Samways – is a 400bhp/1,100kg multiple race winner in the hands of the late Tony Dron in European historic racing. For several engineering reasons, the regulations stipulate Dunlop historic crossply tyres that were designed 70 years ago. The handling difference between the old crossply tyres and any current road-going tyre is as shocking as it is indescribable. In a fast turn, a car takes 'a set'. This is terminology for the angle at which the car eventually leans in a fast bend. The contact patches of the Dunlops then tip over, reducing grip dramatically, whereupon a 'second set' and a drift happens.

16: Exclusive test on one-off Lamborghini 'Diablo Jota' and regular Diablo SV.
17: Factory test driver Valentino Balboni and RG talking about torque.
18: Ferrari 330LMB on regulation Dunlop crossply tyres for historic racing.

power, less weight, and upgraded suspension and brakes. Balboni handed me the keys of the 'Diablo Jota' and got into the passenger seat. I drove out of the factory and into the surrounding countryside. I wanted to drive quickly but also wanted to quiz Valentino on his vast knowledge of Miuras. My pace on the roads varied from sedate to brisk. I didn't want to worry him. At some point, he suggested that we pulled over for a driver change. Balboni knew that my pace was not revealing the capabilities of the Diablo. Straight away, Balboni

LOST IN FRANCE

Time for another travel story. I love all European countries and this time; the destination was France. This is the country that gets in the way when you drive to Italy and therefore worthy of comment. I was ably assisted by my partner Judy Coop. We had been together since the 1980s. Judy tamed me and taught me how to behave – for which I shall be forever grateful. She was an art teacher, artist, historian, UK Blue Badge Guide, English Heritage Guide and Paris Guide. She also had a dress hire business called 'Posh Frocks'. Reading the travel story today, the words bring a smile to my face. As someone who is used to Italy, I see France as being closer to the UK culture than the Italian way of life. Nevertheless, I love France for being French. Italy is almost an island with the Alps acting as the northern barrier. My job was to take a few snaps and write 1,500 words. We had a great time. We went on many trips through France to Italy. Judy's encyclopaedic knowledge of Paris and its art and history educated me. Sometimes I would assist her when she took groups of Americans to Paris. Happy days. But now to end on a tragic loss. Sadly a few short years later, Judy's young life was cruelly and suddenly ended by catastrophic cerebral haemorrhage.

INFLATION

Work just kept coming, and upon my return to England, Ferrari-ness continued with a Talacrest-supplied 250LM track test. I prefer track-testing racing cars on tracks to swanning about on public roads in flashy road cars. The call came to present myself at Brands Hatch Circuit to pitch an unlikely racing Ferrari Testarossa against a racing De Tomaso Pantera. The verdict goes to the quicker car, and this is all dependant on specification and preparation, so it could go either way. In this case, the lighter and more powerful Pantera got the nod.

This reminds me how easy and low-cost it used to be to get on a racetrack. Sometimes we might test a car on the public road but use a racetrack free of charge for a photo shoot. Free of charge because we would use the circuit's lunch break for car-to-car photography. Recently (2019), I was at Donington Park with the John Danby race team, race testing Simon Watts' Lotus Cortina. The respected author and motoring journalist Johnny Tipler was there with a photographer to write a story on the car, and naturally give Donington a good mention. I asked race control if we could do the usual lunchtime thing on track for one lap with the Lotus Cortina following the camera car at about 30mph. A slow shutter speed makes the car look quick. They gave

19: Judy Coop – a life cut short.
20: Monaco and a travel story through France with co-driver Judy.
21: The famous Hotel de Paris, Monte Carlo.
22: Lotus Cortina run by John Danby Racing.
23: Early 1980s Donington. Formula 5000 test. Peter Crutch watching.
24: Car-to-car photography. How it was done before it became dangerous.

me the phone number of MSV's head office, which I duly called expecting 'yes, no charge'. Their reply was, "Yes, that will be £1,500." I responded saying that I thought £15 would be too much, so no thank you. Unsurprisingly, Donington missed out on a complimentary side bar in the story.

FORMULA ONE AND A JET FIGHTER

There are some things in life that you never forget. My first Formula One drive was about to happen. I had little experience with powerful single seaters, however, in the early 1980s, I had the briefest of runs in a Formula 5000 Lola T332. A Formula 5000 is a Formula One car with a larger engine. On this F1 test day in 1998 at Donington, Paul Osborn brought along Pierluigi Martini's 1991 3.5-litre F1 Minardi-Ferrari M191. Osborn looked at me, shook his head, and said, "You are too big. You won't fit in the car. You can't drive it." Pierluigi Martini is a tiny person, and the narrow carbon fibre tub, steering wheel and pedals fit him tightly so that he doesn't get knocked about by the high G-forces."

Suddenly, my Formula One debut looked dead in the water. "Let me try." I begged. I squeezed my 5ft 10", 12-stone (77kg) frame into the car. Here are half a dozen reasons why Osborn's comments were correct:

1: My head blocked the air-box and would be battered about causing blurred vision by being directly in the airflow. 2: My body and pelvis were squashed and terribly distorted. 3: My shoulders were wider than the cockpit opening. 4: My legs and knees were hard against the steering wheel, and painfully against the monocoque, and crushed against each other. 5: My squashed arms and wrists were too long and could not move back enough to operate the gear lever or the steering wheel. 6: Worst of all, my size 12 feet could not operate the pedals because the steering rack was in the way.

"Well?" asked Osborn. "Absolutely fine," I replied. He told me that I had five laps, although with the absence of a pit board, I did six. Here are some numbers: 700hp, 500kg, 1,400hp/tonne, 0–100mph and back to a dead stop in about five seconds and three-G cornering and braking forces. The drive was painful and excellent at the same time. At speed, I was blind because my helmet was buffeting in turbulent air, causing a high frequency battering. I had to dislocate my joints to operate the controls. At F1 pace, there is zero time to rest. Corners come at you quickly and constantly. A photo of the car cornering on three wheels shows that I must have got some heat into the slicks. Whatever, I

25: Donington 1998. F1 Minardi-Ferrari 3.5-litre 700hp/500kg on three wheels.
26: Have you got one in a larger size?
27: Crash helmet in the air stream.
28: RG with squadron leader Paolo Testolin for him to drive a racing Ferrari F50.
29: "What happens if I press this button".
30: F1 Alfa Romeo and an Italian Air Force Tornado at RAF Cottesmore.

had now driven a Formula One car. A huge thank you to Paul Osborn. If ever you are lying wounded, and under fire in no-man's land, I would crawl out and save you. It is my measure of how much I like someone. I mention another person later in this book, for whom I would do the same.

After an F1 test, how could *Auto Italia* raise the bar? Easy, simply get the following people on board for a quadruple test: the RAF with exclusive use of their Cottesmore airbase, the Italian Air Force with one of their Tornados, an Italian squadron leader, a Formula One Alfa Romeo, a Lamborghini Diablo and a Ferrari 355. What a day. Soon after, we put the Tornado pilot (squadron leader, Paolo Testolin) in a Ferrari F50 race car at Donington. Did we really do all that? The pictures tell the tale. What a year. Or was it? My personal life was in disarray, but that is another story. I buried myself in my work hoping for better days.

1999
Multipla and Columns

The year begins by scrutinising the radical new Fiat Multipla due to be launched in the UK in January 2000. Just as any discussion regarding a swan quickly mentions that the big bird can break a man's arm, so it is with the Multipla and the word 'ugly'. Those who have lived with the vehicle, the press, the judges for 'Car of the Year', and the New York Museum of Modern Art, understand this amazing vehicle. Our five-man team with ample luggage criss-crossed Italy in a most efficient manner. Back in the UK, we had a hot Multipla. It was chipped by Red Dot's Augusto Donetti to give more power plus some handling upgrades. Filled with eager passengers, it was quick. I was reminded of the 1959 Abarth Fiat Multipla, which was the cheapest way to scare the largest number of people. Today in 2022, I keep a 2003 Multipla in Scotland parked in the driveway of our Scottish residence, overlooking the Western Isles. It makes the house look occupied. The Multipla still works perfectly. In time, it may become an Abarth Multipla.

1999 was also the year in which I added 'Columnist' to my Chief Test Driver credentials. The columns needed to be unlike the rest of *Auto Italia*. To wake up the reader, my writing style for regular road and track tests included deliberate deviations, some light-hearted banter and a few quotes. For the columns this style of free writing needed to be *de rigueur* for the whole piece. The subject matter of the columns needed to be loosely connected to motoring or Italian lifestyle. Any negative comments are best turned into positives. For instance, if you tour Italy, you will see many derelict buildings. This is due to complicated and bureaucratic inheritance laws

and peculiar planning laws. You will also see many partly built and seemingly abandoned new buildings. Building without planning permission is common in the knowledge that every few years an amnesty is announced legitimising the illegal structures. Also there is a system where planning departments can approve the illicit structures for a fee. For new-builds, planning permission can always be rescinded unless there is a roof present. Therefore, you may see a roof on pillars, but no proper walls. It is standard practice for a building's completion to require a buyer's money. This sounds like a negative, so here is a solution that makes it a positive. "Italians are masters at starting construction projects."

My greatest journalistic pleasure was acquired from writing travel stories, with columns coming a close second. After many years, *Auto Italia* abandoned the publication of columns, although for 20 years, I had another magazine outlet for columns and test-drive features that lasted until 2021. I never had to look for writing work. It always came to me.

A DOG AND A FERRARI WITH 3 WHEELS

Another early start: wheels rolling at 4am to catch the 6.30am red eye from Stansted to Turin. Waiting for us is a car from the Fiat press fleet. We visit several places for future stories and end up at the De Tomaso factory in Modena. The entrance gates are open. The place looks deserted. It is over 40 degrees C. The oven-hot air is so still that the tumble weed is too tired to roll. A dog is sleeping in the shade of a tree. The hound lifts its head. Like tourists we park in direct

1: Fiat Multipla in Scotland.
2: Augusto Donetti and RG at the Turin test track. I am trying to look like I understand how he chips a car's ECU.
3: Chipped Alfa 156s.
4: One of millions of half-finished buildings in Italy.

sunshine. Ours is the only car visible. The dog strolls over to us knowing that he can join us to gain temporary access to the air-conditioned office. We enter with the dog and see a few men working on a handful of De Tomaso cars. The workers' cars are parked on the other side of the building in the shade. Half a dozen new Guaras are being assembled. Don't think 'production line' think cars on axle stands. The Guara had no market, the company should have revived the Pantera. The De Tomaso brand has earned its place in the supercar line-up and needs eager new owners. The latest I know is that a Chinese company bought the brand and may make a 'new' Pantera. I hope the marque survives. The factory had no research and development department. Customers did the R and D and a surprising 7,000 De Tomaso Panteras were produced.

Back to 1999 and several cars were at the fast Chobham test track including a Ferrari F355. At the time, the British Army often used the test track. I noticed a long tank transporter being worked on near an unofficial track access point. Trees line the track, making all the turns and quick sweepers blind. There is a fast opening radius bend leading onto the main straight, a bit like the Parabolica (now named *Curva Alboreto*) at Monza — good for corner exit speed. I was flat out in the Ferrari cornering at very high pace watching the tarmac unfold within my limited line of sight. At well over 100mph, my view was much shorter than my stopping distance. Out of my line of sight, the long tank transporter was entering the circuit via an unofficial access point. It was about to block the entire circuit because its turning circle was so huge. No way could I stop in time, especially whilst cornering. The transporter was gradually closing my last escape route — a narrowing gap between itself and the trees. In a nanosecond, my choice was to hit the transporter, or hit the trees, or go for a tiny narrowing gap. Instead of braking, I was flat out to squeeze through that diminishing gap before it closed. The tank transporter driver would not have been aware of the Ferrari until after it flashed by under the nose of the transporter.

I just made it by a whisker, although the fun was not over.

We decamped to a tighter infield corner for some action shots. This is when the car needs to be clearly 'loose'. Professional photography is so important to any magazine's profile. Rain or shine, photographers often lie down flat on the ground, called belly shots in the jargon. They frequently do this in what I call, 'the death zone'. Cornering hard towards photographer Phil Ward, the front suspension collapsed, sending the speeding three-wheeler in Phil's direction. He got the shot, and I missed him. A lower ball joint had failed, no doubt due to mistreatment from a previous road tester. It would not have been fair to Ferrari to publish the photo at the time. Anyway, 22 years later, here it is. No one died, and it was a gentle reminder that things can go wrong.

5: A completed De Tomaso Guara at the factory.
6: Guara chassis under construction. Financed but failed 4x4 project behind.
7: Nasty moment for the photographer.

ITALY AND SWEARING

Being the test driver, I was volunteered to do all the continental chauffeuring from venue to venue. I was expected to know every road in Italy without resorting to a map. In pre-sat nav days, I never even knew where we were going, as I did not have the addresses or a map, because I was driving. If I took a wrong turn, the rest of the team in the car – who were unoccupied – would remind me how useless I was. Oh, what jolly japes. At the venues when meeting Italians, I did the talking if their command of English was poor. Words and phrases in the English language are global. Italians understand many English words, but few can form a sentence or fully comprehend English conversations. I had to remind our team to watch their language. Our team members sometimes voiced their thoughts thinking that their hosts could not understand. If a member of our team included certain internationally known words in their private conversations like, swear words, chaos, idiot, stupid, etc, the Italians in earshot certainly got the gist. If the team had a difficult question to ask, it was always easier to out-source the difficulty to me, even if I had a mountain of work to do. In the evening, translation duties would continue with the restaurant menu. We packed in as many visits and tests as possible.

Some trips combined travel stories where I describe the good, the bad and the ugly of Italian life. My words were aimed to inform non-Italians that the apparent stereotype that everyone in Italy is enjoying a care-free life in the sun is not always what it seems. Then there is the regionality, something few non-Italians appreciate. Much of Italy is mountainous, and for centuries this limited inter-regional travel. Add that Italy was not a unified country until 1871, and you can understand why the regions vary so much. Factory visits to manufacturers and specialists kept us in touch with developments. Visiting hidden private collectors is not easy as they tend to keep their heads down, fearing visits from the tax police, the *Guardia di Finanza.* You can only find the collectors or specialists if you have local, insider information and have been vetted successfully.

SPORT PROTOTYPES AND LEGS

Waiting for me at Silverstone Grand Prix Circuit is Colin Poole's Osella PA1 2-litre Sports Prototype. I also tested Peter Rigby's Osella at the Nürburgring Nordschleife.

8: Testing Peter Rigby's Osella at the Nordschleife. RG tested several cars there, including exotic Ferraris, sometimes in icy conditions.

14

15

16

9 to 15: Co-driving with Simon Watts in some of his amazing cars run by JDR.
9 and 10: Lola T298 powered by BMW 2-litre M12, 320hp and weighing 500kg.
11: Lola-Nissan B2K/40 3.5-litre ex-Le Mans.
12: Porsche 968 Turbo RS 500hp.
13: Chevron B26 Cosworth Ex -John Watson, Jody Scheckter.
14: BMW 3.5 CSL Batmobile 1971 Spa 24-hour class winner.
15: Datsun 240Z IMSA 350hp/950kg race winner.
16: Every picture tells a story. A happy one in this case.

Colin's Osella at Silverstone came with some downforce, 300hp and weighed only 575kg (522hp per tonne). This was also the test day for Silverstone's gargantuan Historic Festival. This meant being on a busy track with the world's best and fastest sports prototypes. Big banger Ferrari 512M, Lola T70s and the like were my company. The little Osella monstered the monsters. Overtaking was by mugging the big bangers into the corners. While they were busy on the brake pedal, the Osella was still at full throttle.

Here is a snippet from the original test: "The 1970s was a dangerous era. Many drivers never made it into the '80s. The cars were powerful, and their lightness and simplicity gave them their speed. Compared with today's cars, safety was laughable. Exposure to the unsilenced exhaust permanently damaged hearing. Sat in the 575kg Osella with the steering rack pressing on my shins, the column against my knees, a suspension wishbone in my ankle, and nothing in front of me, I knew that I would not walk away from a crash. The only way for the marshals to extract me from a crumpled tangle of aluminium and fibreglass would be to cut my legs off first. They wouldn't be any use anyway."

In 2022/3, I still race similar cars. For example, Simon Watt's ex-Jody Scheckter/John Watson Chevron B26. Other cars recently raced and looked after by John Danby Racing include a Datsun 240Z IMSA spec (320hp and fabulous), an Aston Martin DB4 Lightweight (400hp and faster than one could imagine), an Aston Martin DBS V8 (500hp and surprisingly easy to drive in the wet), a Porsche 968 Turbo RS (500hp and obviously quick), a Lola T298 (320hp BMW M12-powered 2-litre sports prototype), a Lotus Cortina (always sideways), a Lola B2K/40 (ex-Le Mans and powered by a 3.5-litre Nissan motor) and a BMW 3.5 CSL Batmobile, (ex-Spa 24-hr winner in period, and so nice to drive). Plus, my own Jaguar E-Type. All have achieved podium results be they outright, or in class.

BONNY SCOTLAND AND A WEE LASS

Alfa Romeo knew how to sweeten hard-nosed motoring hacks. The launch of the 166 was at their usual Scottish sanctuary where, in pre-*Auto Italia* days, I attended the 1989 UK launch of the 164. This venue, close to the most northerly point in Scotland, gave drivers the freedom to drive fast and hard. It was at a time and a place when you could. It was also a magical place.

Alfa Romeo flew me from London to Leeds, whereupon I boarded what looked like a flying shed. It touched down on a beach close to a castle, not far from the North Pole. A dark green Land Rover Defender completed the short commute. Greatness is achieved by attention to detail.

Ackergill Tower is on the beach and set in a 3,000-

acre estate. It is also a fabulous five-star hotel. The layout is to make guests feel like they are invitees to Scottish royalty rather than hotel guests. The few journalists invited were treated to a fabulous dinner in the great hall accompanied by great open fires at each end of the dining hall, and of course bagpipes, which I like. We were then invited to the late-night bar where there is another menu – not a food menu but a whisky menu, with hundreds of single malts and blends from which to choose. The single malts were fabulous. I tried just one, other journalists were more adventurous. I have never seen anything like Ackergill Tower before or since. The next morning on the Highland test route was amazing. Mission accomplished.

Few drivers make the jump from racing to rallying or vice versa. I was also reminded that I would never make that jump when, previously, I sat in the navigator's seat of a works Ford Escort driven on a forest rally stage by none other than the legendary and always sideways Roger Clark (1939–1998). He comforted me by saying, "As long as we are not looking out of the rear windscreen, we will be okay." My rallying deficiencies were further reinforced when works aces Malcolm Wilson and Gwyndaf Evans did the same thing with me in more modern Works Ford rally cars. Like motorbike racers, rally drivers don't have any of the "what if…?" gene that is loosely present in the brains of most racing drivers.

Another Scottish occurrence happened in August 1999. There was to be a total solar eclipse of the sun. The zone of totality was mid-English Channel, halfway between the Isle of Wight and the Normandy Coast. I was invited onto my friend 'Captain' Warwick Bergin's gentleman's motor yacht, Seafin. Warwick's boat – or ship as I call it – is an 80ft luxury vessel licenced for 40 guests. Built in 1960, it was once the property of the Profumo family. The Profumo affair was a major scandal in twentieth century UK politics. Look it up. Oh, if only boats had ears, eyes and could speak. I am sure I saw the ghosts of Christine Keeler and Mandy Rice-Davies below decks. We were bound for mid-Channel to

intersect the zone of totality. I love using the travel expression, 'bound for'; it implies risk. Arriving at mid-Channel, the sunny day switched to ghostly night as the sea turned bible black. There were five of us on board: The captain, his partner Judith Ellard, her friend Jane Watson, film director Helen Ostler, and me. In 1999, on board Seafin, I met Jane, a bright wee Scottish lass. I didn't realise it at the time, but over the next few years, this petite, astute and appealing individual was going to house-train me and change my life for the better. This was going to have an enormous effect on my personal circumstances, my work life and my sporting life.

17: Seafin. The 80-foot 1960 ex-Profumo gentleman's motor yacht.
18: Captain Warwick Bergin looking for ships. He also rode a 500hp motor cycle in Central London.
19: Doing what you do on a yacht.

MASERATI AND AN UNFORGETTABLE LAUNCH

When Maserati launched the 3200GT, it was the beginning of the marque becoming mainstream. We were invited on the press launch, sending me and photographer Michael Ward on a flight to Florence to pick up a yellow 6-speed manual version. This next bit could send me to prison, which is okay. As mentioned earlier, my private school education was perfect preparation for incarceration or torture. Allegations of a 175mph drive on public roads are hereby denied. Any photographic evidence will mean that we were in Germany to do that. Also, photos can be photoshopped, plus I might have had cramp in my right leg preventing it from coming off the accelerator pedal, or it wasn't me, or the driver was a look-a-like, or I made the whole thing up. Whose idea was it to write this behind-the-scenes book anyway?

Back in Italy, we drove to lovely Lucca to shake hands with the mayor. We traversed the Apennine Mountains to emerge on the coast at our base in Forte dei Marmi, which translates roughly as, Strong Marble. The mountain range behind the coastal towns is called the *Alpi Apuane,* Apuane Alps in English. This is where the world's best marble is mined. The renowned Carrara marble is named after the nearby town of Carrara. At our hotel in Forte dei Marmi, Maserati sent a vintage Fiat 626 bus to transport us to Carrara. These buses were built between 1939 and 1948. This was the bus of my earliest memories in Cetraro, in Southern Italy. My family was relatively wealthy and regularly commuting from the London to Calabria. The title *'Don'* was always used when addressing a male in the Giordanelli family. I learned the difference between the UK's and Italy's social class systems. Cetraro is on a rock overlooking the sea and the coast road. From the lofty town square, children could see the local bus approaching from miles away. This provided plenty of notice of it winding its way around the tight uphill turn that led onto the main street and up to Cetraro's Piazza del Popolo where it stopped. At the tight turn, when the bus slowed to a crawl, the

20: 265km/h on a Maserati 3200 GT high speed test drive.
21: On the way to Carrara to check out the marble.
22: The Automatic version was better than the early manual 3200.

little kids – me included – would run and clamber up the rear ladder that led to a roof rack, to hitch a lift along the main street. The thing I remember most vividly is that I was the only one wearing shoes. I digress… Back to 1999. Boarding the Maserati-supplied vintage Fiat bus was emotional. I always remember the window winders and their effortless action despite their high gearing – just one turn of the handle for full operation of the big windows – very clever. Proper design, and therefore created by an engineer, and not by a designer.

The bus takes us to the nearby marble mine in Carrara and points to a Tom-and-Jerry type hole in the marble mountains. Then a drive into the tunnel, hewn through solid rock, we travel deep, deep into the mountains, eventually arriving at a void of white marble as big as Westminster Abbey. This white cathedral, encased by billions of tonnes of marble, has been fitted with a full-size fashionable bar. We balance nibbles and aperitivi whilst trying to come to terms with our location. In Italy absolutely no one ever partakes of alcoholic drinks without a snack. Everyone is equipped with a Maserati cape because mountains can leak. This was quite the most dreamlike thing to ever happen on a car launch.

After an hour, we retreat to a workers' restaurant at the entrance to the mine. Italian restaurant culture is unlike that in the UK. Plastic chairs and tables, bright strip lights and football on the TV are a good sign. A menu translated into English or German is a bad sign. The best sign of all is a restaurant with no menu. Never judge an Italian restaurant in Italy by its appearance. Judge it by recommendation or by the number of locals present. It is all about the food, not the look.

MORE TESTS AND HOOLIGANISM

Back in the UK, and a twin test of a Lamborghini Espada vs a Ferrari 365GTC4 had the usual high quality action photography. Both were slightly sporty but sensible four-seaters. The magazine test published a photo of the Espada drifting. I liked that. It was great, inappropriate and therefore necessary. An Espada going sideways looks as ungainly as a power-sliding Rolls Royce.

FIA rules – to be quicker than the Ferrari. Time for a couple of naughty stories: it was in 1963 when it is alleged that I borrowed an E-Type Roadster from a car dealer who had left it at my mother's Rossi garage business. I was 15 years old at the time and returned the 150 mph E-Type unscathed and un-noticed, but I was now hooked on E-Types. At the time, most of the cars on UK's roads were old, slow, and crude. It is also alleged that from 14 years of age, I used to borrow my father's 4.2-litre Humber Supersnipe, fill it with school friends clad in striped uniforms and drive it on the A316 at 100mph, a speed just possible on the long downhill gradient towards Twickenham Rugby Stadium, given the usual prevailing south-westerly wind. The speed was perfectly legal in those days as there was no speed limit on that – now 40mph – road. The borrowed Humber was always returned in perfect condition, and my father never noticed.

Apologies again for the digression. Back to the 250GTO and Lightweight E-Type (one of 12). The team arrived at Terry Hoyle's workshop in Maldon, Essex, where the cars were waiting. A quick call to our insurers to cover the cars (£4 million for the GTO and £1 million for the E-Type). In today's money that would be GTO £7 million and E-Type £1.8 million. This shows the real investment as today a GTO is now £50m and the E-Type is £12 million.

23: Sideways in a Lamborghini Espada.

24: In the 1970s, it was compulsory for Andrew Dumont and RG to constantly race each other.

25: RG School boy driver aged 14, allegedly.

26: Father's 1954 Humber Supersnipe 4.2-litre.

27: Pricey pair. £12 million and £50 million.

28: £50 million GTO on a knife edge.

29: £12 million works lightweight E-Type.

30: Ferrari GTO at speed.

Looking at the feature today, the sight of an Espada cornering on full opposite lock was certainly not what Ferruccio Lamborghini had in mind. This reminded me of a previous adventure. Many years ago, I had two Rolls Royce Silver Shadows on long-term loan. My good friend, artist, sculptor and E-Type tearaway Andrew Dumont and I were constantly speeding about. We had a road race in the Rolls Royces. I have yet to see anything as inappropriate as a pair of synchronised drifting Silver Shadows.

Back to 1999, and I particularly liked the next twin test because it involved a Ferrari 250 GTO and its racing opponent, the Lightweight Jaguar E-Type. In period, the highly developed Ferrari beat the E-Types. However, today the E-Types have been developed – within the

A HILLCLIMB AND CHEESE

The Vernasca Silver Flag Hillclimb is a fabulous event. Thanks to Claudio Casali and his colleagues at CPAE – the local car club – the hillclimb has been revitalised. Since 1996, this 'Italian Goodwood' has been a huge success. *Auto Italia* was the first non-Italian publication to give the Silver Flag revival international publicity, helping to transform it to global recognition. Forget UK Hillclimbs with their short narrow runs, this is an 8.5km blast on closed public roads. It is not a competitive event. Drivers are free to go as fast or as slow as they please and take passengers if they choose. For drivers or spectators, the ambiance of the Vernasca Silver Flag in unique.

My first trip there was in 1996. Since then, I have driven at the event Tony Berni's *(Berni Motore)* Abarth 1000SP sports prototype, an Abarth 207A, an Alfa Romeo GTAm Turbo, an original Group 5 GTA, a Maserati Barchetta Corsa, a Lamborghini Miura SV and a Lotus 26R Works Elan.

The Panini family has the Hombre farm just outside Modena that produces the king of cheeses, namely parmesan. The family had previously made a fortune

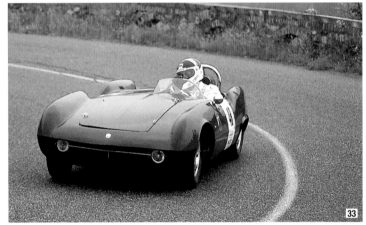

31 to 33: Driving Tony Berni's Abarth 207A at the Silver Flag hillclimb.
34: The Vernasca town square and a few of the 250 entrants' cars.
35: RG driving the 500hp Bertie at the Val Saviore Classic hillclimb.

36: Car-to-car photography of Drummond Bone's Maserati Barchetta from the Lotus 26R on the way down the hill at Silver Flag. Jane driving.

37: Andrew Brown getting the shot in the square at Vernasca, the top of the hill.

38 to 41: The ex-works Lotus being driven hard up the hill.

from books, comics, magazines, stickers, trading cards and other items through its collectibles and publishing subsidiaries. Oh yes, and it is the home of their museum housing the largest collection of rare Maseratis. Matteo Panini gave the *Auto Italia* crew a factory tour to see how the cheese is made. In 1996, thanks to two Italian astronauts, Parmigiano Reggiano became the first all-natural raw milk cheese to be launched into outer space. Later Parmigiano Reggiano was adopted as an official space food, valued for the bone-strengthening calcium, high protein, low fat and other nutrients, it contributes to astronauts' diets. Back on Earth, the Modena Cheese Police regularly visit parmesan factories to check on things, and I duly wrote a cheese story.

HORACIO AND HIS CARS

The Pagani Zonda looked like nothing else. It was the brainchild of the Argentinian Horacio Pagani. I visited the factory a couple of times and chatted with this agreeable engineer and designer. We went through the fine details of the structure and the torsional rigidity figures as well as the huge amount of development in the wind tunnel. Just as in Formula One today, he pointed out how a small change at the front affected the rear, and how a tiny scallop on the lower rear quarter made such a difference. I got on well with Signor Pagani, so much so that he let me into a secret regarding the carbon-fibre and steel tubing used in the roof structure of the early Zondas. One of the highest quality steel tubing, when considering the weight/strength ratio, is Reynolds 531. He said that it would be better to keep this a secret because non-engineers would say that the Zonda is made from recycled bicycle frames. They would not understand that a component introduced in 1935 and used for cycle racing could be utilised in a car – so, don't tell any non-engineers. I test drove some Paganis in Europe and in the UK. On one test, I had cramp in my right leg again as I couldn't get it off the accelerator and quickly reached 180mph. Obviously, this must

42: A blower Bentley powering up the 8km hill.
43: Auto Italia's Simon Park with TV presenter Francesco Da Mosta.
44: The king of cheeses. Parmigiano at the Panini farm 'Hombre'.
45: A trio of Zondas outside the factory.
46: Horacio Pagani and RG discussing aero and steel tubes.
47 and 48: Zonda on test.

have happened in Germany. Oh..., what would we do without the Germans?

ITALIANS, WW1, AND A BIKE RACE

I was now flying regularly to Italy to gather features for the magazine. Being there on business is different from going on a holiday where your main connections are with people in the hospitality industry who are familiar with the strange ways of foreigners, like having a cappuccino after 11am. In Italy, a cappuccino is a breakfast thing, like a breakfast cereal in the UK. Rounding off your dinner in Italy with a cappuccino would be like ordering a bowl of cornflakes with which to finish your evening dinner in the UK. You can attend courses on how to do business with foreigners. Things like – when seated with Arabs, never show the sole of your shoe. Things like *feng shui* and loss of face when dealing with the Chinese. Business with Italians requires an apprenticeship. You must meet a few times, have several lunches and dinners, and eventually be able to speak informally. Only then will future arrangements mean anything. Even then, *"si"* may not necessarily mean yes. Urgency is a northern European trait. I love this quote by an Italian prime minister: "No problem is so great, that it will disappear by itself, given the passage of time."

One of *Auto Italia's* rigorous automotive and industrial itineraries included a trip to a city with flooded streets – Venice. Anyone with a soul should see Venice, preferably in the quiet season, if there is such a thing. Situated on islands you either cross a long road and rail bridge or sail across the lagoon in a boat. We chose the worst way to arrive by car. At the Venice end of the bridge is a grid-locked roundabout and two multi-storey car parks. The big city's tiny population (70,000) is swamped by the millions of visitors who pour in. We did all the standard tourist things you do in Venice, i.e. clutter the stunning city without spending any money.

Next stop the lovely town of Bassano at the foot of the Alps. It has a beautiful wooden Alpine bridge with well-preserved bullet holes, complete with an explanatory

plaque, blaming the beastly French or the equally beastly Austrians, who fought here in WW1. Just up the road is the very well-stocked Bonfanti motor museum.

Pedal to the metal, the multi-talented Multipla munches the miles to Modena. What looks like a black and yellow Ferrari 360 Modena quickly fills the rear-view mirror. On 'Prova' plates, the black paint turns out to be the corpses of a billion flies. With a tail wind, we touched 195kmh (122mph), allegedly. Without the clear signage in the UK, it takes some time to realise that you are driving the wrong way down an Italian one-way street. Totally unperturbed, oncoming cars will make room for you and help you, where in the UK exactly the opposite happens.

Just outside Modena is Maranello where we intend to visit the Ferrari museum, Galleria Ferrari. As we get close, our way is blocked by traffic. In fact, all roads are blocked because the Giro d'Italia bike race is passing through. The Giro d'Italia makes the Tour de France look like a walk in the park. Anyone interested in continental cycling must read the book *Gironimo* by Tim Moore. Police cars race through the town, police motorbikes too. Some of the speeding police riders standing up on their motorbike pegs to get a better view. Then a gap. We see low-flying helicopters approaching. As the roof-skimming, camera-laden whirlybirds get close, so we see a fast-approaching wall of colour. The bikes tear the air as they hiss through the town. Two or three camera motorbikes weave amongst them. Behind that, a 40mph sea of heavily logoed new Fiats with hundreds of spare bikes on their roofs. An array of more support vehicles brings up the rear, then as quickly as it happened, it passed. All is quiet. Locals release the plastic tape. It flutters to the ground, and within seconds all is normal. We visit the Galleria Ferrari; like everything that Ferrari does these days, it is unashamedly slick.

Less slick but nice and friendly is the private museum of the Stanguellini family. Open by appointment only, Francesca Stanguellini, granddaughter of the founder, showed us round the little museum at the rear of their Fiat dealership just outside Modena Central.

Stanguellini registered the first vehicle to drive on the Modenese roads. MO 1 resides in fine condition in the museum over 100 years later. In central Modena, the once greenfield Maserati factory has been surrounded by the city. We are shown the new production line of 3200GTs and are given a Quattroporte Evoluzione with which to go away and play.

With the weekend approaching, we drive down past Piacenza for the Silver Flag Hillclimb. We book into the Hotel Arda and go out to eat in a transport cafe full of lorry drivers. There is no menu, which means the food will be authentic. It is superb and the bill is tiny. Unlike the UK, in Italy all socio-economic classes eat the same huge variety of dishes prepared from healthy, basic, raw materials. Italians are blessed with longevity for a reason. Looking fit is essential. Your appearance is more important than your health, luckily the two tend to go together. Italians also have the world's lowest birthrate, statistics which contradict the stereotype. However, Italy's diminishing indigenous population is a disturbing demographic.

We dash to Turin to meet a man with a fine collection of Formula One cars. He eyes us with caution, convinced we are criminals, under-cover police or tax inspectors. He then softens. Our apprenticeship starts with a sumptuous dinner. The waiters and chef come

49: The 'new' Ponte Vecchio at Bassano del Grappa.
50: Bullet holes on the buildings remain visible, evidence of the fierce fighting in WW1.
51 to 53: RG acting with the F1 Minardi-Subaru.

out to discuss a recent Grand Prix. They talk about tyre and track temperatures and grip decay of different tyre compounds. Next morning, with our apprenticeship completed, we are given a rare F1 Minardi-Subaru 3.5-litre flat-12 to feature. We take it to a nearby racecourse (a horse racecourse that is) and take pictures. I write a feature on the Minardi-Subaru without having the opportunity to drive it. Then, two hours the wrong side of Turin we meet another man with the largest collection of works Lancia rally cars. The anoraks in our team discuss chassis numbers.

2000
A Mad Test and Wales

After a few routine tests, along comes one of those extraordinary twin tests. The special twin test was at the old Transport Research Laboratory in Crowthorne, that has now become a new housing estate. No doubt the same fate will happen to the BBC Top Gear track and airfield at Dunsfold. On this day at Crowthorne, we had a Ferrari F40 pitched against a Ducati 996 SPS Carl Fogarty replica. The magazine regularly included motorbike tests, courtesy of motorcycle expert Alan Cathcart. While I have ridden thousands of miles on several motorbikes and motor scooters, I am no expert. With the help of pro bike tester and racer Bruce Dunn on hand for the serious biker stuff, the action started. I suggested we shoot the F40 drifting sideways alongside the Ducati doing a wheelie.

The *Auto Italia* team is a happy one, with regular jibes and mickey-taking banter. The photo exists somewhere but I taunt the editor that he is photo-fussy. As mentioned before, he will always publish a pin-sharp routine chocolate box photo rather than a less than perfectly composed dramatic shot, like a sideways tyre smoking F40, millimetres away from a race bike on its back wheel. I tease him that he also sees the words in the magazine as something annoying that get in the way of the pictures. I suggested printing grey shading between the photos to save the cost and time with writing any words. He thought that was a great idea. I also repeated my proposal that the photos in a story

1: Biker RG.
2: Bruce Dunn in action.
3: Power-sliding the Maserati Barchetta.
4: Risky business: F40 on power, Ducati on one wheel.

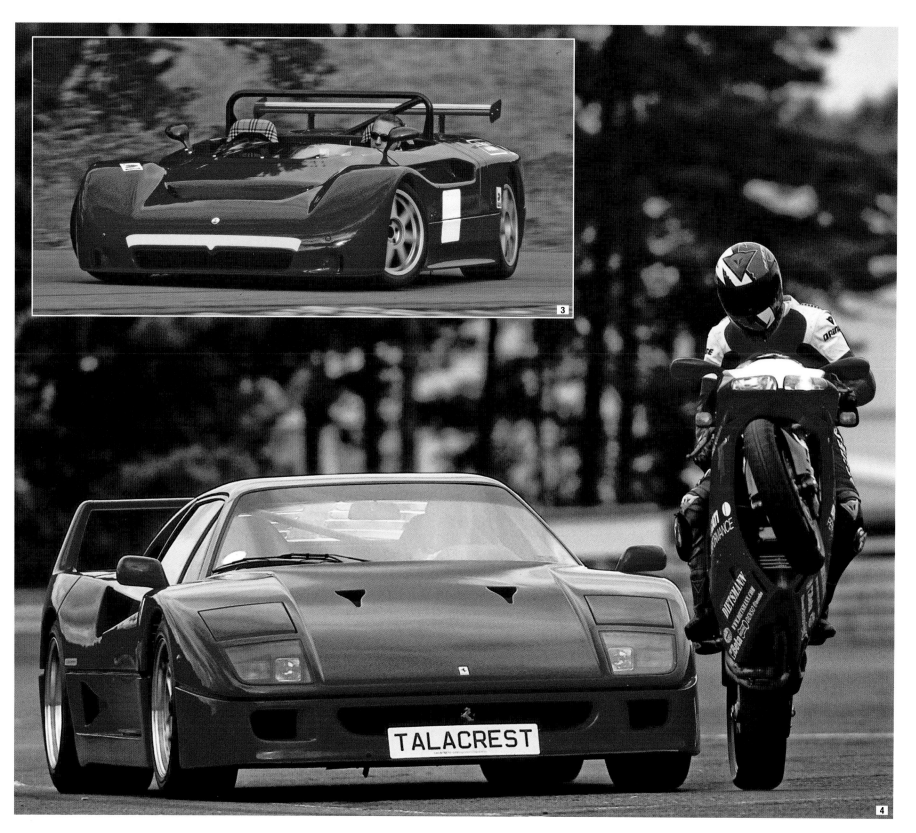

should have a connection with the words. He thought this to be a silly idea. The original manuscript for this book contained 135,000 words. For commercial reasons I had to reduce it to about 85,000 words. When challenged, Phil always finished discussions with, "Stick to the driving Roberto." Don't tell anyone, but he was right about the 85,000-word limit.

The test track surface at Crowthorne was ridiculously abrasive and quickly tore the rubber from the F40's fat wheels. Bruce Dunn did his acrobatic stuff with the Ducati, after which I took it for a road test. A photo was published that received some complaints because I was riding the Ducati without wearing biker gear. I have been driving racing cars since 1966 and never hurt myself. Had this been a lifetime of motorcycle racing, this would not be the case. The younger you are, the more risks you take, and the more you have to lose.

It is always a pleasure to drive a turbo car, be it for testing or racing. When the call came that Drummond Bone's Maserati Barchetta Corsa was at our test track,

I was there in a flash. Like Carlo Facetti's car described in 1993, this is one of 17 cars made in the early 1990s by Maserati when it was in the hands of De Tomaso. The one-make European race series ran in 1992/3. Drummond raced this rare machine competitively in the *Auto Italia* Championship as well being a quick regular with it at Italian Hillclimbs. It was at a pre-Italian hillclimb jovial dinner when my future wife, Jane, and I first met Drummond and his friend the late Angus McLean. Three Scots and me, it was a riotous Scottish evening that set a permanent bond.

I once wrote a column about the world's countries, listing them in order of likeability. I needed a country to be bottom of the list, a *bête noire*, and I knew that I had pushed the envelope too far. For mistaken political correctness and to avoid more death threats, I needed a soft target and chose Wales, even though I quite like Wales and the Welsh. In Snowdonia during the 1970s I had some adventurous summer climbs logging the remains of crashed military aircraft. On a freezing mid-

5 and 6: Silver Flag regular Sir Drummond Bone with passengers in his Maserati Barchetta.
7: Mountain climber RG.

8: In 2000, a 'they cost the same' feature.

9: The ill-fated Brian Brown straps me into the Nanchang CJ-6 'Chinese Spitfire'.

10: Best that the CAA don't see what we did.

winter climb, in deep snow, my friend Andrew Dumont and I reached the summit of Snowdon via the steepest route, in a blizzard, on the shortest day, with near zero visibility, only to find a small group of distressed climbers at the summit. One had a broken leg, another had died, and night-time was not far away. These were pre-mobile phone days, so you are on your own, boyo. Anyway, we survived, and I had great times in Wales.

Replying to a complaint from an irate Welshman about denigrating his country by me saying, "It was only a joke", is like a Nazi using the "I was only obeying orders", excuse at Nuremberg in 1945. I also received a death threat when I criticised hunters in Southern Italy for shooting rare birds on their north-south migration route. The complaints taught me to moderate my writing. For 20 years, I also had a regular column in a Dubai-based weekly car magazine. I was their European correspondent and had never been to the Middle East or to any Islamic country. Envelopes were pushed appropriately because I never received a fatwa.

A CHINESE SPITFIRE AND DEATH

Time for another highlight. This was a comparison test between a Chinese machine vs an Italian with a difference. In the year 2000, for the same outlay, about £80,000 (£136,000 in today's money), you could have either a Chinese war bird, namely a Nanchang CJ-6, or a Ferrari 275GTS. Only one way to decide and that is to give both a good thrashing. The pilot, of what I called the 'Chinese Spitfire', was Brian Brown who had massive experience, flying since 1979. The Nanchang is a copy of the 1940 Russian Yak-18. The test was at an airfield in Yorkshire: we stayed overnight in a hotel. In the morning, knowing that it would be a busy day and that we may skip lunch, I had a full English breakfast. Upon arrival at the airfield, pilot Brown unexpectedly suggested that he took me aloft for some aerobatics. The Nanchang is rated at 6G for positive, or 3G for negative-G manoeuvres. No way was I going to miss such an opportunity, so me and my recent fry-up strapped in for some aerobatics. We performed all kinds

of crazy airborne manoeuvres. It was great and I kept my breakfast. Check out the photo of the aircraft flying just above Andrew Cooper's speeding Ferrari. While this was a highlight test for me, it was also a poignant one and a reminder of the risks that we took. Sadly, sometime later pilot Brian Brown died when his Hawker Hurricane crashed at the Shoreham Air Show.

TWO FERRARIS AND A CAR WITH NO STEERING WHEEL

Two Ferrari 275GTBs were next at the test track: a road car and a racer. The race car was an ex-NART, while the road car was the property of Geoff Williams. While the 275GTB saw some upgrades to 4-cam engines (275GTB/4) and *Competizione* aluminium bodies (275GTB/C), the best thing about the car is its looks. At one of *Auto Italia's* track days, I had the race version to demonstrate and for giving readers hot rides. This is 1960s styling at its best. Later, I tested another 275GTB/C at the Nürburgring Nordschleife. Today, their values are measured in £millions depending on spec, model and history. In the early 1970s, a tired-looking 275GTB went through the Brentford car auctions. It sold for £800 (£12,600 in today's money).

A silly comparison test pitched a Lancia Delta integrale against a Caterham Superlight R. The

11: Ferrari 275GTB/C at the Nordschleife.
12: Noisy NART Ferrari 275GTB/C. At speed, trees approaching.
13: Untethered snapper, and no steering wheel.
14: Caterham Superlight R. Easy car to drift.
15: 'Envirorally' founder Robert Clarke with RG and Clara.

Caterham made the integrale feel like a Rolls Royce. If you are a closet biker but don't fancy broken bones or death, then a Caterham Superlight R may be right up your street. This Caterham was up my street only because it was in my driveway, as I had it on loan for a few days. For some years, many photos were courtesy of pro snapper Andrew Brown. At the test track, Andrew perched himself untethered high on the rear deck of the Caterham to get some wide-angle, high-speed shots that included the driver, the speedometer and the track ahead. This required me to build up speed with near-zero-G to keep Andrew aboard. Once up to speed, any input to steering, brakes or throttle would send the photographer, who was kneeling or standing on the rear deck, flying. The Caterham Superlight R is fitted with a quick-release steering wheel. Naturally, I thought it would make an anarchic shot if I removed the wheel at high speed and held it aloft, the speedo needle would confirm our velocity. The shot was taken – albeit blurred due to panic – but I could not refit the steering wheel. Any braking would have killed the photographer, and the speeding car was getting ever closer to the trees at the edge of the track. At the very last moment, the steering wheel clicked back into place. A miniscule application of

steering angle saved the day as the car eventually came to a gentle stop. Andrew was a good action photographer but was sometimes late supplying the images, which irritated the editorial team. Does anyone know why artistic people and deadlines are sometimes mismatched?

GREEN THINGS

In the year 2000, I visited the Fiat Pomigliano d'Arco factory in Naples to test and write a story on several hybrid eco cars. The model chosen was the Multipla as it had plenty of room under the flat floor for all the eco gubbins. There were four versions: Electra Power, Blupower, Bipower and Hybrid Power. The writing was on the wall for internal combustion engine (ICE). I wrote the story, but in the back of my mind, I questioned Fiat's gargantuan effort. While the engineer inside me was interested, I couldn't get excited and wondered how much this research was costing. The point is that Fiat was experimenting with many alternative power options. The company was thinking and working at least 20 years into the future. That means that right now, Fiat is thinking and testing vehicles for 2042 onwards. Today, the talk is of all-electric cars. The ICE is history. However, while the EVs are already here, a global and green charging infrastructure from renewable energy is something that is far into the future.

In 2021, I drove some brand-new electric cars and some electrified classics at Dunsfold for a new motorsport venture named *Envirorally*. I accept that some classics will be electrified: hopefully only a few common models that were mass-produced in vast numbers. If you electrify a classic, you won't go to heaven. Electric motorsport is growing, and *Envirorally* is in a growth industry.

A warning for hooligans and drifters: rear-wheel drive electric cars are challenging to power-slide. A combination of lateral-G and torque causes a car's rear end to step out. With an ICE engine, this can be balanced with the correct amount of throttle opening (i.e. torque) and the right amount of lateral-G (steering angle). You may be aware that – unlike a petrol or diesel car – an electric car delivers massive torque instantly. This make balancing a slide with an electric car unusually difficult. The electric motor, or hydrogen power will eventually replace the fossil fuel engine. Perhaps the word 'replace' should have been revert. In the 1890s, electric cars were popular. However, the classic car with its ICE will survive indefinitely. Some may even have better investment potential than previously.

THE ICE MAN AND NO CARS

The team was now hunting for stories across Europe as Italian car specialists and collectors are global. We assemble at an overcrowded Stansted Airport and I am reminded of the words of the writer Anthony Price, "The Devil himself probably redesigned Hell in the light of information he had gained from observing airport layouts." For this story, Italy and mostly Austria were our targets. A visit to MS Design who make fibreglass body kits satisfied the automotive feature. I also included a few snippets of Austrian history but there was another story about a 5,300-year-old dead body that I found to be far more interesting than plastic bodykits. This is where I go very much off-piste.

In 3,250 BC (i.e. 5,300 years ago), a man was killed. Shot with an arrow and found on top of the Ötztal mountains at an altitude of 3,210m (10,530ft). The circumstances suggest that he was being chased before perishing. In 1991, his body was found perfectly preserved in ice by two German climbers. The ice was beginning to melt. The dead man was given the name Ötzi from its location. Deciding which mountain police Force should be called was a problem as the location was on the Austrian-Italian border. This border – like many mountaintop borders – is delineated by the water divide. If rainwater flows towards Austria, then this is Austrian territory. If it flows towards Italy, then you are in Italy. Politics and war also confused the issue because this border crept southwards as the Austrians (with German help) fancied the southern slopes and – no doubt – eventually a port on the Mediterranean. In

World War One's southern front, where Italian troops fought the Austria-Hungarian Empire, there were 4.5million deaths and casualties, after which, the border was reinstated at the water divide. Anyway, it turned out that Ötzi was 100m inside Italy. He would eventually go on display in the South Tyrol Museum of Archaeology in Bolzano, Italy. Before this, Ötzi went to the museum at

16 and 17: Murdered 5,300 years ago, the ice man found behind the car shop.
18: Rapallo Riviera tyre test.

the University of Innsbruck in Austria where he had a comprehensive examination and a life-like statue made, which is also on display. The examination uncovered a detailed story of Ötzi's lifestyle, his diet, his last two meals, his health, age, weight, height, looks, genetic analysis, blood tests, clothing, tools, his murder and so much more... They also examined the pollen content in Ötzi's gut to reconstruct his route. The study had concluded that in his last 33 hours, Ötzi had travelled from low-lying areas with warmth-loving trees, to high-altitude zones, 3,000 meters high. He possessed 61 tattoos, and this is the earliest known record of body art. He was also receiving acupuncture treatment for his ailments over 2,000 years before any acupuncture history in China. Research suggests that modern man arrived about 300,000 years ago, making a 5,300-year-old Ötzi much like one of us. Oh, for a time machine...

ITALIAN RIVIERA, SOME BADGES AND DESIGN

A trip to test some Italian tyres by Marangoni took place near Rapallo on Italy's Eastern Riviera. I was given two cars appropriately shod. Winding around the picturesque coastal roads with blue sea on one side and beautiful mountains on the other was not easy. The views are stunning, and the road is bendy. This is singer-songwriter Jay Kay's favourite road. Touring the areas of Portofino, Santa Margherita, Rapallo, Genoa (the home of Christopher Columbus) and Lerici (where Percy Shelley drowned) takes your mind off the tyre-testing job. When your hosts then base you in a five-star hotel, you can't help liking their products. More bribery arrived in the form of a lightweight rain jacket that I still wear 20-odd years later. What more proof can there be that the company's industrial activities are praiseworthy?

With the Riviera job done, we had an Alfa Romeo Sportwagon at our disposal to motor down to Modena to visit the American Bruce Qvale, who did a deal with the shrewd Alejandro de Tomaso to build a new Mangusta. We toured the new factory and then Qvale took us into his office. We chatted and he then produced a big sack containing hundreds of new De Tomaso badges, saying that they were useless. While the crafty Signor de Tomaso sold the Mangusta rights to Qvale, he cleverly masked and withheld the rights to use the De Tomaso badge. Without that household name, Qvale's new Mangustas – although fine sports cars – were dead in the water. Poor chap, tucked up like a kipper: to use a favourite old London expression.

Back on the road in our press Alfa Sportwagon, I rant about the window switches. For years, these were fitted to many Alfa Romeo and Fiat models. Lift the switch upwards to motor the glass down, and vice versa. How does such design idiocy happen? Does this designer still have a job? Does the person who signed-off the appalling window control still have a job?

A DINO AND A STORY

At the test track, and a Ferrari 246GT Dino is waiting for me. Okay, I know..., pedants will point out that a 246GT is a Dino. It is not a Ferrari. Enzo named the Dino after his son who died aged 24 from muscular dystrophy. In the 1980s, my friend and Mustang racer Terry Sullivan had to abandon the restoration of his 246GT, so I got the job. When you restore a car, you have a different relationship with it compared with one that you just drive. In 2000, my father-in-law-to-be John Watson – knowing

19: Qvale Mangusta V8 Modena road test.
20: Father-in-law-to-be John Watson with his Lotus Eleven in Scotland.

my work – confessed a secret to me. He was a proud Scot and sportscar enthusiast, sailor and light aircraft pilot. Who else would buy a brand-new Lotus Eleven racing car to drive on the road? Back to John's secret, he was ashamed that he had destroyed his brand-new Dino 246GT. It was one of the first new Ferraris in Scotland. In the late 1960s, on a freezing cold day, the A78 gave little grip, John's high-speed crash saw the end of that 246GT. He told me that the insurance paid him, but he was left feeling mortified. He showed me all he had left, which was the leather wallet containing the factory booklets and documents. "Leave it with me," said I, thinking that the insurers may have sold the wreck on to a restorer. I contacted that fine chap Peter Everingham of the Ferrari Owners Club and bingo! The car was indeed restored and living in Australia. The new owner was contacted, and the leather wallet (worth thousands of pounds to the new owner) was despatched free of charge. John told me that it was like a weight being lifted from his shoulders. His guilt was gone. The car lived on complete with its original paperwork and history.

THE PRINCE OF WALES AND SOME LAWYERS

Time for a topless England vs Italy contest at the test track: Aston Martin DB6 Volante vs a Ferrari 275GTS. A fine British brand against the nearest thing Italy has to royalty, namely Ferrari. The Italian royal got the vote. No bias here. The Ferrari was simply superior at everything. It also looked better. Chopping the top off an already ponderous-looking DB6 ruined the neat styling of the DB4 and DB5. You would have to be HRH the Prince of Wales to prefer the DB6 Volante. However, in this case, HRH would not look right in a Ferrari, so His Highness is excused.

Three more stunning racing cars were next at the test track: two Ferrari P4s and a Chevrolet V8-powered Can-Am Spyder. However, all was not what it seemed, as these were all replica kit cars available from NF Auto Developments. To copy is certainly to flatter. As previously mentioned, where major manufacturers

were once unperturbed by replica car builders, they now unleash their lawyers to stamp them out. Today, everything is much stricter. At least the UK still clings to some diminishing automotive freedom. In Italy and certain other countries, any modification to any car, or indeed any replica, can expect it to be sequestrated and crushed.

21: Dino 246GT and Alfa TZ restorations at Rossi Engineering. My father and Colin Earl behind the Dino. Dave Hood with the TZ.
22: Ferrari vs Aston Martin test.

TUSCANY, A DUEL AND A PRIEST

A tour of Tuscany next in a new Alfa Romeo 166. I sped past the little Tuscan town of Vinci, the birthplace of the world's cleverest man. If I had a time machine and were allowed to visit just one person in history, it would have to be him. From infants, we are brainwashed and guided to either the arts or the sciences. Nobody can be artistic and technical. Leonardo ignored this by utilising both sides of his cerebral hemispheres. Apart from using my time machine to visit Leonardo, I would bring him forward to the present day. A bar in Florence would settle him in nicely, followed by a world tour. I would then ask him to design things that we would use in another 400 years' time – in the year 2525, if man is still alive.

Further in Tuscany, I arrived at captivating Cortona (Italy's oldest city) close to the Tuscan/Umbrian border. In the UK, motorway tailgating annoys the man in front. In Italy not tailgating the man in front of you, annoys the man behind you. Eager to get to my hosts waiting poolside at a secluded Tuscan villa, I pressed on. Again, one of the guests included Jane Watson whom I had previously met on the ex-John Profumo motor yacht, Seafin. Jane lived in Kensington and enjoyed fell-running in her Scottish homeland. She is also a good sailor and, like her father, she is a motor racing enthusiast. Little did she know that in a few weeks' time she would be my pit crew at Spa.

23: Jane at Spa.
24: Before we had electric maps we had paper maps

Tuscany has been a magnet for well-mannered Brits for centuries. Back in the days of 'the grand tour' it was the same – Byron, Keats and anyone who was anyone did Tuscany. In a way, there are two Tuscanys. There is Tuscany (8,900 sq. miles) and then the region immediately to the south. This equally attractive region is called Umbria (3,300 sq. miles) and it has been discovered. Way before the Roman Empire, the Etruscans had a fine civilisation and lifestyle here. They respected women. Women owned property and were treated as equals. The Etruscans didn't like fighting, so they used to hire mercenary armies to do the killing. The unreliability of this system eventually played a role in their demise, although their civilisation lasted 700 years. Until relatively recently, Italy was comprised of separate states. In 1861, at the time of Italy's unification, only 2.5% of the population spoke the language we now call Italian. The Tuscan dialect was chosen as standard Italian. The Umbrian university city of Perugia is a perfect place for a language course. The hilltop city centre – like so many – is refreshingly pedestrianised and civilised. There is a car park lower down the hill with an escalator that takes you through the restored underground Etruscan city before finally popping up in the main street – Corso Vannucci. Then, there is the Umbrian/Etruscan town of Orvieto with its massive double helix staircase down a huge well 54m (177ft) deep. There is Orvieto's brilliant gold mosaic facade to its cathedral. Siena has its pleasingly crazy 'no rules' Palio horse races around the main square, Piazza del Campo. The Palio is to horse racing what Motorhead is to a string quartet. The winning rider is a hero, and the crowd carries him aloft. The rider who comes second is the scoundrel. He could have won but didn't. The crowd beats him up as punishment. Whenever I come second in a motor race, I always think of the Palio.

San Gemignano, Gubbio, Todi, Cortona, Assisi, Florence... the list is endless. If all this sounds a bit 'born again', then so be it. After all, the word Renaissance translates as born again. Leonardo was right in the thick of the world's greatest cultural revolution. Michelangelo, a fellow Tuscan – and a young rival – was there too. In Samuel Johnson's words, "A man who has not been to Italy is always conscious of an inferiority." Economically, Italy is eighth in the world's GDP table of 213 countries. This is surprising considering the huge black economy and the ungovernable South. As a comparison, the UK ranks sixth. My Tuscany trip was rounded off by giving Jane a lift in the Alfa from Tuscany to Turin Airport, although first via a couple of days on the Italian Riviera, for more travel story information.

Back in the UK. I arrive at the Surrey test track to be greeted by the sight of a Ferrari 250SWB. This was another Talacrest car. I described it as a rorty chuck-it-about kind of 1960s hot rod with a beautiful face and an eager heart. Once upon a time this 250SWB was a 250GTE. Its chassis was duly shortened and a new alloy body fitted. It would take an expert of miraculous genius to spot the difference. There is no subterfuge here, its history is transparent, and the chassis number tells the tale. I notice that while the £50 million 250GTO is the crowd puller, the £8 million 250SWB is perhaps a

25: This fake Ferrari 250SWB 'hot rod' was track tested by RG at Chobham. The imposter was exposed when the real one turned up.

26 to 28: Ferrari 360 Spider with a sociable Italian priest encountered during a road test in the hills above Maranello.

more gallant choice. A bit like the Spitfire and the Hurricane. The big-ticket Supermarine Spitfire attracts a crowd like a 250GTO, while the Hawker Hurricane is like a 250SWB and is appreciated by the aficionados. This reminds me, but don't tell anyone. In 1941, my father (aged 19) had a duel with a Hurricane in the Desert War. The Hurricane shot up his army truck. Two men killed and my father slightly injured. The pilot made a rare mistake in having a second attack, thereby losing the surprise element. Dad figured that the pilot must have been like him, i.e. young and inexperienced. On the Hurricane's second strafing attack, my father emptied his last magazine of a machine gun at the low-flying Hurricane as its cannon shells threw up the sand. Unexpectedly, the aircraft was hit, probably on its oil or coolant system. It made off into the distance trailing smoke. My father – a law student and lieutenant in WW2 – related to me why two educated teenagers who could easily be friends should engage in such a duel. As with many war veterans, it was not easy prising war stories from my father.

No duelling today as our team enter the portals of the Ferrari factory in Maranello to pick up a 360 Spider. We head up into the hills for a photo location. I find a roadside churchyard. All is quiet. I park. We start taking

pictures. An old Italian priest clad in black robes emerges from the church. We expect a bollocking, but this is a Ferrari in Italy. *"Ah bella machina,"* says the priest. *"Sono venuti qui dieci anni fa – gli americani.* ("They came here ten years ago – the Americans). *"Aspetta ti faccio vedere"* (wait I shall show you). He scurries back into the church to emerge wearing a red Ferrari cap and carrying an old American magazine. He then sits in the 360 Spider. Only in Italy, we thought. "I am 92 years old. It was easier to get in and out ten years ago," he recollects. With our photo shoot completed, he invites me to partake of his home-made liqueur. This is a common activity in Italy because shops sell bottles of 100% alcohol so that you can turn fruit or veg waste into liqueur. The priest's liqueur is cloudy, strong, sweet and most agreeable. Thankfully, Italy is free of puritanism, which was nicely defined by the critic H. L. Mencken (1880–1956). "Puritanism, the haunting fear that someone somewhere may be happy." The priest was born in 1908 so he will now be supping his hooch with his god. When my time comes to access those pearly gates, it will be convenient to have this ecclesiastical contact on the inside. For anyone who doesn't have someone inside the gates, be sure to take a cordless angle grinder with you.

2001
Change and Two Zondas

In 2001, I closed my car business department of Rossi Engineering. It was involved with classics, exotics, racing cars and an amazing Amphicar in which Anthony Bisiker (ex-Mungo Jerry Band) and I explored some of the River Thames in Twickenham, Richmond, and Sunbury-on-Thames. After 23 years, the closure of Rossi Engineering came as a relief. Financially, the company washed its face but was never going to make money. However, I knew that I could not rely on writing income, so I qualified as an ARDS race instructor. As previously mentioned, I was accepted as an expert witness by the Law Society regarding classic car and racing car issues. I signed up for the legal work, partly to carry on with my paternal family's history in jurisprudence. It paid well, and I had some successful cases. I never really enjoyed the work so gradually abandoned it. I may pick it up again one day. Who knows…? My greatest enjoyment will always be with workshop tasks. I love working with my hands. Workshop tasks are also good exercise for the brain. In a tenuous way, hands and brain are also employed when writing on a laptop, although they say that a sedentary job is worse for your health than smoking. How authors of old managed to write eloquently with only quill and parchment, I have no idea.

Twenty minutes from my workshop is the Chobham test track. Two Pagani Zondas were ready to test. "Why two?" I hear you ask. If the 6-litre car with its 0-60mph in 4.1 seconds is too slow, there was a 7-litre car available, which will save you 0.4 seconds for a 3.7 second rubber-burning dash. Pagani went on to make 16 versions of the Zonda before marketing the new Huayra, which currently boasts ten versions. Allegedly, and I dare not say where, I once drove a Zonda at 180-mph — well below its top speed — and it was as steady as a rock.

TURIN, MUSHROOMS AND DEATH
Off to Italy again… Imagine the scene, four of the team are in Turin, in the Ristorante Bastian Contrario, on a hillside overlooking Turin. On a long self-service table, there are 69 different dishes for the *antipasto* (the starter course). The restaurant owner told me not to choose from 69 starters, but to try all 69 starter dishes. One of our team, unaccustomed to foreign muck, was not impressed. He reckoned only 62 of them were any good. Next, a pasta course, followed by a second pasta course, each one served from an entire hollowed out parmesan cheese round. After that came various meat and fish dishes with fresh vegies. Desserts and cheeses followed with various wines and finally the whole thing was rounded off with espresso, grappa and other *digestivi*. It was also a custom to hand around the table a large covered wooden bowl with several stubby outlets. The number of outlets matched the number of people at the table. Inside the bowl was a hot alcoholic liqueur that took your breath away. Just as in the UK, a bottle of port is passed around a table in the correct direction, and without rest, so the wooden bowl did the same. Food also enthralled the conversation. Discussions from Italian foodies as to how an altitude change of 50m will affect the quality of *Parmigiano* cheese were thoroughly considered. Fiction tells us that the ancient Romans used a vomitorium for those special

1: Zondas at the test track.
2: Rossi Engineering's restored DB4, 5 & 6. Just before the 1988 market downturn.
3: Rossi Engineering's Colin Earl (Mungo Jerry Band co-founder), Anthony Bisiker (band member) & RG with two restored Alfa SS coupes.
4: Restored Abarth 2200 Allemano Spider. RG, Bisiker, Earl & Ben Dorling.
5: Rossi Engineering sea trials on the Thames at Twickenham. Anthony Bisiker at the helm.
6: When they were young: Anthony Bisiker, Jonathan Patrick & RG.
7: 40 years later. Same guys. Same shed. Same watering can, and still with an E-Type Jaguar.

evenings. Apparently, to get things moving, they also used to carry a bird's feather to tickle the back of the throat. I am sorry but research by my son Dino finds these stories to be false.

Our budget airline jet flew us to Turin for less than the Stansted car park charge. One of our ports-of-call was once Turin's first international airport, now a flying club HQ and test track. Owned by Fiat, the Aeritalia airfield was also used regularly by Abarth for testing. For some years, this Italian test track was our second home. A retired local puts out some cones. Nobody pays him. He does it for the mushrooms. He comes and goes at any time. He tells me that he knows where and when the best mushrooms appear, and that he keeps the information secret. He tells me that he doesn't just pick a mushroom but cuts it off, just above ground level, ensuring that it will regrow. While mainland Europeans gather wild mushrooms, the British – me included on this subject — with their wild fungi phobia, go for bland supermarket mushrooms. The mushroom picker told me about truffle hunting with either a trained dog or pig. He said the dog is better because if a pig finds a truffle, you have a fight on your hands to wrestle truffle from pig. As any Italian will tell you, the French know absolutely nothing about food or wine. We rubbished French truffles and noted the superiority of Italian truffles that cost £2,000 per kilo (in 2001).

On the Aeritalia track, we are doing brake tests with an Alfa Romeo 156 fitted with countless sensors. Then an array of standard and after-market brake discs and pads were fitted. I flog around the track getting up to exactly 120km/h and then stamp on the brake pedal. Then repeat and repeat all day. G-readings and pedal pressure come up with some results. Conclusion, it was difficult to beat the original braking efficiency.

Suddenly the unmistakable approaching sound of a competition car spins our heads. A 1970s Fiat 131 Abarth rally car arrives, spins its wheels and slides about from grass to tarmac. The driver is a well-known ex-Abarth engineer and rally driver who has an Aladdin's cave of Abarth cars and parts at his home

9 and 10: The unique Giro d'Italia Abarth 031 V6 being restored.
11: Giuseppe Volta and RG.
12: Lancia LC1 in the Macaluso collection.

8: Giuseppe Volta drifting a Group 4 Abarth 131 at Aeritalia – the former Abarth testing facility.
13: Lancia Delta S4 in the Macaluso collection.
14: Inspecting the secret track-only FXX prototype.
15: TVs 'Wheeler Dealers' Mike Brewer at Ferrari delivering pizzas. Allegedly.

workshops. We visit. We tour his tidy place open-mouthed. Abarth watchers will know that we are talking about the late Giuseppe 'Beppe' Volta. Volta was a human dynamo. Sadly, I refer to Volta in the past tense. In 2017, aged 71, he stopped on an autostrada to help a stranded motorist and was killed instantly by a passing vehicle.

Back in 2000, in his immaculate and spacious underground workshop, I peek under the bonnet of a Fiat 131 being restored. Beppe mentioned that the American actor Paul Newman was related to the car. I was surprised to see a V6 under the bonnet. Further investigations revealed the gearbox to be a Pantera-type ZF transaxle located at the rear.

Still near Turin, we visit the well-known Macaluso collection whose toy box is too big to describe. The collection included a Lancia LC2, a Formula One Ligier, a DTM Alfa Romeo 155 with two spare motors, a Lancia-Martini 037, some Martini integrales, an Alitalia Stratos, some 124 Abarths, a Renault 110 Alpine, a works Monte-Carlo Rally Mini Cooper, Roger Clark's Escort, a Lotus Cortina, a prototype Ferrari F40, a 131 Abarth, a works Renault 5 Turbo Rally, a works Audi Quattro, some classics – a Merc 300 SL, a Bizzarrini 5300 GT, an Aston Martin DB5, a Ferrari 275GTB, countless spares… While the Macaluso collection is above board, some car collectors in Italy are low profile for tax reasons and as an anti-theft precaution. Secrecy is common with cars hidden from the authorities to avoid the hefty annual tax payable on all valuable possessions.

We nip down to Maranello. Ferrari gives us a factory tour. The trackday-only FXX prototype was being prepared for a production run of just 30 examples. I then spotted TV's Mike Brewer touring the factory in a van, presumably delivering pizzas. We pop into the Maserati factory in Modena to inspect the production line and have a meeting. Reading between the lines, I suspected that Maserati is to return to GT racing. Looking back, it did indeed happen.

RIVIERA AND MORE MADNESS

With a couple of days to spare, I visit the charming Riviera town of Rapallo and check into the delightful Rosabianca Hotel, bang in the middle of the promenade and a favourite of Hollywood legends of old.

We visit nearby Portofino – a one-time fishing village now embraced by the glitterati. In the 1970s, I remember parking my Jaguar on the deserted harbour frontage. Now pedestrian only, there is a compulsory underground car park. Apart from the boats of the super-rich, there is not much to see in this quasi-Disneyland with its film-set building facades that – in this case – are real. Unless you have a 40m gin palace moored in the harbour, enjoy the cafe-life, imagine it 100 years ago as a fishing village, or in the 1960s/70s as an *avant garde* bolthole for the cool, and leave.

Time for a mad twin-test at the Surrey test track. Madness – What is it? Let me test you: would you ride a motorbike with an 8.2-litre, 502hp V8 engine? Like it says on my t-shirt "I can resist everything but temptation." Warwick Bergin can't resist temptation either. He bought the brand-new Boss Hoss, the world's biggest baddest motorcycle. I went with him to Belgium to collect the American import. We part-exchanged his 5-litre supercharged motorbike for a specially tuned 8.2-litre version. If you think 502hp is a bit much for a motorcycle, there are now some turbo versions making 1,600hp. He used this mad machine as his daily Central London transport. Your job in the twin test was to choose between a Ferrari P4 replica and a 502hp bike.

There are no performance numbers for the Boss Hoss. At 1,000hp-per-tonne, and driving through only one wheel, a 0-60mph time would require skills that I do not possess. Warwick left the Boss Hoss with me for a few days as I offered to insulate the exhaust manifolds that burnt riders' legs. The riding position is legs-akimbo to clear the V8. When I dropped it off back at his Pimlico apartment, the exhaust manifolds still set my jeans on fire.

Decision time – you would have to be mad to choose the bike. But this is a mad test. The Boss Hoss must be

16: Glamorous Portofino on Italy's Eastern Riviera.
17: 500hp 8-litre Boss Hoss. The words on RG's T-shirt say: "I can resist anything but temptation."

18: Testing a 147 with new Dunlop Sport Maxx tyres at the Nürburgring.
19: Alfa Romeo 75 'Ring Taxis' on the notorious Nordschleife.

the craziest bike in the world. It easily wins the Mad Test. "Moderation is a fatal thing… Nothing succeeds like excess." Oscar Wilde.

SICILY AND THE NURBURGRING

To quote a line from the 1974 film, *The Godfather*, "This was an offer I couldn't refuse." Alfa Romeo offered to fly me to south-west Sicily to test some UK spec right-hand drive "Car of the Year" Alfa 147s. Alfa was brave to set testers loose in Sicily with the endless yumps on the fast Sicilian roads. There were tortuous hairpin bends, fast undulating country roads, steep narrow gradients, towns and flat-out motorway blasts on dry, wet, muddy and earthquake-broken surfaces. Add some sheep, dogs and mischievous road-racing with other motoring hacks and you have a quick way to get to know a car. What I didn't get to know was Sicily. That is the thing with press launches. Treated like a king, but you do as you are told and behave professionally. It means that when you find somewhere captivating – like Sicily – you want to return with a loved one to explore the place properly. To understand Italy, you must see it all, including Sicily.

On a separate trip driving from Italy to the UK, in my own Alfa 147 fully laden with holiday stuff, I just happened to be passing the Nürburgring and thought it discourteous not to participate. It was also an opportunity to report back to Dunlop on what I thought of the Sport Maxx tyres they gave me to test. A couple of laps around the Nordschleife left me most impressed with the Dunlops and the handling of our Alfa Romeo.

GAS CHAMBER ON TOUR

My friend Peter Crutch had an amazing collection of rare Alfa Romeos that he would regularly loan me. I borrowed his Group 5 1300 GTA for a track test and for a Round Britain Rally organised by the MSA (now MSUK). The route included fast quiet country roads, laps of several race circuits and a hillclimb. It was like a civilised version of the French Tour Auto. GTAs are fabulous cars, although Peter's GTA, while it functioned, needed much sorting. For instance, it had horrendous bump steer, due – no doubt – to the top wishbone angles being out of line with the steering arms. This meant that as the suspension rose and dropped over any surface undulations, so the road wheels would steer left and right, even though the steering wheel was stationary. Five minutes of this persecution and the driver is either exhausted or dead. It also had another trick up its boot lid. Aerodynamic flow is complicated. If the bootlid has no rubber seal or fits badly (both in this case), then exhaust fumes are drawn into the boot compartment and hence into the cabin. Air and fumes move from an area of high pressure (usually outside the car) into an area of low pressure (usually inside the car). Opening the windows offers little help because side windows can let more air out than they let in. Five minutes of this and the occupants are again either exhausted or dead. The Round Britain Rally was three days of torture. It made me and my navigator/co-pilot Jane, sick for a week.

I also transported Peter's Group 5 GTA to Italy for some hillclimb events. Gassed on the way up the hills, but the downhill returns were done Italian style, in neutral with the engine switched off. I also had a hillclimb run in Drummond Bone's Maserati Barchetta Corsa. The 8km Vernasca Hillclimb begins with a 3km straightish section where the Barchetta must have been at over 150mph. The aerodynamics were lifting my crash helmet enough for strangulation. I have no idea how much the actual car was lifting due to blurred vision from buffeting. I remember Drummond telling me that the front spoiler had been temporarily removed to aid transportation.

Motorsport in Italy is sociable and involves huge dinners between the driving days. One such dinner was unforgettable. The first course arrives. It is small and lovely. This is often the way. Then the next course, and so on until – on course number eleven – a pudding course arrives together with a menu for the evening. We read that course number eleven is the *Dolce Intervallo* (Interval Pudding). Yes, we were only at half distance. Another eleven courses followed. A twenty-two-course dinner is difficult to forget.

The Val Saviore Hillclimb is a far more gruelling, and far more serious climb than the fast Vernasca Silver Flag Hillclimb as the Saviore ascent is much longer and

20: The MSA Rally included roads and race circuits.
21: The Peter Crutch GTA Group 5 tour also included UK hillclimbs.
22: Peter Crutch's 'gas chamber' starts the Round Britain MSA rally.

climbs to the top of an Alp. That evening it rained. When I say rained, on the top of this Alp, the air turned to water. Such was the deluge, that no word has been invented for this occurrence. I took cover and watched Drummond get into his Maserati Barchetta (Italian for little boat). Had it been an actual boat it could not have floated because it was full of water. As Drummond set off, it was like watching a friend on a pier being washed away by a tsunami.

WHY DOWNFORCE IS DANGEROUS

Time for a big banger... If you have watched the iconic 1971 film *Le Mans* starring Steve McQueen, or the brilliant 2019 film Ford vs Ferrari you will recognise the Ferrari 512S. The Ken Miles character in the 2019 film is inspired. The Porsche 917 and the Ferrari 512S could reach 225mph. With their primitive 1970 aerodynamics, they were flying on the ground. I have already mentioned a 512M test. This track test was of the earlier 512S, which relied purely on mechanical grip. Its aerodynamics were targeting low drag, perhaps with some stability, rather than new-fangled downforce, that was not even in its infancy.

In late 2019, I raced some sports prototypes that have downforce. There is an often-used expression to encourage drivers who are new to downforce to enter corners at seemingly impossible speeds. It is, "To have trust in the downforce". For instance, at Paul Ricard Circuit, at the end of a very long Mistral Straight, there is a near 90-degree Signes Corner. I was racing Simon Watts' 160mph 2-litre Lola T298 powered by a BMW M-12 engine. Arriving at a corner at 160mph felt wrong, but I knew I could take Signes without braking. John Danby Racing's data showed a constant full throttle each side of the turn, with only a 0.4 second lift at the 50m board to help turn-in. This gave a mid-corner speed of about 140mph. Simply lifting off the throttle for 0.4 seconds produced much retardation via aerodynamic drag and then tyre scrubbing during turn-in. This resulted in a 20mph drop in speed at the apex. All was okay as there is the world's largest tarmac run-off area if things didn't

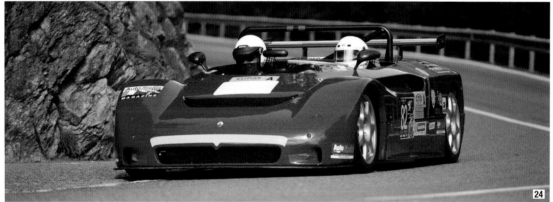

23: Maserati Barchetta, Drummond Bone & RG at high altitude before biblical rain arrived.
24: Val Saviore Hillclimb.
25: RG throwing the Barchetta at a tight turn.

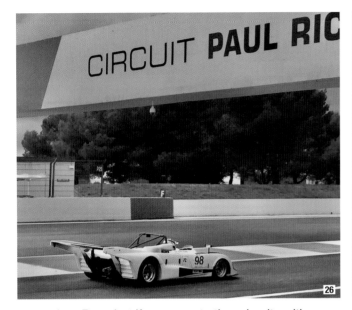

go to plan. But what if you are at other circuits with limited run-off areas? Running off any other track at 160mph is going to end badly. Downforce only works if a car is travelling forward and close to the ground. If a downforce car lifts due to any contact, or if it travels sideways or spins, it will takeoff. This renders things like gravel traps irrelevant.

Equating speed with fun is a common misconception. The 1970 512S would be more fun than a modern Le Mans car. Of course, danger with old racing cars exists but in a different way. Old race cars were designed for speed, not driver safety. However, downforce is dangerous because – for several reasons – it can diminish or disappear. Downforce introduces cornering speeds that are too high for 99% of fast turns. However, if you offered any race driver – me included – a choice of two cars to race: a fast dangerous one, or a slow safe one, the fast dangerous one would always be chosen.

A LETTER AND THE PASSAGE OF TIME

Next at out test track was the 1970 Alfa Romeo T33/3 sports prototype of Jon Shipman. I was instantly covetous as the T33/3 is another favourite. Anything that reminds me of the real Targa Florio is of interest. Carlo Chiti was the Autodelta team manager and was a great guy. Alfa Romeo chose to separate the Autodelta race team from the Alfa Romeo company. They did this so that if Autodelta failed, it was not Alfa's fault. However, if/when Autodelta won, Alfa aligned with 'their' race team as winners. Unlike Enzo Ferrari, whose orders were delivered down a chain of command, Chiti would talk to all his staff and mechanics. He graduated in aeronautical engineering from the University of Pisa in 1953, when he was already working for Alfa Romeo. In 1980, I was racing an Alfa Giulia Sprint GT (equipped with 40DCOE Webers) against hordes of more powerful Lotus Cortinas. I needed some help and asked Chiti if he could oblige. He supplied me with an official Alfa Romeo letter stating that while the Sprint GT came as standard with 40DCOE Webers, larger 45DCOE Webers were offered as factory optional extras, making them race-legal for historics. Not many people know that.

Let's return to the Alfa T33/3. Its success was thanks to the over-engineered mistakes of the earlier T33/2. Basically, it was a conventional steel spaceframe car weighing 650kg and powered by a 400hp 3-litre V8. This results in a power-to-weight ratio of 615hp/tonne. The 3-litre cars like this Alfa 33/3, the Ferrari 312PB and Matra M660 went on to beat the big-banger Ferrari 512S, 512M and Porsche 917 even at the fastest race circuits. I described the Alfa T33/3 as a 400hp go-kart. All I needed now was a Ferrari 312PB to test-drive. It

26: RG racing a Lola T298 at Paul Ricard in 2019.
27: Drifting a Ferrari 512S on 'wooden' tyres.

was coming…

Ask a small child to draw a car and you get the 3-box shape; or so I thought. In 2019, at a launch for a new Jaguar SUV, I asked the Aston Martin and Jaguar designer Ian Callum if that would always be the case. He replied that toddlers are already drawing mono-volume shapes. The three-box saloon car like an old Cortina or Fiat 124 saloon has now become cool. When cars become classics, the intricacies of performance and handling are irrelevant. Take a Ferrari Boxer for example. At the Boxer's launch, motoring journalists (me included) pointed out that the engine was mounted above the gearbox giving it a high centre of gravity at the rear (C of G), which would upset the handling. Please excuse the following technical sentence. If you cut a car into slices – like a loaf of sliced bread – the C of G of each slice is in a different place. If you join all the C of G points into a line, this imaginary line is called the 'mass centroid'. Having a mass centroid that is parallel with ground level is ideal for reasons too complicated for this story. The Ferrari Boxer's mass centroid is low at the front of the car, and high at the rear. Pushed to the limit, a Boxer will probably spin the on turn-in. As a classic car, it matters not. A Boxer is now like a 1930 Blower Bentley. It no longer needs to compete with moderns. It is a fabulous classic, and that is good enough.

A BUSY THURSDAY

Time for an eventful Thursday with appointments at two race circuits plus an evening engagement in Kensington. At 8.30am I arrive at Goodwood for a Ferrari UK jolly run by F1 racer Peter Gethin. A fleet of

28: Alfa Romeo T33/3, a 400hp three-litre V8 go-kart. Another personal favourite.

new Ferraris and Maseratis are waiting. One of the instructors is Richard Attwood, 'Dickie' in period, and now a nickname only for friends and family. Yes, Attwood, the Porsche 917 1970 Le Mans winner. He always teases me about things Italian and I always ask him if his knighthood has arrived.

Another Le Mans veteran with a Porsche 917 is David Piper. Piper lost part of one leg in a crash whilst filming *Le Mans* in 1971, starring Steve McQueen. Piper was my chauffeur driving a Ferrari P2 racing car until the noise-police waved the black flag.

I forgo an Italian-style lunch at Goodwood to dash to Thruxton for an afternoon meeting with Pat Blakeney, the Thruxton race school boss, chief instructor, racer, circuit fixer, and today also the ARDS Chairman. While I had been giving private race instruction for some years, I sought an official qualification. My examiner was Pat Blakeney. He drove, while I acted as his instructor. At one point, Pat rested his elbow on an arm rest, which I immediately spotted and suggested he desist. I was pleased when Pat gave me the nod. I could now work part-time at Thruxton and any other circuit whilst continuing with motoring journalism and other stuff. Thruxton Motorsport Centre is a great place. One day, a

group of Italians arrived for an 'experience day'. Pat commented that he knew there must have been a reason to employ me. There is much banter and camaraderie between instructors. Many became friends.

Thruxton also worked for manufacturers. One such job included a few days taking a fleet of new Honda S2000s on a round-Britain-tour of race circuits. The purpose was to act as demonstrators and minders for dealers and buyers to try out the cars. We started at Knockhill Circuit in Scotland and gradually worked our way south via many race circuits, finishing up near London at Brands Hatch. I noticed that as we got closer to London, so the track driving skills of the guests deteriorated. I put this down to population density. The quieter and more wide-open the roads, the more they are like race circuits. With my Goodwood and Thruxton appointments over, I dashed back to Adam and Eve Mews in Kensington for an evening launch party for Jane's new human resources company. A busy Thursday.

A ONE-WEEK DIARY, AND A METAL MAN

Time for another trip to Italy to gather gossip, write reports, and scoop some scoops. Here is a snapshot, but first, I must issue a warning. I have been advised to

29: Richard Attwood, 1970 Le Mans winner and still at it...
30: RG with David Piper, ex-F1 and ex-Le Mans racer.
31: Mrs Giordanelli in girl clothes.

32: Works Lancia 037 on test at Aeritalia in Turin.
33 and 34: Supervisor sits where Senna sat.

remove the following observation seen at Turin Airport as it is not PC. Unfortunately, it reflects the shocking attitudes of the time. However, this event happened, I apologise in advance for any offence or trauma it may cause. Offensive statement begins: We knew we had landed in Italy when we saw the person guiding our jet to its parking space. At Heathrow he would be clad in reflective clothing, steel toecap boots, gloves, goggles and holding illuminated table-tennis bats, plus a flashing beacon on his hard hat. At Turin Airport, a young female in a chic Armani ensemble and heels guided us in with her bare hands. Offensive statement ends.

Monday

The Fiat press office supplied our five-man team with an Alfa Romeo 156 JTD and a white Fiat Doblo van. Peter Collins left his camera equipment cases on the ground in the airport car park that was now two hours away. He returned and his stuff was still there! We arrive at the Aeritalia test track (once Turin's main airport). My three tasks are to carry out some more brake testing in a Fiat Marea loaded with sensors, test-drive a Lancia 037 rally car and drive a concept car, the 'Stola' Porsche Boxster. Other people are there doing their thing – the ex-Senna

Lotus Formula One Lotus 98T1 from 1986 in its JPS black and gold livery is being prepared for a run. *Auto Italia's* Peter Collins (a walking talking reference book) reckons it to be a 'qualifying special'. I tease him how he questions the authenticity of virtually every historic racing car. He giggles. I have never seen him without a smile on his face.

It was the first time I had driven a Lancia 037. Engineer, Abarth and rally guru – Giuseppe Volta brought the car to the track and spent ages driving sideways on the abrasive surface. The 2-litre engine has a nominal 325hp. Volta relates the story that 1,000hp was often dialled-in and that the motor could momentarily deliver 1,500hp if fed with illegal fuel (allegedly). Then it was my turn. Verdict – fabulous. The 037 was a world-beater because it is so quick and so easy to drive.

Back to the Stola concept car. Stola makes them for car manufacturers. Based in Turin, Signor and Signora Stola personally delivered the Stola version of the Porsche Boxster – the Stola S82 to the track. Apart from re-bodying the car there are many mechanical changes, including a 3.7-litre twin turbo 470hp conversion. It's good to see concept cars that work and this one

35 and 36: Metal man takes RG for a ride on the wild side.
37: Stola Porsche chat with the company owner.

rocketed down the test track.

After a very long day, it was time to pack up and get back to our hotel. I always feel relieved when it's all over. Guests get their cars back in good condition. Dangers have passed and the job is done. It was all over for the day. It was time to go. Nothing bad can happen now. I am not going to die today. Then we started talking to an old bloke in biker leathers (he was about the editor's age). You know when motorcycle/sidecar racing comes on TV, sometimes with images of crashes and what looks like a rag doll flying? And you know when you say to yourself, "They are bonkers. You'd never get me on one of those." Well, I've always said that too. However, knowing I always say yes to everything, editor Phil Ward volunteered me for a ride on the wild side.

Franco Martinel (1941–2018) had competed in 36 Isle of Man TT races driving sidecars and survived. This racing sidecar legend was a Turin taxi driver and a hands-on engineer. We chatted. "Have you ever been hurt?" I asked. He pointed to many parts of his body recalling all the metal plates and screws holding him together. Apart from his machine's power unit, he made just about everything on this outfit, which stood a tad over one foot high. The engine is a Krauser 500cc two-stroke producing 170hp. The whole thing weighs only 170kg, so that means a power-to-weight ratio of 1,000

hp/tonne. With a mistaken preconception of just a gentle run in a straight line down the runway and back, we never bothered with helmets or leathers. My safety kit came from a pair of Ray Bans and stout brogues.

Lying on a hard flat shiny surface, my fingers curled into a couple of slots and with my legs poking out the back, I had no idea what was coming. The acceleration was so strong (0–60 mph in two seconds, 0–100 in five) that it was like a horizontal version of hanging by my fingertips from a rising hot-air balloon with someone else hanging from my legs. Finger and arm muscles were under severe attack. Face-first and after two seconds at about 70mph I was considering letting go because I figured that at 70mph, I would not get as injured as I would coming off at 140mph. The runway surface is the most abrasive I have ever seen – like a sea of black spikes.

With a life expectancy of First World War soldiers at the battle of the Somme, old biker/sidecar racers are rare. Franco was old and tough. I wondered how I would cope with metal holding my bones together. Crazy things happen in this job, but I never saw this racing sidecar trip coming. Those bikers really are bonkers. However, Franco Martinel came up against legendary Italian bureaucracy in that after 70 years of age, he could not renew his race licence. I feel that it was this forced

38: Fiat G90/1 jet fighter at Fiat Centro Storico.
39: Like a car only smaller. RG and minder in a Stanguellini driving round Modena.

retirement, this officialdom, that steered him to decline and an early death at 77 years of age. Otherwise, he might have continued racing or retired. But whatever..., it would have been on his own terms.

Tuesday

There is a classic car show at Lingotto, but it's Tuesday and they don't open until 3pm on Tuesdays. Near the building used for a rooftop car chase in the 1969 film *The Italian Job,* we visit the Biscaretti Car Museum (now the *Museo Nazionale dell'Automobile*). Excellent and recommended, with enough stuff to keep our anorak team going for a while. Then round the corner to Fiat's slick Centro Storico Museum. Not very big, about the area of a football pitch, the Centro Storico has designer images of the Fiat story. Don't expect to see everything Fiat ever made. We see the 1924 22-litre, 320bhp, 235km/h Mefistofele record car. We see the 1933 diesel-powered Littorina train. In the aircraft department, we see countless models of Fiat planes as well as a favourite, a 1954 G91 R/1 jet fighter. These proper fighters – as opposed to jet trainers – were once employed by Italy's extraordinary aerobatic team the *Frecce Tricolori.* They now use latest Aermacchi aircraft. In the ship department, we notice a cutaway model of the Italterra cargo ship specially made for

transporting cars to export markets. The Centro Storico Museo is a reminder that 'cars' are only a small part of the Fiat empire.

Leaving Turin, the team heads for Modena. Andy Heywood, boss of UK's McGrath Maserati is to quiz Adolfo Orsi, whose family once owned Maserati. Then on to Stanguellini who were 1950s and 60s competition car builders, just east of Modena Centre. They have their own private museum. We plunder it for a future story and take a 750 Bialbero racer out onto the public road. Unbelievably, the miniscule 475kg car competed at the Le Mans 24 hours. We visit a couple of supercar restorers and specialists and see so much craftsmanship. We also find a Ferrari scrap yard.

Wednesday

The next day is the 25th of April and the Liberation Day national holiday. Halfway through the Second World War (in 1943), Italy – with two million military personnel – changed sides and declared war on Germany. In 1941, Russia also changed sides, adding a further 11 million troops to join the Allies, making a total of c50 million to defeat Germany's 14 million soldiers. Back to Italian Liberation Day and everything is closed, so we re-visit Matteo Panini's parmesan cheese farm to photograph some Maseratis on the farm's internal roads.

Thursday

I park Adolfo Orsi's 1965 Maserati Quattroporte next to an old farmhouse for static photography. The car's first owner was one of my favourite actors, Marcello Mastroianni (1924-1996). In its heyday, the QP was the world's fastest four-door car. Fast cars could cruise the uncrowded autostradas at their top speeds, shrinking Italy and Europe considerably. Adolfo Orsi took me for a spin in his Quattroporte. He drove quickly for the action shots. Back at his house, many of his walls are covered in movie posters. We have an argument regarding the name tag on the Alfa Romeo GTAm. Orsi says it stands for GT *America*, while I say GTA *Maggiorata* (Italian for enlarged). The argument continues, "Yes, it is. No, it isn't." etc. Orsi is a historian, a walking talking

encyclopaedia on Italian cars. Thinking that he must know more than me, I surrender. However, a recent Google search says that I am right.

We arrive at the De Tomaso factory in Modena and pull some cars out of their museum. We head off onto the public roads to test a Guara Coupe and do some car-to-car photography. The factory is still the sleepy old place it was. However, the Guara has given a handful of people some employment. Having driven the Guara Coupe, we get pushy and ask to try the prototype Guara Barchetta. To get the drive, I sign away all my worldly goods. I am then to comply with a weird Italian law regarding open-top racing cars on the road. This means that I am required to wear a crash helmet. The factory cat had recently and rightfully peed into a dusty old

40 and 41: Setting up a photo shoot on Panini's farm.
42: Maserati man Adolfo Orsi in a hurry chauffeuring RG.
43: RG in a Maserati Birdcage down on the farm.

44: RG complete with 'cat's' helmet road testing the De Tomaso Barchetta on Prova plates.

helmet that was lying on the floor. On with the 'prova' plates, I test-drive the Barchetta, looking like a fool wearing the ancient, stinking, first-generation, massively heavy, full-face helmet. We have a very tight schedule. Smelling of cat pee, we dash to Brescia to look at Igor Zanesi's collection of rare and beautiful Maseratis including lots of Maserati motorbikes. Then back to Turin and the Hotel Crimea.

Friday
An easy day. Drop off the trusty press cars, head for the airport, leave sunny Italy and back to England with enough editorial material to keep the five of us going for quite a while. I join the gridlocked M25 on a wet Friday evening and question the meaning of life.

GOODWOOD AND LUXURY
The next task is a luxury day at Goodwood circuit hosted by Ferrari. The guests for this top corporate event are separated into four teams of five people for their day of driving Maseratis, Ferraris, go-karts, skid-pan car and helicopter flights. The original Tiger Moth flights were cancelled as two years of continuous rain had water-logged the two grass runways. By moving mountains of earth, the Duke of Richmond has since solved the flooded runway issue, making it possible to operate heavy aircraft like a DC3 Dakota from the grass runways.

Goodwood is wired for sound on a permanent line to the local Council's Noise Police HQ. Any hint of sound and the Noise Police will swoop in and close this beautifully restored and important piece of motorsport

heritage. The noise limit at Goodwood requires cars to be as silent as the quietest road cars.

F1 driver Peter Gethin ran the show and former Porsche 917 driver and Le Mans 24 Hour veteran, David Piper gave hot rides on this corporate event. Piper told me that he came to motor racing late – in 1954 with a Lotus, when he was 24 years old. Coincidentally Graham Hill, the two times F1 World Champion, Le Mans 24 Hours and Indy 500 winner did not get a road driving licence until he was 24 years old. Today's UK protégées start karting officially at six years of age for practice and eight years of age for racing. Although as previously mentioned, in some countries, I have heard of two-year-olds practising.

My chauffeur for the next car – the Ferrari 360 Modena, was Le Mans veteran Richard Attwood. Jacky Ickx was one of Ferrari's legendary drivers, his daughter Vanina had recently won a race at Spa Francorchamps in a Ferrari 360 Challenge car. The car I am strapping myself into at Goodwood is that car. The 360 Challenge cars are specially made racers from the factory. A day of luxury to remember. "The saddest thing I can imagine is to get used to luxury," Charlie Chaplin.

SEXISM AND HISTORIC RUINS

When historic car racer Sally Mason-Styrron arrived at our test track with one of her fine collection of race cars, call me old-fashioned, but I couldn't help noticing that she was female. Today it is PC to be gender-blind and everything-else-blind. So be it. Therefore, I must apologise for noticing Sally. I had previously met her when testing her ex-Maranello Concessionaires Ferrari Daytona racer. Now she is at the track with her delightful 1950 Ferrari 166MM Barchetta. As historic racing has become an aggressive sport, to be competitive today means much crafty engineering plus much cost and considerably more risk. Wisely, Sally now uses her exceptional cars for genteel historic events rather than all-out racing.

Back in 1908, Brooklands circuit was the birthplace of women in motorsport. Females in motorsport include: Lella Lombardi, Michele Mouton, Vanina Ickx, Corentine Quiniou, Sabine Schmitz, Maria Teresa de Filippis, Desire Wilson, Maria de Vilotta, Pat Moss and Susie Wolff. Apologies for countless omissions. The list I am looking at includes about a thousand names. What is more, the list is only of the pro-drivers. It does not include the motorsport world of amateurs or drifting.

45: Mr and Mrs RG inspecting the heavy-duty runway at Goodwood.
46: Sally Mason-Styrron, RG and Ferrari 166 Barchetta.
47: Ex-wife Mary Giordanelli with Graham Hill in 1968.

48 and 49: Former Rossi Engineering's Kirsty Widdrington laying rubber and making smoke.

Women in drifting competitions are super rare. Kirsty Widdrington is a total petrolhead and a popular figure in UK Drift Championships. She is ex-Rossi Engineering and an ex-Ferrari mechanic. One of today's most famous women in motorsport is Jamie Chadwick. Her racing CV is amazing and deserves a look. She has tested F1 cars for Williams and recently signed for the Italian F3 team Prema Powerteam.

Having spent much time at Brooklands, I am saddened that such a place of great historic interest has not been funded to be better preserved. While the Brooklands site and the museum exist – and well worth regular visits – the industrial, architectural, and corporate post-war vandalism over the original site is a shame. Money-no-object it should be returned to its heyday with fitting improvements, in-keeping with how it should have evolved. Think of Monza, which opened in 1922. The banking is not used but has been restored, while a revised track layout ensures an excellent racing venue. Think also of Goodwood today to understand my thoughts. I shall stop now before asking why archaeological sites like the Roman Forum and countless ruined castles have not been restored. They were not built as ruins.

I LIKE TO BE IN AMERICA...

Russ, an American airline captain, once entrusted me with his 1959 Jaguar Mk.9 to rebuild the engine. I did so and he drove his Jaguar around the world. So impressed was Russ with my work that he offered to finance me and set up a classic car business in Fort Lauderdale, Florida. He even invited me to be the best man at his wedding. Suddenly, one of life's crossroads was staring me in the face. And unlike other crossroads, this one was signposted. Here was a money-no-object arrangement, and a new life for my family. Despite huge pressure from Russ, I declined the offer. Since then, I have never been sure of my sanity and still wonder how my life would have changed. I guess I just wasn't hungry enough to leave what I had in the UK and Europe. How does this concern track-testing?

In 1974, Russ bought a brand-new Ferrari Berlinetta Boxer. Knowing that I was a racer, Russ entered me for a Ferrari trackday at Goodwood with his new Ferrari BB. I learnt that trail-braking into Lavant Corner does not work with a Boxer due to its propensity for lift-off oversteer, roll-oversteer and turn-in oversteer. The same thing happened with it at Silverstone if I entered Becketts too quickly. 25-years later, when motoring journalism put me on tracks in Ferrari Boxers, I was already familiar with their habits. Talacrest supplied a couple of versions for me to go down memory lane. The carb-fed BB and the later fuel-injected BBi became obvious targets for investors when in 2011, the used-car prices fell to below £50k. Then by 2016, they had risen to £350k. It was obvious to me that a 12-cylinder two-seater Ferrari was always going to be an outstanding investment.

THE ENGLISHMAN WHO MADE MASERATIS

Five Lancia integrales in various states of tune were next to test. Then something special: it was a real pleasure to chat with Maserati 250F expert, the late Cameron Millar. The Maserati expert Steve Hart, who was also involved, was there to help run the car. Cameron Millar was a true gentleman and war-time Squadron Leader who later in life scooped up thousands of parts from the Maserati factory, enough components to make 12 of the famous 250F racing cars. We had Cameron Millar's ninth 250F (CM9) at the track. It was magnificent. No roll cage, seat belts or fire protection. It is amazing that public perception once thought that it was safer for a driver to be thrown clear than stay inside a crashing car.

In the early 1970s, Ferrari set the sports racing world alight when he launched the little 312P. Described by many as a Formula One car with the wheels covered, the 312P was an immediate winner. This test-drive was a big one; another box ticked. The Ferrari 312P is like an Alfa Romeo T33/3 or TT12 but just that little bit better. If you are used to racing Touring Cars or GT cars and then drive a Sports Prototype, you are in for a shock. Everything is different. Any changes in speed or direction are instantaneous. Think of how quickly a fly can change direction and then compare it with a swan's manoeuvrability – that is the difference. Being in the open air really helps you to understand aerodynamics. Slipstreaming is felt colossally, aero battering from other cars too. Braking is in another dimension, but here is

the thing, you don't need to brake as much because your mid-corner speeds are now so much higher. There is little opportunity for a rest. By a rest, I mean one second to check mirrors or instruments. If you were a sane person, you would also feel more vulnerable as you have nothing in front of you, and 650kg behind that is ready to squash you. Sports Prototypes are physical to drive. Not because the controls are heavy, but because of the busyness and constant high-G that comes at you from all directions. To run competitively requires the fitness of an athlete. Sure, an unfit person could drive one, but the level of fitness would determine the time before a mistake would occur. Five minutes at race speed would consume a normal person to the point where the brain would be malfunctioning.

Today in 2022, I am asked to share a sports prototype in long races, yet I am not an athlete. I cope well because, I have been racing for a lifetime. Question: How long could you concentrate at your maximum potential while your heart is at its maximum beats per minute (BPM)? In a motor race – especially in a downforce car – a heart rate monitor will show that your BPMs are indeed at max. Imagine playing a physical game like say squash for an hour, whilst someone is constantly firing mental arithmetic questions at you that you must answer correctly and instantly. Hesitate or answer incorrectly and you are in the hospital or worse.

The next track test was large. The little Ferrari 312P was physical to race, while the next monster waiting for me was as gentle as a lamb. This took me from a vehicle weighing 0.65 tonnes to a 40 tonnes juggernaut, namely a fully loaded Iveco/Ford Eurostar Cursor 430 articulated truck. This was a first for me. Time to fire up the 10.3-litre turbocharged engine and think about the 12-speed semi-automatic gearbox. Trying to get a feel for the handling was alien because the softly sprung driver's cabin is suspended independently from the stiffly sprung chassis, so I never managed drifting in the 40-tonne truck. Truckers deserve the respect and facilities that they receive in France and not be ignored as they are in the UK.

50 and 51: RG drives an Iveco HGV.
52: Giant killer. Ferrari 312P – like an Alfa T33/3 but slightly more refined.
53 and 54: RG and Maserati 250F builder Cameron Millar.

52

52

54

2002
Art – and Trial by Television

My first glimpse of Ferrari's new 550 Barchetta was by detective work. Outside the casino in Monte Carlo, I saw a large crowd. Further investigation revealed that people were doughnutted around the new Barchetta. It looked good in the sunshine, but what if it rains?

The marketeers at Ferrari had to make a stab in the dark when they made the 550 Barchetta. This is an open-top 550 Maranello. The only weather protection would be sunglasses. However, there is a hood. Not a folding version, obviously. There are some makeshift hood-sticks that poke into the body. A small piece of black cloth is then draped over the sticks. The final shape of the erected hood could not be photographed as the photographers feared that the image would damage their cameras. I looked at the hood in erected mode, long and hard. I squinted my eyes and cleared my head of conventionality and concentrated. I put myself in the place of a famous post-modern art critic like Hal Foster. Eventually, concentrating as artistically as possible, I stopped laughing and reckoned it might be 'courageous'. After all, Leonardo da Vinci's friends laughed when they saw his Mona Lisa. And the artist Joseph Turner (1775–1851) became a recluse because some said his later paintings were blurry. In reality, Turner was going blind. The only way you can know if something is of true artistic value is with the passage of time.

Ferrari had to calculate how many of the 499 Barchettas should be right-hand drive UK-spec cars. After reading Douglas Adams' *The Hitchhiker's Guide to the Galaxy* and the answer to the 'Great Question' regarding life, the universe and everything, the Ferrari marketing department arrived at the same answer as the Deep Thought computer, i.e. 42. One of those 42 was kindly supplied by Joe Macari to our test track. Ultimately the hood thing will be of no consequence. After all, do we criticise the hood on a 1950 Ferrari 166MM Barchetta or Jaguar XKSS? No, we don't.

Another Italian trip, this time we had a new Lancia Lybra Estate 2.4JTD. Lancia's UK reputation was destroyed by TV watchdog-type programmes. The late 1970s early 1980s Lancia Beta models were fine cars. They had their power units bolted to a subframe that was in turn bolted to four captive nuts in the cars' floorpans. At the time, Italy was using rubbish steel from the Soviet Union. The rear captive nuts holding the subframe rusted, causing the subframe to move. Game over. For a welder, this was a relatively easy fix. However, it was not to be. The UK's mainstream newspapers got their Lancia-killing knives out and the consumer TV show, hosted by Esther Rantzen put the boot in. The new Lancia Betas were recalled and crushed and Lancia withdrew from the UK market.

Ford escaped persecution because their rust problem was in the 1960s when consumer protection was simply a case of *caveat emptor* (buyer beware). The front suspension top strut mounting points on most Ford models of the 1960s quickly rusted through. Welding new top plates to the McPherson strut mounting points was almost a service item. The press was unaware, and Ford escaped persecution of a trial by television.

A UNIVERSITY AND A POINT

The town of Egham is at the bottom of a hill in leafy Surrey. Ferrari UK Maranello Concessionaires is based there with Virginia Water and Windsor Great Park on the other side of the prestigious hill. Halfway up the hill is a university. Royal Holloway College of London opened its doors in 1849. The stunning Founders' Building was unveiled by Queen Victoria in 1886. It is still the focal point of the campus and was our photo location. We proposed readers with a question. Would you have the brand-new Ferrari 456MGT or would you have the old classic car, the Ferrari Daytona 365GTB/4? What a daft question, I hear you say. At the time (2002), they cost about the same money. Today, 20 or 30 456s would cost the same as one Daytona. It is quite fashionable today for some of the UK's motoring journalists to malign classic cars because they don't drive as well as new cars. Obviously so, but if you have empathy or nostalgia, or the need for some time-travel, you know that judgement to be missing the point.

A WEEK IN ITALY AND WINSTON CHURCHILL

Sunday

It is Sunday and I dash from Oulton Park to catch a late-night flight to Turin. A Lancia from the press office is waiting for our team at the Italian airport. If you have ever wondered why Turin does not look Italian, it is due

1 and 2: The Ferrari 550 Barchetta is essentially an open car. Spotted at the Monte Carlo Casino. The hood is too horrible to show.
3 and 4: Ferrari Daytona and 456GT at the Royal Holloway College.
5: Midway through WW2 Italy changed sides. My father swapped his Italian uniform for a British uniform.

to the French who annexed it and the whole Picdmont region in 1802. Then in 1861, it became the first capital of Italy when the country was unified and became a nation. Until then, as you may know, Italy was a collection of independent states. The term 'Italy' has existed since pre-ancient Roman Empire as a geographical expression. The name Piedmont derives from its location near the foot of the Alps: pied (foot) mont (mountain).

Monday

We have plenty of time to drive the Lancia to the Aeritalia test track for 10.30am. Have you noticed that it is generally when you have plenty of time that you are late? We got lost and grid-locked in heavy traffic, so we arrived an hour late. Since the 9/11 attack in the USA, the Aeritalia test track has armed soldiers on the main gate. You can only get in if your name is on their list. If it isn't, you phone someone inside, who then writes your name on their list and you are in. The only exception is the mushroom picker who is exempt from bureaucracy, because in Italy, foodstuffs have the ultimate priority. For example, in WW2 when ancient British Swordfish biplanes torpedoed and destroyed the Italian naval fleet at anchor in Taranto harbour, it was in the evening at dinner time. Consequently, all the Italian sailors were in Taranto's restaurants, so no one was injured. Priorities save lives.

Back to our trip to the Aeritalia test track. My job on the magazine was to be a chauffeur on foreign trips, navigate whilst driving, test the featured cars on road and on track, write the stories, be an interpreter, convince car owners to allow me to thrash their cars and take all the blame if anything goes wrong. Therefore, it was obviously my fault that we were lost, in a traffic jam and late.

Much of life is about contacts. Augusto Donetti became a great friend. Augusto was based in London, but he and his family, are from Turin, a Torinese. In London, Augusto – a race driver whenever he gets the opportunity – ran Red Dot. This company specialised in selling brake

products. Augusto also marketed engine up-grades with various ECU chips. I am coming to the point because Augusto's family owned Frenitalia who were based in Turin and manufactured braking components for major outlets. Frenitalia frequently had exclusive use of the huge Aeritalia test track and would invite us to come and play with some cars. They were also well-connected with the classic and competition car scene. This was a vital lifeline for contacts.

Abarth rally legend Giuseppe 'Beppe' Volta was there burning rubber as usual, this time in a 'works' Fiat 131 Abarth Rally. Red Dot was there for us to test some brakes on an Alfa 147 and a Smart. The German 'Brake Pad Police' were busy with EU homologation tests for a set of Red Dot pads, which costs Frenitalia a fortune. All car parts sold in Italy must be homologated, which explains the absence of UK-style motor factor outlets or classic car suppliers who sell pattern parts for most vehicles. Be thankful (for now) that in the UK, if you want parts for your MG, Jaguar, Mini, etc, all parts can be remanufactured by specialists and are readily available. This is not possible in Italy, as non-homologated repro parts are not permitted.

6: Lancia and Abarth cognoscenti gather at Aeritalia test track.
7: Sliding a works 131 Abarth.
8: Four-year-old RG in Italy testing the wing strength of a Siata.
9: Data logging with Augusto Donetti.
10: Cisitalia 202 Berlinetta.
11: Gippo Salvetti's unique Pininfarina 2500 Coupe.

The 131 Rally had been pirouetting on the abrasive surface until the tyre cords were clearly visible, but when it was my run, the tyres exploded. I got the blame. For the evening, we are taken to dinner in a remote suburb of Turin. While 'location location location' are the three most important factors for any property market, in Italy the location of a restaurant is of less importance. Italy is all about local knowledge. We find a blank door in a long blank wall, on a long blank stretch of road. We open it, and inside is a massive and busy restaurant.
It was like a door into another world.

Tuesday
Our next appointments are near Milan. We stay in Pavia – a pedestrianised historic centre, very civilised and typically Lombardi. Timing is as important as local knowledge. Arrive at a popular restaurant at 7.20pm and you will be told to wait outside, as the place in empty, the staff have yet to arrive. Arrive at 8.10pm and the place is packed and you won't get in.

Wednesday
We dash through the early morning light from Pavia to Como for our next appointment. Eventually, we roll onto the forecourt of Classic Motor and drive off in a couple of cars for future features. A Siata Spring, which is a 1970s Fiat 850 that looks like Noddy's car. Not exactly my thing and best driven in public wearing a full-face helmet with a black visor. However, as a four-year-old, I thought a Siata was great. Somewhat better is the Cisitalia 202 Berlinetta – a good effort for 1949. Time for a pavement café, this time lakeside in Como.

We motor to Milan for a meeting with 'The Blue Team' set up by Gippo Salvetti – taking its title from the nickname of his father's race team. The Blue Team is not a race team but a small club of about 20 enthusiasts who meet up every Thursday to talk Alfa Romeo. Salveti's own private collection comprises of over 130 cars, mostly very rare Alfas.

It is huge, I have seen smaller aircraft hangars. I feast my eyes on a fabulous Alfa Romeo cooker, which in the

176781•MI

11

1990s, cost the equivalent of £14,000 (£27k today). Salvetti hands me the keys to a super rare 1950 Alfa Romeo 6C 2500 Sport Pinin Farina. Voted the most beautiful car at the 1950 Geneva Show, it wafted along like a mature countess. In 1950, Italy was having its long flirtation with communism and Alfa Romeo gave one of these cars to nice old 'uncle' Joe Stalin. He killed 20 million people in his work camps but he wasn't a fascist, so that's okay. The Blue Team is a non-commercial organisation and does not normally enter shows or competitions. Like so many Italian collections, it is concealed and below the radar.

Thursday

Arrive at the Maserati factory at 9.30am and pick up a new car. Photographers Ward and Collins panic and worry as the morning sun turns to fog as we drive out into the countryside. We park in a pedestrian zone during market day. We break some laws, but no one objects. Workers are at work. Kids are at school. The locals, mostly the retired, surround the Maserati. *"Che bella machina."* On the way back to the factory, we use the Maserati as a camera car to photograph our Lancia car-to-car on the motorway.

We tour the rapidly expanding Maserati factory and then have a meeting with a possible future columnist. We interview a young Italian female journalist to be 'Our Man in Italy'. We motor from Modena to Monza for our next overnight.

Friday

It is the warm-up day for the Monza weekend when Ferrari celebrates in public with a huge race meeting. Every racing Ferrari that can move is there. There are countless screaming red F1 cars. The public car parks also have a distinctly red hue. Last year it was Mugello, this year Monza has been chosen. A weekend of red madness, red happiness, red extravagance, and red-blooded enthusiasm. We arrive a day early because we are trying to talk our way into driving some top-end red cars. We also need to talk

our way onto the sacred track at its most special time – both activities being particularly difficult. Imagine a bunch of foreign magazine staff turning up un-announced at a major live race meeting like the British Grand Prix or the Silverstone Classic and trying to talk their way unintroduced (and free of charge) into car-to-car on-track photography. I know no one at Monza, yet I get the job to talk my way 'cold' into going on track with a race car and a camera car at Monza's busiest weekend.

The chain of command is long. After knocking on numerous doors, 17 individual permissions; 11 from Monza officials and six permissions from people connected with the cars, we took to the track free of charge with two racing Ferraris. We had a rare 330GTO, a Competition Daytona and our camera car.

Anyone who has driven a 250GTO will tell you that you must keep the 3-litre motor in its narrow power-band. The solution would be more engine capacity. Ferrari made four 330GTOs with 4-litre engines and I got into this one at Monza. With just the pitlane exit marshal to convince via much two-way radio dialog, we were finally on track. After a full day of permission meetings, I was exhausted and relieved. However, the photographers were having heart attacks worried that the daylight was vanishing. The flash-assisted photography did the job, bringing reality and atmosphere to what we achieved unrehearsed and un-pre-planned at Monza's busiest weekend. We network, we shake lots of hands, we leave and celebrate our photo-shoot.

Saturday

I am not even going to attempt to describe *'Tutte le Ferrari a Monza'* (literally all the Ferraris at Monza). The show is indescribably self-indulgent. Ferrari is well and truly on top and not ashamed to show it or enjoy it. In 2002, Ferrari F1 was doing what Mercedes F1 was doing in 2020. There were also countless 'stock car races for millionaires' – called the 360 Challenge. We network and leave.

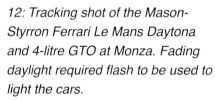

12: Tracking shot of the Mason-Styrron Ferrari Le Mans Daytona and 4-litre GTO at Monza. Fading daylight required flash to be used to light the cars.
13: The GTO poses in front of the disused Monza banking.
14: Luca di Montezemolo with RG's Sanremo neighbour and motorsport executive Claudio Berro.

Sunday

With a big crowd watching, the monster grid of 360 Challenge cars, the demolition derby gets underway. For the spectators it's great, for the drivers and/or owners, it's madness. The pit lane is a teeming scrum. Wounded racing cars blast through the crowded pits. Later, the *tifosi* in the grandstands cheer the big red helicopter carrying Schumacher, Barichello and Badoer as it lands on the Monza starting grid, right in front of the grandstand. As if descending from heaven, our waving heroes jump into three open-top Maserati Spyders for a lap of honour and the Sunday party-proper begins. Montezemolo, Cantarella and Todt go walkabout.

Three of the high-pitched Grand Prix Ferraris scream past the grandstands. Schumi, Barichello and Badoer stage an exciting F1 race – pit stops and all. The *tifosi* go wild. With Schumacher, Barichello and Badoer doing their tyre smoking F1 doughnuts and the big red party at Monza on full song, we depart for Turin and our flight to London. After eight days, our worries and concerns disappeared. Nothing went wrong.

At home, my father asks how things went. "Was everything okay? Did you have any trouble?" He was a great fan of Winston Churchill and collected his books. This is despite three years in North Africa, during which time Churchill tried to kill him. In his book 'Their Finest

Hour', Churchill wrote, "When I look back on all these worries, I remember the story of an old man who said on his deathbed that he had had a lot of trouble in his life, most of which never happened."

FREE RIDES AT DONINGTON PARK

It is the *Auto Italia* trackday at Donington Park Circuit. Many of the *Auto Italia* Championship and Alfa Romeo Championship cars are there with passenger seats fitted. Meridien Maserati bring along a Ghibli Cup race car. Max Wakefield's Ferrari P4 replica looked fabulous in its Scuderia Filipinetti livery. Max is ex-army and has a racing car collection. He is also the most fearless person I have ever met. One of his homes is Chillingham Castle where he had a great trick. I saw him place Michael Ward, facing forwards, on the handlebars of a powerful motorcycle scrambler. Max whacked the throttle open and kept the scrambler on its back wheel at speed, still with Michael on the handlebars, through forest tracks. I declined Max's kind offer to be similarly terrified. Back at Donington, Drummond Bone was giving rides in his Maserati Barchetta Corsa. John Rutter brought along multiple Stratos machinery. It was a great day and free of incidents. Claudio Casali, the organiser of the glorious Vernasca Silver Flag Hillclimb, made the journey from Italy. At Donington, he hitched a ride in my Alfa GTA Turbo with 633hp-per-tonne. The day was unprofitable for *Auto Italia* but a worthy PR stunt.

RALLYING AND POLITICS

One of the trips to the Aeritalia test track in Italy included a story on the Fiat 131 Abarth rally cars. Think of them as Italy's Ford Escort rally cars. The innocent-looking 131 was a simple three-box saloon that – even when new – looked dated, but worked brilliantly, winning the World Rally Championship in 1977, 1978 and 1980. Keep those results in mind. The Lancia Stratos looks more modern, yet it won the world title in 1974, 1975 and 1976. Politics from Fiat's top brass and marketing department dictated that the mass-produced 131 should replace the rare Stratos on rally podiums. There were

times when the works drivers piloted both the 131s and the Stratoses. So how did they compare? I have tested both. The Stratos is the darling. It can be quicker than the 131 but needs considerable skill to extract the best from it. The 131 was the workhorse and could be instantly chucked about with impunity. Abarth authority 'Beppe' Volta told me that he, and most of the works drivers, preferred the 131. Cars like the 131 Abarth are so much more appealing to drive and it takes seconds to understand them. A Stratos is stunning to look at but difficult to control. Which would I choose? The Stratos wins. Oscar Wilde said, "The true mystery of the world is the visible not the invisible."

BUILDING A FORMULA ONE CAR IN A SHED

Another Formula One car to test but it is not what you are thinking. The engines in today's 900hp F1 cars may be powerful but F1 enthusiasts dislike their silence. Noise is a major part of the deal. F1 screamers from earlier eras like the 3-litre, 3.5-litre, 1.5 turbos and 2.4-litre engines made iconic hullabaloos, with outputs up to 1,500bhp. However, from 1961 to 1965, F1 engines were only 1.5-litre making 150–225bhp, and here I am about to test one. It is an LDS, powered by a familiar Alfa Romeo 1,500cc twin cam engine. Think of a 1960s Formula Ford 1600 and you won't be far wrong about the LDS F1. Amazingly, the last F1 cars to be built in a shed were by the heroic Ken Tyrrell, who won three F1 Drivers' Championship – into the 1970s. Anyone can drive a 1961-65 Formula One car. Once into the 1970s/80s/90s era, you need experience. Only a handful of drivers can be effective in a current F1 car.

LANGUAGE AND TWO SCHOOLS

Our team could get by in Italy by only speaking English, but it helps enormously if at least one of our group speaks Italian. Italians preferred chatting with me in Italian than stumbling with limited English. The standard procedure was to see who spoke the other person's language better. As a small child, I was bilingual but in

15: Wheelspin in the Bertie Turbo at Donington.
16: Lancia Stratos 'Jolly Club' Group 4 at Aeritalia.
17: RG in the F1 1,500cc LDS Alfa Romeo.

later years was always aware of a growing deficiency. As my wife-to-be Jane and I were considering a permanent move to Italy, we signed up for two one-month intensive language courses at Perugia University. Jane already had some command of Italian. I have family connections in Perugia and know the place well. Perugia has a race circuit nearby.

Frequent trips to the *Autodromo del' Umbria* at Magione kept me in touch with motorsport. I love race circuits on weekdays. The local race school '*Scuola Piloti Henry Morrogh*' was busy and deserved a magazine feature. Henry's race school has since expanded to other Italian circuits. Henry is an Irishman who emigrated to Italy and brought up a family there. Henry sent me out in one of his Formula Fords. I asked him what the difference was between race schools in Italy compared with the UK or Ireland. He said that in Italy, many of the students come to the school to show the instructors how to drive. His race school also had a couple of the old two-cylinder 19hp Fiat 500s. Henry told me that they

were there for anyone who had trouble changing gear on the Formula Fords with their non-synchro Hewland gearboxes. As the Fiat 500s also had no-synchro gearboxes, Henry would send a troubled student out in the Fiats on the local roads to learn how to change gear smoothly. The following F1 drivers are all ex-Henry Morrogh: Elio de Angelis, Eddie Cheever, Andrea de Cesaris, Piercarlo Ghinzani, Emanuele Pirro and the 1977 World Champion Jacques Villeneuve.

A LIVE CIRCUIT AND A DEAD ONE
Another day, another race circuit. This time it is in the UK at Mallory Park. Known as the friendly circuit, it also boasts the best café food in the UK. I had three cars to compare: two 1965 Alfa GTAs and a 1964 Lotus Cortina. These were simple, communicative cars that you could race flat out immediately.

Off now to the Rockingham Motor Speedway, all brand new and squeaky clean. With its banked oval and 13 different inner race circuit configurations, it was like

18: Back to school at Perugia University.
19: Irishman Henry Morrough and RG at Magione Circuit.
20: RG checking out the Italian race school.

21 and 22: Rockingham International Speedway with a Johnny Herbert Ferrari F355.

23: Our last podium at Rockingham. A two-driver race. RG and Simon Watts.

24 and 25: Testing Alfa race cars at Mallory Park.

being in the USA. It was opened in 2001 at a cost of £70 million. It could seat 55,000 spectators. What could possibly go wrong? Well, for 17 years it worked. Race car transporters would arrive with precious cargoes. The grandstands provided picture-perfect views of whichever circuit was in use. Then there were some financial issues. Today, transporters, trucks and cars are there only because the place has been demolished, relegated to the parking of vehicles. Rockingham Motor Speedway was in perfect condition when it was destroyed. What a waste.

One of my many trips to Rockingham included a look at F1 driver Johnny Herbert's Rockingham Experience. This is where customers could drive a Ferrari F355 Challenge racing car on slicks. The Rockingham banked oval was intended for use by American oval race cars. Such vehicles are built for the job and can cope with the huge increase in tyre temperatures that banking delivers. The lap record for the 1.392-mile oval stood at an average speed of 211mph. For everyday use, only two of

the high-speed eight-degree banked turns are used before diving into one of the infield layouts. A banked turn adds a huge increase in cornering speed because some of the centrifugal force on the car is trying to move Northamptonshire. Imagine a corner banked the wrong way and how it would affect the car.

I was gentle with Johnny's cars as I didn't want to smudge the recently painted concrete wall that lines the top of the banking. However, to give you an idea of what is required from a driver, I shall relate some race car testing that I carried out there in 2017 with a 500bhp Porsche 968 Turbo RS. The first banked turn is taken flatout because it follows on from a slow infield turn – easy. Then full throttle down the start-finish straight to be presented with Turn-1, a slightly tighter than 90-degree turn. The Porsche had no appreciable downforce, so I was reliant solely on mechanical grip from the slicks. Slicks don't work unless they are properly hot, so at least two or three warm-up laps are required before going quickly. The John Danby Racing Team that I was with were using data, which analysed information after each run. With data, a driver has no place to hide. Given no downforce, I was taking the Turn-1 apex at 120mph. There was no slip angle from the tyres, so I knew I could go faster, even though it was scary. This is where a driver must forget about the concrete wall that is only inches away. After passing an apex, tightening the line is something that a driver never does. Next time, I took a deep breath, went into the more-than-90-degree turn faster than felt safe, and – with a slight lift – the data showed 135mph at the slowest point on the apex. Then back on the gas to the exit point almost brushing the wall. I could just about feel some slight slip angle. There was no safety net. It felt wrong but my lap time tumbled enormously. Had this been a track test for a magazine story, I would not have pushed so hard. Every time I go on track, I think of the object of the exercise. The next step for a race set-up would have been Turn-1 without a momentary lift of throttle. Given enough technique it might well have been okay; but I ran out of track time. Not a problem now as Rockingham's banked Turn-1 is now rubble. I shake my head at the corporate vandalism.

FAST CARS AND DAN DARE

Once a minor global player, in 2002, a survey placed Lamborghini in third place for a study in 'Supercar Brand Awareness'. A visit to revamped factory to test the new Murciélago reinforced not only brand awareness but a technical leap forward. More importantly, the workers' restaurant was fabulous, with a huge TV screen at one end. It was a clever way to eliminate absenteeism due to a football match. Workers were able to down tools and watch the game in the factory, rather than phone in sick.

Cesare Florio was the Lancia rally team's manager. Lancia launched the awesome 1,000hp Delta S4 into Group B rallies. The company even had a more ferocious monster in the pipeline: the Delta ECV. Two of our Italian contacts (Giuseppe Volta and Claudio Berro) were involved in the original project, presenting a reconstructed ECV to the public in 2010 at San Marino. The Group S Delta ECV was more powerful and 20%

B Engineering whose factory bordered onto the Bugatti works at Compogalliano. When 21 chassis tubs were left over from the production run of 139 Bugatti EB110s, the obvious thing to do was to heave them over the fence into the B Engineering factory next door. The 200mph barrier had become history as 230mph was the new 200. In 2002, the 1992–98 McLaren F1 cost £600k (£1million equivalent in 2021), with the 2004 Edonis undercutting it at only £500k (£820k today). I can remember when £1million was a lot of money. It will now only just be enough for a Hermes Birkin handbag, which at £1million, is a bargain compared with a Mouawad 1001 Night Purse costing £2.75m.

Also at the track was Tony Calo with his one-off Michelotti Pura concept car. Photos of cars and boats can be misleading as they may offer little idea of the size. The Pura was tiny and looked like something from a 1950s sci-fi comic. It weighed only 675kg and was made in 1988. Think of an early attempt at a trackday car like a Lotus Elise or Renault Spider, although the Pura preceded both by many years. I was expecting the Pura to be fitted with a modest power unit. However, its longitudinally mounted Alfa Romeo 75 Turbo Evoluzione engine pushed out c200bhp, well below the Alfa Nord's twin cam's 350hp potential. Given its miniscule frontal area, with the right gearing, that equates to a potential 200mph top speed. This is where a test driver needs a very small brain. The 'what if' factor must be absent. My small brain must be larger than I thought, as I refrained from attempting such high speeds, leaving that to Dan Dare.

PRIVATE JETS AND TOWING

Road trips are a favourite as they avoid the agony of airports. Which reminds me, there is an exception. That is when Alfa Romeo charters a jet and flies you to Italy and back via a private local airfield, Farnborough in this case. Alfa's amiable press officer Neil Warrior explained that a private jet was not extravagant if you factor in the numbers of passengers involved, countless logistics, and Club Class tickets on scheduled flights. On a sad

26: Lamborghini Murciélago Italian road test.
27 and 28: Ex-Cesare Fiorio 600bhp Delta S4.
29: Edonis supercar based on a spare Bugatti EB110 chassis.
30 and 31: Michelotti Pura concept.

lighter. These were killer years, and Group B and the stillborn Group S were banned. Lancia ordered the destruction of the S4 and the ECV, leaving just 40 examples of the S4 for posterity. A rare Stradale version: the personal car of team manager Cesare Florio was waiting for me. With 4WD and only 500hp it was driveable and I handed it back with the tyres still on the rims.

The B Engineering Edonis was a new Italian supercar. Supercar inflation has happened. As we are into the 1,000bhp territory, the new name for monstrously powered machines is hypercar. Fringe hypercar makers that survive are rare. The Edonis was made by

note, on June 1st, 2009, Neil Warrior was on board Air France flight 447 Rio-to-Paris when it crashed into the Atlantic. All 228 souls were lost.

Back to the road trip. This time Jane and I transported my Alfa Romeo GTA Turbo race car. In those days I had an open trailer, towed by a Classic Range Rover. We motored through Belgium, Luxembourg, Germany and Switzerland, eventually arriving at our base in Fiorenzuola for some Italian hillclimbs. While the car won many UK races, it was on the Italian hillclimbs where we had the most fun. Racing is a demanding sport which can deliver immense satisfaction, while the hillclimbs were more like social events. Such trips made good magazine stories, which helped with expenses.

In Bassano, the plan was for me to head south-east with the team to Venice, making several stops on the way, to gather material and photography for future stories. Meanwhile, my co-driver Jane was charged with heading north-west and solo, towing the rig (Range Rover, trailer and race car) to the top of a distant Alp for the Val Saviore Hillclimb on the following weekend. Jane had zero experience with serious trailering. A one-minute course followed, "Turn the steering wheel the wrong way for reversing. Use this low-ratio lever for steep climbs. Here is a map. Goodbye."

After the Venice expedition, the team headed for our hotel at the top of said distant Alp. The hillclimb course started at a valley bottom and finished at high altitude. On the way to our lofty destination, I wondered how Jane could ever manage with the long and tortuous journey with only a rudimentary map. At autostrada toll booths, she had to get out of the vehicle to collect the tickets. For the 'throw-the-money-into-a-basket-stops', she utilised good aim from the wrong side of the Range Rover. This was nothing compared with what was about to happen.

Turning away from the valley bottom meant a climb so steep, narrow, and so complex that the Range Rover's transfer gearbox would have to be permanently in its low ratio mode, crawling at 10-mph during the 4,000ft ascent. Did Jane remember anything from my one-minute course a few days previously? The Range Rover's engine was the basic 112hp original Italian VM 4-cylinder 2.4 turbo that was designed for marine and agricultural purposes. Visions of the Range Rover and Alfa race car lying crumpled in a ravine disappeared when, there parked at the top of the Alp was the rig, with Jane on the hotel balcony enjoying an aperitif. I should never have doubted her, or how quickly she learnt things. She tells me that her HR work means that she can see round corners. I can't do that but as a race instructor, I can see five seconds into the future. As for the alfa on the hillclimb, with its monstrous power-to-weight ratio, it disregarded the incline and rocketed up the mountain three times with ease to collect another trophy.

DRAGSTER

It is always uplifting to do something new. How could I say no to Santa Pod in a dragster? This was as a passenger in a Top Fuel 9.3-litre supercharged 'Rail',

detuned from 2,000hp to only 1,000hp and with a passenger seat squeezed in between the engine and Susanne Callin, my 18-year-old Swedish dragster pilot. I have professed that sub three seconds for a 0-60mph is unpleasant. The dragster managed it in one-second. From a 0-mph standing start, the rear of this long dragster is already doing 70mph as the back wheels cross the start-line. If you want to know what it is like, sit on a chair on a railway line with your back to the oncoming Intercity Express. The thing is, because the action is all over in such a short period, you don't have time to be frightened. In his deadpan 'Kimi Räikkönen-esque' Nordic accent, team boss Johan Hässler pointed out the intentional weak links in the long space-frame chassis. "When crash, it break into three pieces: It break here (he points). The motor fly away. The front break here (more pointing). The driver stay in this piece and fly away." I nodded and said, "Oh, that's OK then."

Down at the Surrey test track was a Michelotto-modified Ferrari F40 with a modest power increased from 478hp to 520hp. Remember this is a car with no driver aids or electronic safety nets. Making an F40 more powerful is a bit like shortening the wings on one of my favourite jets: an F-104 Lockheed Starfighter nicknamed the widow-maker. Question, is there a jet with wings shorter than nine feet? Which reminds me; my cousin Bruno Cerbelli was an F-104 pilot, a brilliant 12-string guitarist and a smoker. While the F-104 failed to assassinate him, cancer killed him in his 40s. The good die young.

32 and 33: A novice receives a one-minute course on towing a racecar in the Alps.
34: Preparing for the Val Saviore hillclimb.
35: Starfighter in the Commendatore's garden. Enzo Ferrari liked them too.
36 and 37: RG gets a ride with top fuel dragster racer, 18-year-old Susanne Callin.
38: 520bhp Michelotto F40.

2003
Jodie Kidd at Goodwood

Next was Goodwood for one of Henry Barczynski's Maserati Days. Henry was a legend in live broadcasting. In Formula One, all the teams had his Gigawave on-board camera systems. Sadly, Henry died in 2021. Back to 2003 and my job with Henry was to give hot rides in various cars as well as some race instructor duties. The supermodel, UK Team polo player and one-time BBC Top Gear track champion, Jodie Kidd was there with her Maserati 4.2 Cambiocorsa Spyder. High-end manufacturers often take a celebrity under their wing so that the celeb can be seen in their cars. Today, they are called influencers. Jodie completed some quick laps, with me pointing out Goodwood's intricacies. In later years, Maserati invited both of us to race in their Trofeo series.

SCHOOL AND HOUSE HUNTING

The year began with a winter road trip to Perugia University for our second month's intensive course in Italian. My partner Jane was enrolled in the intermediate class while I was in the advanced group that comprised much history and culture. *Auto Italia* featured the details of this university that specialises in Italian for foreigners (or for displaced Italians who need a top-up). For this travel story, I added a separate feature on the local Grand Prix driver Mario Borzacchini (1898–1933). He had countless success, but he is little known outside Italy. He died at the 1933 Monza Grand Prix. It was one of the blackest days in racing history. In one day at Monza, three Grand Prix drivers lost their lives: Giuseppe Campari, Mario Borzacchini and Count Stanislas Czaykowski. Motor racing's killer years lasted right through to the 1970s.

Change also happened for me when my partner Jane and I had been looking to sell my share in a family home in Cetraro, Southern Italy and buy somewhere else. But where? Sicily? Tuscany? Umbria? Then a team trip took me to Sanremo. It is in western Liguria, close to Monaco and the French border. This lively Riviera town with its 60,000 inhabitants is where – thanks to UK St Albans restaurateur Terry di Francesco – we met Sanremo car collector Nuccio Magliocchetti. Nuccio drove me from sea level, up mountain roads used by the Sanremo Rally, to a restaurant at San Romolo alt 1,200m (4,000ft). This is a trip that takes a long time, unless you are in a works Fiat Abarth 131 rally car being driven by a local expert at full chat. Nuccio is a race and rally car enthusiast, rally driver, yacht broker/chandler, light aircraft pilot and more. We lunch near the top of the mountain in a superb restaurant. The Dall'Ava restaurant is owned by the family of the recently deceased WRC rally driver Orlando Dall'Ava. Orlando was always happy, although hard of hearing, no doubt due to a lifetime in noisy rally cars. He died in 2019 aged 77. His restaurant walls are covered in rally photos and memorabilia. The family will continue to run the restaurant. It is a favourite. After lunch, I wandered to a viewing point overlooking Sanremo and the blue Mediterranean. It was one of the few days when Corsica was clearly visible on the horizon. I phoned Jane and said, "Sanremo is the place."

We had a goal, but we were a long way from achieving it. It wasn't going to be easy, especially as

1: Jodie Kidd and RG at Goodwood in a Maserati.
2: Sanremo Casino, a magnet for the local Russian community.
3: Nuccio in a hurry in another 131 Abarth.
4: Dall'Ava restaurant at San Romolo, high above Sanremo.
5 and 6: Nuccio's Abarth 131 Rally in the mountains.

burning bridges in the UK was not on the agenda, so please wipe your eyes, as no sympathy is necessary. If it had not been for *Auto Italia* work, who knows where we might have ended up…

THE 9/11 ATTACK AND THINKING

At the Chobham test track, we had Ferraris aplenty. The star of the day was the 1963 250LM brought along by Terry Hoyle. Goodwood Revival watchers will remember it as the car that had the big Stars and Stripes flag on the door in honour of the near 3000 people who perished during the 9/11 Twin Towers attack. The 250 LM is a priceless icon upon which many books have been written. F1 driver Jackie Oliver raced it at Goodwood and in a published conversation with reporter Charis Whitcombe, Jackie summed up the 250LM admirably.

At the test track, my Psion palmtop was on fire as I fed it with countless notes and *aide-memoire*. I also took numerous pictures for reference. I don't think I have ever had writers' block. I like the expression, "Even if a writer is staring into space, he is still working."

FORMULA TWO

At the Turin track was a 1977 Formula 2 Ralt-Ferrari. This Minardi-inspired Ralt came about after a Giancarlo Minardi – who was yet to build cars in his own name – had a conversation with Enzo Ferrari. The idea being that a short-stroke 2-litre V6 Ferrari was capable of high-rpm, thereby making more power that the 4-cylinder opposition from Cosworth and BMW. Ron Tauranac built two chassis for V6 Ferrari power. The car I tested at Turin was the ex-Elio de Angelis car. While the Ralt-Ferrari produced some reasonable results, it never set the F2 world on fire. The Ferrari V6 engine was underdeveloped and too heavy. However, as a historic car it is a star. A true time-warp car – it is totally original and unrestored, including the Scuderia Minardi Everest team logos.

7: Ferrari 250LM at Goodwood.

8: RG driving the F2 Ralt-Ferrari.

9 and 11: Lotus vs Alfa Romeo at Mallory Park.

12: Modified 850kg, IMSA Ferrari 308 on test at Chobham.

13: Outlaw flat four Fiat 600 with 220hp

UK, USA AND FRANCE

I was up early to arrive at Mallory Park Circuit to track-test two age-old adversaries: George Bryan's Lotus Cortina and Simon Drabble's Alfa Romeo GTA. The Cortina is the easier and cheaper car to race-prepare. However, the GTA is the darling. At the time, Simon Drabble was juggling a busy job in the City of London with his UK and European racing; not to mention raising a family in Hampshire. Today, he has his own company – Simon Drabble Cars, his passion finally becoming his occupation.

The team returned to the Chobham test track in Surrey for another look at the Lamborghini Murciélago and to try out two crazy Fiat 600s. While this looked like a regular twin test, we tested one Fiat 600 in Italy at Vairano and one in the UK and then joined the two stories together. The original Fiat 600s came with 21hp. In Italy, we had a conventionally Abarth-ised 120hp car presented by Fabio Gementi. However, at the Surrey test track, we had something quite different. How about a 220hp Fiat 600 used for drag-racing? The Greek Cypriot owner arrived with his own private army who

helped with the project. They looked like hard men who would bite your head off for no reason. Research shows that the maddest of all are the Italian maniacs who put a V12 Lamborghini engine into a tiny Fiat 500. But then I spotted in *Road and Track* that a V12 Lamborghini engine has been fitted to a motorcycle.

An American Ferrari 308 IMSA was the maddest test of the day – USA, land of the free. Compared with the tight technical regulations of European racing cars, our Italo-American Ferrari demonstrated a refreshing and liberated approach to racing. The Italian stereotype of disarray is at odds with their car culture. Italians are possibly the most obsessive people in the world when it comes to originality. Show this 1976 308 IMSA to an Italian and he will see it as vandalism.

American SVRA rules permit more modifications than European super-strict FIA rules. This wild 308 found its way to the UK via Paul Osborn to its owner David Higgins. Including a massive roll cage, the whole thing weighed only 850kg, while a standard 308 weighs 1,385kg. A 535kg weight reduction can only be achieved by a start-again-from-nothing approach. I would love to park this car in Paris's Place de la Concorde outside the offices of the FIA.

SPAIN

Auto Italia was invited to Spain by the Austrian designer Christian 'Hrabi' Hrabalek. Hrabi had two cars down in Sitges that were crying out for a twin test for two reasons: both the Dino 246GT and the Lancia Stratos had Ferrari V6 engines and both were yellow. Photo locations were many: the sea, the sun, the empty roads. Unusually, we were spoilt for choice. We chose a deserted cement works but after a while we were asked to leave. I told the security guard that we had been thrown out of better cement works than this. I then took the cars for a run along the gorgeous coast road – blue Med on one side, rock face on the other. The Ferrari 246GT was the sensible car. The Lancia Stratos (Stradale version) was the mad car. I prefer madness. But with a caveat: not in yellow. Only Stradale blue or in works rally livery.

We motor off to nearby Barcelona and do tourist things. Phil and I spot a UFO but – for obvious reasons – we don't tell anyone. Then off to nearby Circuit de Barcelona-Catalunya to try and get me into a Formula One Ferrari. On the way out of Barcelona, I accidentally run a red traffic light, right under the noses of two motorcycle cops. They stop our car and are about to write a traffic violation ticket. I apologise and explain what we are doing in my best Italian. The officer replies in Spanish, *"Circuito Catalunya, pare probar una Formula Uno,"* as he puts his notebook away and waves us off. Methinks: how pleasant to experience the long-lost art of police discretion.

We arrive at the circuit that is owned by Joaquin Folch. For this test day, historic racer Folch has exclusive use for his own car collection, on his own track. Our target is Folch's 1978 ex-Carlos Reutemann Ferrari 312 T3 that Martin Stretton and his men are spannering. This was to be Folch's first run in his new car, but it was not quite ready for him. By the end of the day, it was good enough for Folch to try some laps.

18

19

14 and 16: Yellow Dino vs Stratos in Spain.

17: Very high-speed tracking with F1 Ferrari where Phil Ward was thrown about to emerge battered and bruised after the high-G turns.

18 and 19: More yellow cars. Testing a Lamborghini Gallardo in Italy.

20: Trouble ahead with the polizia driving the Ferrari 360CS on the Maranello test route.

Things were not looking good for our team who had spent a whole day doing not very much. We did manage static photography and one slow lap of car-to-car snaps. With some interviews, I managed to write a story on the car, the circuit, and some associated history. We had squeezed a reasonable story from the day despite not having a test drive in the car.

ROME

Lamborghini jetted me to Rome for the presentation of the Gallardo. After a launch party in a central Rome hotel, the next morning the press were bussed out of

the eternal city to Vallelunga Race Circuit. *Top Gear* was there with a film crew. The new Lamborghinis had started circulating the track when suddenly there was much tyre screeching accompanied by a lot of shouting. I was on the spot when a journalist exited the pitlane in the wrong direction. He attacked 'his' first corner (i.e. the circuit's last corner) at the same time as another journalist was diving into the 'real' last corner. Two new Gallardos were trying their best to have a high-speed head-on crash. They just failed to ram each other as the car circulating in the right direction opted for a gravel trap rather than the hospital. Then back to Rome for another party and a return flight.

BANNED FROM DRIVING

This time a three-man team consisting of editor Phil Ward, deputy editor Michael Ward and me jetted into Bologna to pick up a hire car. Next stop Maranello and a Ferrari factory tour followed by receiving a road-racer version of the Ferrari 360. The 360 Challenge Stradale test included some laps of Ferrari's Fiorano Circuit. After the track, we motored up into the hills for a proper test for a road racer. This was also the day that Italy decided it was time to begin its zero tolerance on speeding. We had finished our road test and the Ferrari and hire car were trundling slowly back to the factory on wide open and traffic-free country roads. No other vehicles were within sight when ahead was a police road block. No problem, I

20

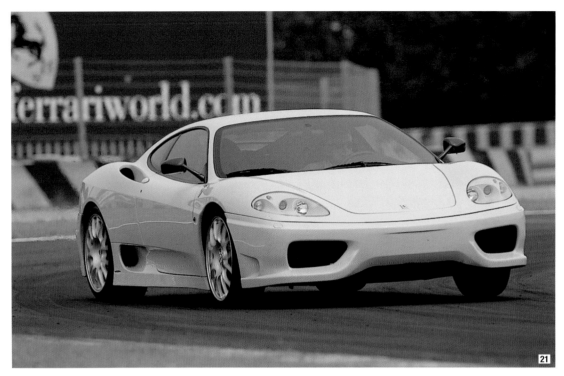

thought, as roadblocks are a common occurrence in Italy to inspect various compulsory documents, check the contents of goods in cars and to check that your income tax records match the value of the car you are driving. However, this was different.

Apparently, a few kilometres back, we had gone through a hidden speed trap at 101km/h (63mph). The speed limit was 70km/h (44mph). The low limit is from the days when ancient heavy trucks with inadequate brakes used to creep down long hills. At 101km/h, we had exceeded the 70km/h limit by more than 30km/h, i.e. by 1km/h more. That extra 1km/h meant a driving ban. Our UK driving licences were seized and we received an on-the-spot three-month ban from driving together with €350 fines each (£500 each in today's money). We were given two pieces of paper: one for me in the Ferrari and one for Phil who was driving the hire car. Only Michael who was a passenger escaped punishment. The pieces of paper permitted us to finish our short journey the Ferrari factory. Fortunately, from the factory, we had Michael who could drive all three of us back to the airport in the hire car.

21: RG testing the Ferrari 360 Challenge Stradale at Fiorano.
22: Prefettura di Modena. After one year, Phil and RG collect their driving licences.

Upon return to the UK, the DVLA issued us with replacement driving licences. After the three-month ban had elapsed, I contacted the Modena police many times via letters, phone calls, emails and via their press office to ask if they could send our licences back to the UK. Dogmatically, the reply was always, "No, you must come here in person to collect them." Italy is great like that. Its bureaucracy keeps millions of people permanently employed in the public sector who would otherwise be on benefit. Phil and I decided that we would indeed collect our licences from Modena, otherwise the Italian system would believe that we were driving without physical possession of a driving licence, which is illegal. We decided to collect our licences at a time in the future, that would suit us.

The Italian licence system is connected to Italian Passport Control. Many months later, when I flew into Genoa, while my licence was still at Modena, the

Passport Control officer scanned my UK passport and reminded me that I could not drive in Italy because my licence was still in Modena. After about one year, Phil and I were in Modena and went to the police department that held driving licences. We were ushered into a Soviet-style office where the walls were lined with shelves containing thousands of dusty files, each bound with a ribbon. "Ah…, you are the journalists from England," said the nice lady looking after the dusty files. I was surprised to see that Phil and I each had bulky files bound with ribbon. As the lady handed us our UK driving licences she said, "You need not have come here in person, we could have posted them to the UK."

LEARNING AND ITALIAN STUFF

Off to Varano Circuit in Italy courtesy of Maserati to spend a couple of days at the track in a fleet of 4200GTs. With me at Varano were supermodel Jodie Kidd, whom I instructed at Goodwood, journalist Emma

23: Sliding around on the wet handling area with a 4200 GT.
24 – 26: Maserati driving course at Varano with Jodie Kidd.

Parker-Bowles (niece of Camilla Duchess of Cornwall and future Queen Consort) and editors Phil and Michael Ward. Our minders were Italy's top instructors. In his intro, ex-F1, ex-Le Mans, ex-F3000 and ex-F3 Champion Enrico Bertaggia told me, "You never stop learning." Naturally, I pinched this expression for my own driver training clients. Indeed, I did learn one trick from Enrico that I shall keep to myself and to my driver-training customers. Enrico lives in Monaco, which is 20 minutes along the coast from our place in Sanremo. What a coincidence when he told me that his favourite restaurant in the whole world is the same as ours, the Ristorante Byblos in the Ospedaletti suburb of Sanremo.

The Modena Historic Challenge was organised by Matteo Panini and held in a stadium. I was strapped into Fabio Gementi's Formula Italia single-seater. In the Modena stadium, my task was to compete in a regularity challenge, of which I knew nothing. Until then, I thought a regularity challenge involved consuming large quantities of prunes. A challenge indeed. My previous occasion in a stadium was in 1966 at Wimbledon where I simply had to lap as fast as possible. Unlike my Wimbledon success, my regularity debut was a failure, but far more importantly, while I was in the area, I learnt some more about balsamic vinegar and parmesan cheese. Balsamic vinegar varies from the dirty water sold in supermarkets, to the vintage delight that costs vastly more. As for parmesan, you should know that the supermarket dust version should only be used for mopping up oil spills on the garage floor. The proper stuff should be grated within seconds of use. It can also be enjoyed ungrated in chunks with bread and a little red wine.

MR FERRARI AND MR LAMBORGHINI

Back in the UK, I had a routine test to carry out on a Lamborghini and a Ferrari. I considered the men responsible for these premier global brands. Unlike Mr Kia or Mr Hyundai who make cars for money, our Italian founders made cars purely to make the greatest

cars possible. I am reminded of a story from a Mille Miglia event. An American's Ferrari broke down on the Italian road rally. It happened to be near a tiny workshop. The mechanic came out and quickly fixed the car. Much relieved and pulling out his wallet, the American asked the mechanic, "How much?" *"Niente."* (nothing), came the reply. "But you did me a favour", said the American. The mechanic replied, *"Non l'ho fatto per lei. L'ho fatto per la macchina."* "I did not do it for you. I did it for the car."

Back to Mr Ferrari and Mr Lamborghini. I think how different they were from each other. Many people know the story of how Commendatore Enzo insulted lowly tractor-maker Ferruccio Lamborghini because Ferruccio complained that the clutches Ferrari used were too small and that the cars' interiors were rather basic. We also know that this inspired Ferruccio to build cars that would be better than Enzo's. The car war started. Ferruccio made the 350GT, which was easily a match for the best Ferrari. Then Ferruccio won the war outright with the Miura. He then twisted the

knife with the Miura SV. This at a time when Ferrari's flagship was the Daytona, a car that drove like a fast truck. At this point, Ferruccio Lamborghini retired, and the rest is history. I used to visit relatives in Umbria regularly, very near Lamborghini's country house.

Ferruccio Lamborghini retired to a farmhouse complete with a farm and vineyard on the banks of Lake Trasimeno. As he made his initial fortune from tractors, returning to tend the land and grow his vines was in his blood. I knew someone who was friendly enough with Ferruccio to visit unannounced. One Sunday, whilst approaching the main door of the house, he could hear some drilling and DIY noises. Signora Lamborghini opened the door, *"Ciao, prego accomodarti."* Come in, make yourself at home. There was Ferruccio in his underpants covered in dust drilling a hole in the wall. Enzo was too aloof to be caught with his trousers down. Enzo Ferrari never let his guard down. Ferrari was that secretive, ruthless aristocrat in dark glasses. Ferrari was remote and aloof, while Lamborghini was one of us.

27 – 30: Back to basics. Formula Italia test at Varano circuit with owner Fabio Gementi.
31: Ferrari 575 GTC poses outside Enzo's house.
32: Lamborghini tractor.

2004
Best Car – Worst Car

Another trip to Fiorano to test the car nicknamed "The Ice Racer". It had languished for 25-years buried in a Finnish shed. This 750 Monza became the property of collector and racer Carlos Monteverde. The 750 Monza weighed next to nothing (760kg) and is powered by a four-cylinder, three-litre 260bhp motor. The suspension is rock solid and it runs on Dunlop crossply historic race tyres. At Fiorano, the pit crew looked at me and I looked back. Normally 80% of communication is via body language. In this case it was 100%. They were looking at me and thinking, "Let's hope this pen-pusher brings it back in one piece." I was looking back at them and thinking, "F*** off. I have raced and track tested hundreds of racing cars. This is just another car." The track-test was done the magazine story on such cars usually includes the history, written expertly by Peter Collins or Keith Bluemel – this time it was the latter. Also, at Fiorano, Carlos Monteverde had his 250 Testa Rossa and Dino 206SP, both being looked after by Gary Pearson. With some tech spec from Gary, the seven-page story was in the bag.

Still in Italy, Alfa Romeo gave me a 3-litre GTV for a week. My travel story was quite ruthless by pointing out any Italian negatives. I meant no harm-indeed, it was my futile attempt for the words to get back to someone in power who might eliminate those negatives. If I only wrote about Italy's positive aspects, the story would read like something from a travel agent's brochure.

I am frequently asked what is the best or worst car that I have driven. To which I reply, "Road car or race car?" The worst race car I have driven won the European Touring Car Championship (ETCC). So how can it be the worst car? The car in question was the Alfa Romeo 156 GTA Super 2000, in making it the fastest car they also made it the trickiest to drive. Alfa Romeo needed a third place or better in the final round at Monza if they were to shatter the might of BMW. Alfa fielded five cars for the race, employing their best drivers, namely: Giancarlo Fisichella, Gabriele Tarquini, Nicola Larini, James Thompson and Roberto Colciago. How could Alfa fail? Disaster came in qualifying when Alfa's three F1 drivers Fisichella, Tarquini and Larina all wrecked their cars. Faced with three piles of scrap, Alfa's best shot was for its mechanics to spend a night cobbling together one car for Tarquini. Tarquini came third and that was good enough for Alfa to win the ETCC. So why was it tricky to drive? It was because if you simply thought about lifting your foot from the accelerator pedal whilst not running perfectly straight, the car would spin. I drove the car at Varano and chatted with the legendary Alfa works driver Andrea de Adamich. He also found it 'interesting', which for someone with an Alfa Romeo supplied race school, is corporate speak for 'horrible'.

Still at Varano race circuit, the Alfa Romeo works team has a 147 GTA Cup race car for me to try. This is a one-make championship where the winner is guaranteed a Touring Car drive. The car was great but even better was having another legend, Giorgio Francia, looking after me, briefing me and strapping me in.

Best and worst road cars? This depends upon how old I am when asked the question. In my youth, speed, acceleration, handling, and affordability were my only concerns. Modified Fords, Alfas, and Jaguars from the 1960s were obvious favourites. I have never been a

1: The Monza nicknamed the 'Ice Racer' about to go on track at Fiorano.
2: RG with Gabriele Tarquini at Mugello in 2022.
3 and 4: Exotic Ferraris from the Monteverde collection at Fiorano.
5: Alfa 156 European Touring Car Championship winner. One of RG's worst racing cars.

I-only-want-a-car-to-get-me-from-A-to-B person. Like the clothes you wear, your car says something about you, even if they cost next to nothing. I have never owned a new car. Special cars apart, in the last 40 years, my daily drivers have included various Range Rovers, topped up with some Alfa Romeos, Fiats and three front-engined Porsches: 924 Turbo, 944 2.7 and 968 Club Sport. I like the mechanical configuration of BMWs, although I have never owned one. I love American cars from the dawn of motoring, right up to the 1970s, be they huge luxury limos, regular vehicles or muscle cars. I have never owned one because I would feel self-conscious driving one in the UK or Europe.

The nearest I got was when I restored and competed in 18 races in the famous Dean Van Lines 1958 Lister Chevrolet. Weighing only 850kg and with 520hp, massive aerodynamic lift and running on bicycle tyres, it was always trying to kill me. The really great thing about that Lister Chevy is that whatever monster I drive now is child's play. I raced at Goodwood ten times: eight times in the Lister, once in Stephen Bond's Lotus 26R, and once in Paul Clayson's Ford Falcon. I have been fortunate enough to race dozens of different cars in hundreds of races. As for test-driving, I have never added up the numbers. While there must be many hundreds, only a few are mentioned in these pages.

I would love to race an Alfa GTAm, but it falls into an unfortunate FIA period where it cannot win a race. At 21 years of age, I had a 1961 Jaguar E-Type Roadster; it doubled as my road car and racing car, winning at Silverstone in the 1970s. It cost £400 (£5,700 in today's money). I recently turned back the years by returning to an FIA pre-63 spec E-Type, for race use, whereupon in 2021 it won a race, first time out of the box. It is my time machine and it's had six podium places from its last six races.

DESIGNERS DESIGNING FOR DESIGNERS

A trip to a design house can be a laugh. Gruppo Bertone is in Turin and its 1970 Stratos Zero is straight out of a period sci-fi movie. This was a driveable

6: German track. German car. Porsche 924 Turbo.
7: I have driven too many great racing cars to list them all. A well-sorted E-Type is one of the goodies.
8: The 500hp/890kg Dean Van Lines Lister Chevrolet. It was always trying to kill me.
9 and 10: The Bertone Stratos Zero is an example of bad design which fascinates me but is a good PR ornament.
11: Ron Simon's walking tour – Nürburgring Nordschleife Karussell. A more than 180-degree banked turn.

concept car. The Stratos Zero could never have worked. Even the designers would have been able to work that out.

The Stratos Zero has no doors. Entry to the Zero is via a hinged windscreen that doubles as a partial roof. The windscreen is almost horizontal. It is very close to your face and your body, extending from your feet to your head. The sitting position is reclined so that you have a good view of the sky. If it is a sunny day, you are barbequed. While the Zero looks remarkable, I presume it was designed purely as a publicity stunt – in which case Bertone is excused.

In the 1960s, during my five years of engineering studies and apprenticeship, I spent three years in a design and drawing office of Fluidrive Engineering Company in Isleworth. Design has always interested me. There are two kinds of design: good design and bad design. Good design is what I expect. It is bad design that fascinates me. Bad design deserves a book.

DEUTSCHLAND, DEUTSCHLAND UBER ALLES...

Back in the UK, the photographer Andrew Brown set up a visit to Germany's Nürburgring Nordschleife (northern loop). At the time, Ron Simons ran the 75 Experience at the notorious circuit. Not to be confused with the

adjoining Nürburgring Grand Prix Circuit at 5km per lap, the Nordschleife, or 'Ring' as it is often called, was purpose-built by a sadist in 1927. Words cannot describe the Nordschleife and photos cannot reveal the tricky gradients and downright dirty tricks of the circuit designer, although Jackie Stewart summed it up in just two words, 'Green Hell'. Today, anyone with a road legal vehicle can pay €25 per lap (€30 at the weekends) or €1,900 for a one-year pass. Yes, there are Ring junkies that can't keep away. On public days, you will see all kinds of cars, SUVs, vans, motorbikes – and minibuses – circulating. The 21km (13-mile) lap has 170 corners, steep gradients and blind brows, lined with steel barriers with no run-off areas.

When I steered our Porsche 924 Turbo into the famous Karussell turn, Jane understandably thought that we had crashed into some road works. At this point, if you are thinking of having a go, you should watch the countless YouTube footage of crashes at the Nordschleife. First-timers (Ring virgins) are normally cautious and safe. Ring junkies with thousands of laps under their belt may also be safe. It is the majority, i.e. those in between the virgins and the pros, who make the most catastrophic mistakes. There are those who have never driven there, and there are drivers with a mad twinkle in their eye who have.

ITALY, COMMUNISTS AND BRAVERY

I was spending much time in Italy. Writing negative things about Southern Italy brings on death threats, so let's criticise the North. There has always been an underlying whiff of the 'Soviet' in northern Italy with far too many business-stifling regulations and senseless bureaucracy. In the post-war years, Russia created the Soviet Union which gobbled up countless countries and created what in 1946, Churchill called, the Iron Curtain. His words were, "From Stettin in the Baltic to Trieste in the Adriatic, an 'iron curtain' has descended across the continent."

Italy's eastern frontier bordered the Iron Curtain and was under threat from a domino effect. The Australian writer and broadcaster Clive James (1939-2019) wrote in his book, *My Russia*, "A Russian will knock down a neighbour's wall and then help him rebuild it, but a little further into the Russian's territory." At this time, Italy had more communists than any other Western European country. There was a realistic threat that Italy could end up on the wrong side of that Iron Curtain. Even today, communism in Italy is strong. You can add socialism to that, although the following quote may upset socialists, but history cannot refute the words of Vladimir Lenin, "The goal of socialism is communism." The Brescia/Milan area is where the money is made. This is where there is the highest concentration of prestige car dealers. It is also the stronghold of the political left, so the communists here are wealthy.

We motor to Maleo to meet the global Abarth guru Tony Berni. Tony decamped from Wales decades ago, to work for Ferrari before setting up his own business. His squeaky-clean premises are a world-renowned base for things Abarthy. Tony took us to visit several collectors for future stories.

We whizz up to Turin to meet up with Gian Claudio Giovannone, the founder of the Senna Foundation, who was on hand with some interesting machinery. The Senna Foundation is a charity that helps underprivileged Brazilian kids. Claudio brought along the ex-Ayrton Senna Formula One JPS Lotus 98 (ch.

12: Tony Berni, RG and Renzo Avidano, Carlo Abarth's number two and race team boss in the 1950s/60s/70s.
13: The Italian Communist Party is still strong.
14: Assorted classic F1 cars at Aeritalia.
15: Phil shooting Maserati interior.
16: Milan cathedral.
17: Concorde on static display.
18: Pagani's self-prepared Formula Renault.

no. 98-1). Built in 1986, its Renault V6 1,500cc turbo motor produces 780hp in just 540kg (1,444hp/tonne). We couldn't resist sitting where the great Brazilian ace once sat. This was a period when the driver sat far forward. With the suspension wrapped around your legs, and the steering rack resting nicely on your shins, you had to be brave in those days.

NICE THINGS

We book ourselves into our usual Modena hotel – which is not in Modena but near Maranello in the little agricultural hamlet of *Settecani* (Seven Dogs). Hotel Zoello is inexpensive, clean and has a great restaurant. Enzo Ferrari dined there in his own booth.

We clash with Swedish journalists shadowing our Modena movements, muscling in on our cars to cover the same stories. We call a truce and suggest a night out in Modena. They take off their Viking helmets and we ask them about polar bears in the Swedish streets and how they dodge suicide victims falling from buildings. They ask when the UK will drive on the right. Funny that, Italians also ask that question.

Next morning, we drop into Lamborghini at Sant'Agata Bolognese for future features. We lunch with Lamborghini, but we still haven't photographed our Alfa GT press car, which is filthy and take it to a car wash. Washing your own car in Italy is a no-no. It's a class thing. I always wash my own cars because I know my place.

We return our Alfa Romeo to Milan, which we decide is our least favourite Italian city. We ask what Milan has done for us. Ok, so the bit around the *Duomo* is nice. And yes, there are some posh shops. *La Scala* opera house and the Science Museum aren't bad either, but we still don't like it. From end to end, Italy is 1,000 miles long, with nearly 5,000 miles of coastline. It's a mad and often infuriating place and we can't wait to return.

ART FOR ART'S SAKE

A few days later, I return to Italy to revisit a hero. I can't think of many of my heroes that are alive except

perhaps one, Horacio Pagani. He did not launch his hypercar company in a post-war industrial boom, where everyone was singing from the same hymn sheet, but in modern times where half the population is employed trying to stop the other half from doing things.

A friend of a friend is the artist David Hockney, who announced, "Art has to move you, and design does not – unless it's a good design for a bus." At this point you should be aware that the new London buses cost about the same as a Zonda. With room for one passenger and some designer luggage in the side pods, the Pagani Zonda is not a bus, but it does mix art, design and engineering.

Indoctrinated from cradle to grave, most of us don't realise that we have been brain-washed to regard art and engineering as worlds apart, like oil and water, Rangers and Celtic, the East and the West, the Left and the Right, the woke and the gammon, the do-ers and the stoppers. In colleges and universities, art and engineering students are kept apart. Those who escape this indoctrination are the exception. Pagani's hero is Juan-Manuel Fangio who could wield a mean spanner and his driving was certainly an art form that moved him as well as those watching. The Concorde aircraft had that magic combination. I realise that I am flogging a dead horse here, because artists will tell you that if an object has any function, it is not art. However, now that Concorde is for static display only, it has no function.

A car designer once told me that the Zonda's styling is like the work of a child. This reminded me of a saying that architects design buildings not for people, but for other architects. The Pagani factory's reception area has some interesting displays. That the head of a car company once had to slug it out in motor racing says much and is a good thing. His 1976 self-prepared Formula Renault from his Argentinian race days nestles in the corner.

The Maserati factory was next and we were given a Quattroporte by Maserati's charismatic press officer Andrea Cittadini. Andrea was always helpful and his invaluable assistance much appreciated. We drove the

QP to nearby Carpi for a photoshoot in the town centre. Things began badly. I got fined €68 (£100 in today's money) by the *Polizia* Locale for driving the Maserati into Carpi's pedestrian-only zone for our photo shoot. The nice policeman said that as we were *gentile* (pleasant), he would wave an additional £100 ticket he was going to give us for parking. As we hung our heads in shame, looked at our feet and apologised, we considered the three previous illegal photo shoots at the same location.

SPAIN, ASCARI AND A HUEY

Dunlop chose Andalusia to launch a new top-of-the-range performance tyre, the SP Sport Maxx. The road-driving in the empty hinterland of Spain was a reminder of motoring pleasures long absent.

Day One

Day 1 began with driving an Opel Speedster (the European name for the Vauxhall VX 220). The Opel/Vauxhall is based on the Lotus Elise. From just south of Marbella on the Costa del Sol we motored 50km inland through the mountains to Ronda. Tyre-testing on public roads calls for observations on ride, noise and stability rather than flirtations with slip angles. It all sounds rather responsible, but we were in the company of 14 other hacks in seven other Speedsters, so the race was on. Eventually we rolled into Ronda and the Hotel de Parador perched on a beautiful cliff top where the journos exchanged tales of derring-do deep into the night.

Day Two

For our second day, bleary-eyed hacks were bussed into the nearby Ascari Race Resort where we had a variety of cars fitted with the new Dunlops. A tyre test without comparative data from several tyre makers means little. More PR jolly than anything else, at least we were able to experience driving on this amazing track. I doubt that many have ever heard of the Ascari Race Resort. It was brand-new in 2004. It was the

brainchild of oil billionaire and motorsport enthusiast Klaus Zwart. Klaus created his circuit and the many facilities on the massive site in what was once an empty valley of near-desert conditions. It is now an irrigated green and pleasant land. At 5.4km in length, it can also be subdivided into several alternative circuits. It can be wetted at the push of a button. It incorporates and emulates the best of the best, for instance, turn 5 is Copse (Silverstone), turn 7 is The Dipper (Bathurst), turn 16 Eau Rouge (Spa), turn 19 is from Daytona. Klaus's track is not for racing. It is an exclusive club with a £100k joining fee but for impoverished writers, it is one hell of a corporate jolly.

The tyre test was rounded off without wheels, via a

flight through the mountains to Malaga Airport in old Bell Huey helicopters. Two Hueys flying in tandem took 20 people from the circuit, over the mountains and then along the Costa del Sol to Malaga Airport. The Bell UH-1, nicknamed Huey, first flew in 1956 and was in production until 2016. Used by the police and military worldwide, including the Italian Carabinieri, with Augusta-Hueys built under licence in Italy. In all, about 15,000 have been built. It was featured heavily in the film *Apocalypse Now*. It is the first mass-produced helicopter to use a jet turbine. The tips of its long rotor blades run at supersonic speed generating the woka-woka-woka beat that only a Huey can make. Apart from the smell of napalm in the morning, I loved skimming over hill tops and through high mountain passes. The rattling clattering Hueys bobbed, weaved and yawed in the turbulence. Flying along the coast gave a bird's eye view of the incredible sprawl of villas and pools. Cruising at 100 knots (115mph) and 1,300ft, the building site went on and on and on.

I worked out why I loved the Huey so much – the same reason that I like cars from the period. You can see exactly how the machines are made: the screws, the rivets, the brackets, the welds, the nuts and bolts, the pre-electronic electrics. Anyone can repair a Huey. It has since been replaced by the UH-60 Black Hawk, that is better at everything. Everything except charm if you can say that about a machine.

19: One of 15,000 Hueys. We had two in Spain.
20: Spain – a selection of cars to test shod with new Dunlops.
21: Ronda. Don't fall off your hotel balcony.
22 and 24: Alfa Giulia Ti Super racing at Silverstone.

BACK ON TRACK

When the request came to race Simon Drabble's rare Alfa Romeo Giulia Ti Super at Silverstone in a 45-minute, two-driver race, I replied, "Yes. Love to." They made 600,000 similar-looking Giulia saloons, but only 500 lightweights like Simon's factory original Ti Super. Think of it as a GTA saloon car. However, unless the Alfa is totally re-engineered at a cost of £200k and driven by a pro, it does not stand a chance of a top-ten place. We did our best and came nowhere. Given a typical 40-car grid, 39 cars (97.5%) will be piloted by losers. It is not like a football match where 50% of the players are winners. Many people do not understand this, neither do those who ask me, "Did you win?" and look at me pitifully if I reply in the negative. Even coming second is a total failure, "First of the losers", being the expression often used by those who have never raced.

AUSTRIA AND GERMANY

Austria, land of music. It was certainly music to our ears when we received a tip-off about a classic car scrapyard. What rust-blooded car enthusiast can drive past a continental scrapyard without rubber-necking? You are dying to stop and explore, but the normal people in your car think you are deranged, so you drive on by. Aficionados know that a scrapyard is an art form, especially if it contains old stock. If Carl Andre's 'pile of bricks', or Tracey Emin's 'unmade bed' – both exhibited

in the Tate Gallery and short-listed for the Turner Prize – are art, then so is a scrapyard.

Heaven is a classic car scrapyard that is not open to the public. Welcome to heaven, which is located about 50km south of Vienna at Josef Schmalzl's Autometal recycling works. From the road, you see nothing but a huge house with a full-size dummy whale in the front garden. Hidden from public gaze, the premises are vast. The dozens of cars in the back yard, or under restoration in the many out-buildings are treasures. After the tour of the enormous classic car scrapyard, we go through a door at the far end of the yard. It's a bit like *"The Lion, the Witch and the Wardrobe"*. We enter Schmalzl's private green and pleasant paradise – a lodge on a lake. We test various Austrian alcoholic

drinks and reorganise the world. Did I just see a whale?

Our next stop in Austria was nearby to visit Franz and Gerda Krump who were on their ninth De Tomaso, currently a Pantera Si and a Guara, which was De Tomaso's last production car. An early Pantera looked great and performed well. The concept worked. Think of a Ford GT40 wearing Prada or Armani and you have a Pantera. The early Pantera GTS is my favourite with a nicely sorted Mangusta in second place. Later-series Panteras got fat and less attractive. Why does that happen?

Gerda Krump accompanied me on a test drive in the Austrian countryside in their De Tomaso Guara. With the Guara, the factory lost the plot. In short, they were making a high-tech track car for geeks that was

25: Austrian scrapyard. To be precise, cars awaiting restoration.
26: Compulsory scrapyard dog checking a 'fuel injected' Fiat 125. A nice dog.
27: Franz Krump watching his Pantera Si being fuelled.

unaffordable. Geeks already had a choice of fast low-cost trackday weapons.

The Krumps took us to central Vienna, which is a lovely place to sit and watch the world go by whilst testing some strudel. If you are a foody, you may know about the claim Austria has to *wiener schnitzel* (breaded veal escalope). As any Italian will tell you, it is Italian and called *vitello milanese* (veal milanese).

Just down the road (350 miles away) is Stetten in Germany, the HQ location of Novitec. This is a tuning house for high-end exotic cars with whom we had built a great relationship. Fast cars apart, Novitec gave us many opportunities to enjoy Germany.

When I wasn't writing, racing or in my shed, I was a race instructor at several locations. One of those tracks was the UK's fastest circuit. Having Thruxton Motorsport Centre only one-hour from home was convenient. Many of the cars in the Thruxton fleet were Italian supercars. There was another ready-made story for the magazine. World War Two (1939–45) was good for UK motorsport as there were countless airfields with perimeter roads

that became redundant. Thruxton's 2.4-mile lap provided fast flowing curves that only a vast area can deliver. Less fortunate circuits have squeezed a long lap length into a small area. Instead of fast corners, many are cursed with innumerable tight turns. Sadly, Snetterton Circuit, which was a war-time airfield, scored an own goal when a tight infield section was added, spoiling what was once a great race circuit.

TURIN, MASERATI AND MONZA

Another trip to the Aeritalia track in Turin and I am faced with an onslaught of cars including famous Lancia works rally cars: a Fulvia, a Stratos, an 037, a Delta S4 and an integrale. It is a busy day.

I mentioned at the beginning of the book how a motoring writer can receive various useful connections and benefits. One such return was when Maserati asked me to come to Monza to test their new race car. With new ownership, Maserati was entering the world of mass production with the 3200GT and then the 4200GT. Figures show that in 1997 they sold 300 cars. The year I

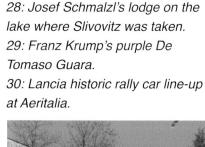

28: Josef Schmalzl's lodge on the lake where Slivovitz was taken.
29: Franz Krump's purple De Tomaso Guara.
30: Lancia historic rally car line-up at Aeritalia.

am at Monza (2004), they sold over 2,500. By 2017 they sold 10,000 and nearly 20,000 in 2019.

Anyway, back at Monza and Maserati Corse is showing off its swarm of snarling 4200 GranSports, racing-prepared for the Maserati Trofeo one-make series. This was to be another unforgettable assignment. The series was in its third year and offered the ultimate in arrive-and-drive racing for gentlemen drivers. The term 'gentleman driver' means a non-pro driver who has attained a high-grade (International C) racing licence, and then buys his or her way into the series. The drivers may be very quick or average, but not slow. The success of the series saw an increase in pro drivers. Jodie Kidd was one of several celebrity racing drivers that Maserati invited to the Trofeo. She was tipped to join Tiff Needell in July 2005 for the round supporting the British GP at Silverstone. I was on my best behaviour, as I could see the possibility of invitations to race in the series, which turned out to be the case.

The preceding day, I had arrived at the Milan hotel to meet my international contemporaries and Maserati hosts. It is at times like this that you realise how English has become a universal language. Italians, Spanish, Swedes, Hungarians, Romanians and others, all communicated in English. Although on this occasion, the Romanians must have misunderstood, as the next morning, they were fast asleep while the rest of the party stood waiting. Add a Milan traffic jam and my transport arrived at the circuit too late for my time slot. I signed-on and changed into my race gear in record time. Knowing that there was a queue and not much time left, the crew indicated *"Tre giri"* (three laps). The three laps ended in a nanosecond with too much information to assimilate in such a short time; I made notes. It was my first time at Monza, and I had a new circuit to learn. It is fabulous and so fast, although spoilt in 1972 by the addition of its first chicane: the *Primo Variante.* This is a ridiculously tight chicane close to the end of the start-finish straight, where cars must slow from their top speeds to near-walking pace and go single file. No one likes it. This chicane causes crashes,

ruins the racing and instigates cars to back up, often with the cars at the rear of a crowded grid coming to a stop. That apart, Monza really is the 'Cathedral of Speed'. There are plans to improve its magnificence. To mark Monza's centenary, there are plans to spend €100,000 to make changes and increase its 5.8km length to 10km. This would include using some of the banking and make the best even better.

Back in the cockpit, the slicks were cold and would need two of my three laps to reach their operating temp. Three laps done and back in the pits, I wondered what information I had missed. Did I have time to push the car hard enough to learn anything meaningful? Er ... no. I needed more seat time.

The next journo test session wasn't until 4.40pm-5.00pm and dangerously close to the time of my return flight. What if we get held up in more Milan traffic? What if I don't drive again? I could simply make something up, cobble a story together. Who would know any different?

I chatted with Maserati press boss and rugby fan Andrea Cittadini and – because I live near Twickenham rugby stadium – he organised an early slot for me to have another go in the race car. I interview some key personnel including a Pirelli tyre engineer, Maserati race engineer Silvio Campigli and their works MC12 GT driver Fabio Babini. The information added much welcome insight to the magazine feature.

Time for my second drive and more knowledge. The track is busy with Maseratis and Alfa Romeo 147 Cup race cars. It was good to be in that frenetic company. In pre-track limit days, the Alfas straight-lined the chicanes with all four wheels in the dirt. Not slowing down makes a massive difference to lap times. My time was up. I bid farewell to the Maserati team and their GranSport race cars, dash to the airport in a chauffeur-driven car, making notes. I wondered if I would ever be invited to race one. Little did I know at the time that I would be invited for eight one-hour races in the Trofeo Championship, as well as several pre-season appraisals of the racing version of the next model, the GranTurismo Trofeo.

31: Monza. A swarm of Maserati Trofeo race cars, fresh out of the box and ready for testing.
32: Rugby fan and Maserati PR boss Andrea Cittadini with RG.
33: At speed through Ascari.

2005
You're Nicked Sunshine

We tested several modern Alfa Romeos that were upgraded by Jano Djelalian, the boss of the London workshop called Autodelta. The company has no connection with the factory Autodelta but the upgrades we tried were good. One day, Phil Ward received a call from Jano that he was organising a supercar run to a dealership in the Swiss city of Basel. As Phil and I could combine the run with delivering a Maserati GranSport press car to Modena – via a stop at the Bologna Motor Show – we agreed. I was volunteered to be the driver of the Maserati. Canonball-type runs are my idea of hell, but I consented. At 5am one morning, our five-car convoy set off from Jano's west London workshop. Jano told me that the Basel dealership was having a lunch party for us. From experience, I raised my eyebrows knowing that we would arrive in Basel at about 5pm local time. I led the convoy, followed by half a dozen very fast cars. Speeding was not on my agenda. While you might get away with a brief burst of rapidity, speeding for a long distance would result in trouble. By the time we entered Swiss territory, all the drivers were bored, their right feet itching for action.

We arrived at the Basel dealership for the lunch party at 5pm local time, i.e., when it was all over. We said hello and goodbye and set off for the Italian border with our Maserati still leading the convoy. There was cannonball-talk of a photoshoot on the famous Stelvio Pass. Knowing that it would take all day, Phil and I quashed that idea. We were on the Swiss motorway that will eventually lead us to the Italian border at Como. I noticed that the Swiss get annoyed and flash their headlights if you misbehave even slightly, so I kept a lid on our quick convoy. Speeding is like farting: your own are okay, those of others are disgusting. Suddenly, and totally out-of-character a Swiss-registered hot hatch hurtled past us on a quiet stretch of motorway. This provocation allegedly sent the four supercars behind me after the hot hatch and, allegedly, overtaking it at huge speeds. I dare not write what those hypothetical speeds might have been, but as mentioned, all the cars were capable of 160mph. I blame the garage food. Junk food causes anti-social behaviour. The hot hatch turned off the motorway and we all slowed down and fell back into line. At the Swiss/Italian border-post I felt a disturbance in the force. The authorities were waiting for us.

As this was the Italian-speaking part of Switzerland, I was our spokesman. A police officer started shouting at me about our speeding. He collected all our passports and took them away. We were all detained. I needed to know whether the police had any evidence of our speeding or whether they were seeking a confession. "We know what you did and the speeds you reached." barked the policeman. After more shouting, I figured that they had no evidence, and – like any criminal – I continually denied all accusations that our bunch of hooligans had been speeding. *"Non eravamo noi",* ("It wasn't us"), I repeated endlessly. I worked out that if the police had evidence, we would have been immediately arrested with no discussion. Time went by and eventually our passports were returned, and we were shown the way out of Switzerland. "I have been thrown out of better countries than this," were the words I was too timid to utter. We were lucky because penalties

1: In the process of annoying the Swiss police while on tour with UK Alfa Romeo specialists Autodelta. 2: Autodelta-tuned Alfa GT and hot shot 147 GTAs.

could have been astronomic including huge fines, prison and confiscated cars. At this point Phil and I parted from the supercar run and set a course for Bologna. That was my first and last cannonball-type run.

The Bologna Show was a rowdy affair. Each stand played its own music at deafening volumes. This meant that you were constantly in range of several bellowing music tracks at any one time. It was torture. Maserati had an MC12 race car that they were wheel-spinning around a temporary track delineated with cones. Their works driver doing the honours was Andrea Bertolini whom I had met several times. He offered me a ride which I accepted – the noise inside a race car being better and quieter than that in the exhibition halls. Outside the show, a non-Italian tried to mug me and failed. Time to move on. We motor into Modena to deliver the Maserati to its makers and are taken on a guided tour of the refurbished Maserati factory. The central Modena factory is a listed building, so during renovation, the exterior had to remain the same with the interior being brought up to date. With all jobs done, we headed home.

NURBURGRING AND SPA

Track tests on the Nürburgring Nordschleife require great care as the place takes no prisoners. A suitably modified Lancia integrale (300bhp) and a modified Alfa Romeo GTV6 (275bhp) were given to us thanks to Ron Simons of RSR Nürburg. These were used by Ron to instruct and to give taxi rides like no other. A hot lap around the Nordschleife with Ron, is the best way to realise how well you don't know the circuit.

Spa-Francorchamps circuit in Belgium is only 85-minutes from the Nürburgring. Ask any racer to name his top five favourite race circuits and I cannot imagine Spa to be an absentee. Waiting for me in the pitlane is a late 1950s Maserati 300S. During the late '50s early '60s, race car development was moving fast. Today's historic racing series are categorised in various periods. The Maserati 300S was made from 1955 to 1958, which means that it is a 1955 design. This puts it into the FIA

6

7

3: RG with Maserati MC12 racing driver Andrea Bertolini.
4: Doughnuts at the Bologna Show with Bertolini.
5: Modified Alfa and Lancia at the Nürburgring.
6: Maserati 300S at Spa.
7: Scottish west coast neighbours, Jane and Jackie.

Period E (1947 to 1961). Obviously the nearer your racing car is to the cut-off date the better. Therefore, you never see a Maserati 300S doing well at races like the Goodwood Sussex Trophy where the cut-off date is at the 31/12/1961. That said, driving any car at Spa is always welcome. All race circuits have booby traps and I always point them out when driver coaching. These are where accidents are most common or most serious. Spa is fast and has two obvious booby traps: Blanchimont (a fast left-hander) and Radillon, the notorious left kink at the top of Eau Rouge. Thankfully, Radillon has been re-aligned as there have been too many deaths and life-changing injuries. The modern 7km Spa is infinitely safer than the old 14km Spa (1939-1978). Have a drive around the fast old circuit, which is on public roads to try to imagine how scary it must have been for the drivers.

WEE JACKIE
2005 also saw the completed restoration of my Miura SV, which was now dashing about the UK and Europe in various motorsport and classic events. Meanwhile, I had an appointment with triple F1 World Champion Sir Jackie Stewart at Harrods in Knightsbridge. My then partner Jane is also a Scot. Her father John Watson

knew Jackie in the 1960s as they were west coast neighbours. Say what you like about the Scots, but they are more united than those who live south of the border. Jane accompanied me to Harrods, a shop she knows worryingly well. At the time, Jackie was the president of the BRDC (British Racing Drivers Club). Jane and Jackie connected immediately chatting about contacts on Scotland's west coast – such is the way with those from north of the border. I took the opportunity to ask Jackie a few questions. The Q and A session was featured in some magazines.

£75 MILLION ON ICE
There are some days that you never forget. One such day was a twin-test at the Nürburgring Nordschleife. The circuit has a museum, inside which were a Ferrari 250GTO and a Ferrari 250LM a conservative £75 million in today's money. We have all been to car museums, looked at the cars and thought, "I bet they wouldn't work if you put them on the road or track."

Very early, one freezing cold morning at minus 5C, and before dawn, we extricated the two priceless cars mentioned from the Nürburgring Museum. The owner was far away and gave us permission to test the cars, provided we had them cleaned after we had finished

8–10: The Nordschleife. £75m on ice. Our orders were – don't crash.
11: At 540m (1,800ft) altitude, winters at the Ring are cold. The downhill sections were lethal, especially on historic race tyres.
12: The Ring has steep gradients.

with them. At the entrance to the notorious Nordschleife, the barrier was closed. The 14-mile track was frozen. At 540m (1,800ft) above sea level, it is influenced by a meteorological continental climate of hot summers, cold winters. The changes in elevation at this circuit located in the Eifel Mountains vary by 300m (1,000ft). In late autumn, early winter, any sunshine is of the very low variety, with long shadows. The hills and trees guarantee that much of the track remains in permanent shadow for months.

After negotiation, we persuaded the circuit officials and no-nonsense RMA trackday organisers to let us onto the closed track with a camera car. Off we went. Track temperature was below that necessary for historic crossply race tyres to supply any grip. The surface varied from slippery to silly. In places, we had sheet ice, which was especially tricky on the downhill sections. I can hear you thinking, "What kind of track test could come from this?" In my defence, I make several points: On separate occasions, I had previously track-tested both a 250GTO and a 250LM, therefore all the knowledge was already in my head. The test at the Nürburgring on treacherous and unpredictable surfaces showed how old-school cars had much more feel than new cars. With the GTO and the LM, you could sense what was happening at the tyre contact patches through

the steering wheel. This type of connection also existed at the brake pedal because the assembly was un-assisted and direct. The slightest touch on the accelerator pedal would send the tail out – no surprises there, but how it could come back into shape was revealing and a testament to the lightness and configuration of the cars. My pre-brief to the team was that if there were to be a crash, it would be better if the cars didn't crash into each other. We also used the little-known Südschleife (4.82-miles) that was in use until 1971 for a ghostly photoshoot. The locals loved scaring us with Südschleife ghost stories. No priceless icon was damaged in this test. With society's ever-increasing risk aversity, I don't think such a £75million test drive on ice would be possible again.

At another wintry RMA track day, race engineer Tim Samways had brought along the late Tony Dron and a fine array of cars including a Ferrari 330LMB, 246S, and F50 plus a Prosport 3000 and a track-prepared BMW M3. The previous day when the track was dry, *Auto Italia*'s Josie Ward hitched a ride with Tony Dron in the F50. She has not been the same since. Snow was falling as we left the Nordschleife. The Samways transporter was due to leave the next morning. It was stuck there for days, such can be the impediments of a high-altitude German winter.

NEW RETRO STRATOS

I got a phone call from Christian 'Hrabi' Hrabalek. You may recall that he was one of the reasons for the *Auto Italia* trip to Spain to drive a yellow Lancia Stratos and a yellow Ferrari 246GT. Hrabi worked in the car design industry. He was fascinated in my radical build of a race-winning Alfa Romeo. Despite some years in a design/drawing office, I never draw anything that I am making. He knew that I was an engineer and that I had chopped up an Alfa until all I had left was half a floorpan upon which to construct the race car. Hrabi wanted to build a retro Stratos and came to my Surrey home one evening to check me out. The title of 'engineer' encompasses a wide range of skills from tyre fitter to rocket scientist. At our meeting, I told him that the designs are in my head and that I build things first and design them later. This is not what any

designer wants to hear. It is not how they think. He realised that I was too pro-active, too hands-on, too Sergio Scaglietti, to be of any help in a conventional design procedure.

Hrabi was determined and eventually I found myself at the Geneva Motor Show looking at Hrabi's finished product. It was a gargantuan effort and there it was. Unmistakably a Stratos and unmistakably not a Stratos, because Gandini's deliberate rough edges had been smoothed away. In the end, Hrabi's Stratos disappeared, as have the retro versions by others. At around £1million, the cost of a new retro Stratos would be similar to an original Stratos. If you can't afford £1 million, Hawk Cars Ltd can sell you a good copy of an original Stratos for a fraction of the price. There are also used Stratos kit cars on the market from £35k. Of course, this is a different market. No one contemplating

13 – 15: Christian Hrabalek's retro Stratos at the Geneva Show.
14: Real Lancia Stratos on the Sanremo rally.

spending £1 million on an original or a new retro Stratos would buy a replica.

700 HORSEPOWER IN THE WET

Off to Snetterton now. Thankfully, it is still an old fast version of the now much-impaired track. The call came to test two Ferrari 360 Challenge cars that run in British GT racing series. Robin Ward's Damax Company was looking after them, while Henry Barczynski's Gigawave company was testing some in-car cameras. One of Damax's GT drivers was Miles Hulford, then 16 years old. Toddlers in karts have a decade of experience by the time they are in their teens. When you think that triple F1 World Champion Graham Hill couldn't drive a car until he was 24-years old, you can appreciate how tough and competitive is today's racing business.

Still at a wet Snetterton, I had one of those test drives

waiting that you don't forget. Albert Einstein said, "Only two things are infinite: the universe and human stupidity, and I'm not sure about the former." People often tell me that motor racing is stupid and I always agree. This makes me stupid, which I already know. It is also stupid to track-test a lightweight 700bhp Ferrari with no driver aids at a cold wet Snetterton Circuit. Brought up without driver aids, for me, this is normality. The car in question is a 1980s creation. This was when the Iron Lady sent her armada 8,000 miles to fight over the Falklands/Malvinas. We saw Prince Charles' fairy-tale wedding to the wrong person. Then a wind blew down 15 million English trees. The Soviets and the Eastern Block saw Dallas and the western world on TV and immediately the Berlin wall and the Iron Curtain were demolished. My bank invited me to its cocktail parties and offered to lend me vast amounts of money (if they

16: Ferrari 288 Evoluzione at Snetterton. 700hp, 546lb ft of torque, 1,000kg, no driver aids and a wet track.

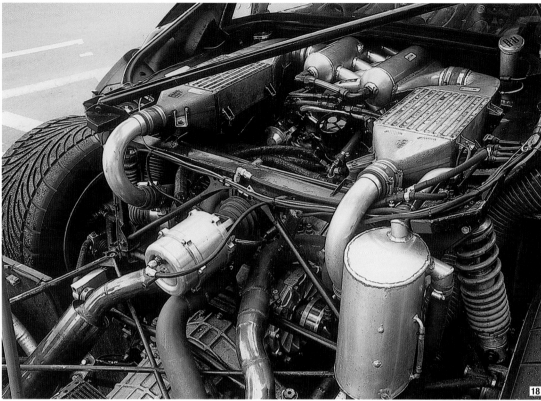

had the deeds to my house). It was boom time and carmakers could do no wrong.

With the F40 still on the drawing board, Ferrari used special 288GTOs as mobile testbeds. In 1988 they made just three production examples of the 288GTO Evoluzione. The power of these brutes reached 700bhp. They were even considering rallying them. How mad is that? Tim Samways Sporting and Historic Car Engineers looked after this red monster for its then owner Harry Leventis. The transporter was backed up against garage 13. Some circuits ignore the number 13 to appease superstitious drivers. Although not superstitious, the thought of 700bhp in the rain was a good reason to consider superstition and ignore it.

Samways and the boys were deep in the engine bay fettling, while driver Peter Hardman sat quietly in the hot seat waiting for his next run. Samways has the laptop connected and is tweaking the MoTec boost map to make the car more driveable. Left to its own devices, boost arrives in a mad rush, just like in the olden days of early turbo cars. Now that we have engine management electronics, we can adjust boost characteristics and thereby the power delivery. This works well on cars that cannot break traction but with 546lb ft of torque in the wet, fiddle as you might, but once you are in that power band wheelspin happens. With about 5k on the tachometer, you simply cannot floor the throttle. No, not even in a dead-straight line. Pressing the throttle pedal is as stupid as seeing how hard you can stand on a landmine before it goes off.

For the non-technical, here is the difference between torque and power. Think of a bicycle. Torque is how much weight you can put on a pedal. Power is how fast you can turn the pedals against a resistance. It is torque that induces wheelspin.

The engine cover is lowered – not that it covers anything, as it is full of holes. This is the only 288GTO Evoluzione in the world that gets exercised properly. Leventis uses it for track-days and is a regular at RMA trackdays, where pro driver Peter Hardman is tasked

17 and 18: The 288 Evo has the record for the most air vents on any car. One of just three production cars intended for Group B racing.

with petrifying the owner's guests.

Power is now 700bhp with just 1.55 bar boost. Charge temperature is the key to turbo power and the 288GTO is limited by the size and position of its two intercoolers. Fitting larger intercoolers in an area with high airspeed is not possible without losing the car's character. If it were, then 2,000bhp would be possible. So today at Snetterton, I must make do with just 700bhp in a car weighing 1,015kg.

The sky is as wet and as grey as the sodden circuit. Waiting for an improvement in conditions might see a worsening and no drive at all. It was definitely raining when Tim Samways asked, "Would you like your go now Roberto?" With coolness more in line with being asked if I would like a cup of coffee, I replied, "Er, yes, ok."

Samways tells me not to look at the boost gauge as it is lazy. "Use the little blue light on the dash," he says. "It comes on a split second before boost arrives."

On the circuit, standing water and puddles tug at the steering wheel before bursting into spray. I flirt with the blue light. It threatens at around 4,800rpm. Changing gear and feathering the throttle each time it winks; I start to use the power and it is world-shrinking. At some time or other, I have to use full bazooka otherwise what's the point? In the first three gears wheelspin is explosive and

of cartoon proportions, requiring much steering correction. The faster you go, i.e. fourth and fifth, the more power it will take. The trouble is that it is virtually impossible to recover the slide if the rear tyres light up at 150mph. Leaping between corners, the Evo swallows up the pit straight and gulps down Revett Straight. Torque causes the nose to rise while aerodynamic forces are trying to keep it down. The editor Phil Ward is one of those victims tortured by Peter Hardman in this car on the Nordschleife. Phil cannot describe it. You either know what it's like because you have done it, or you don't. Words have not been invented that can describe such an experience. I had danced with the devil at Snetterton and managed some full-power blasts, but the rain was worsening. Less is more in this situation, so back to the pits for a debrief. Samways interrogates the data logging to see what I'd been up to. "Hmmm, you had some fun out there." From the traces he could see high-speed wheelspin, rpm and a throttle map showing use of full power. Suddenly the prospect of driving home in my 60bhp-per-tonne road car never seemed so welcoming.

MONZA, MIURA AND MISCONCEPTIONS

Early in 2005, I entered the Miura SV in three first-rate Italian events, the splendid Coppa Milano – Sanremo

19: The restored Lamborghini Miura poses during the photo shoot on the infield at Monza circuit.
20: Miura SV on Milano – Sanremo rally overlooking the Bay of Genoa.

rally, a three-day regularity trial that started with a Monza trackday and ended at Sanremo. Next were two exciting Italian hillclimbs. Unlike UK hillclimbs, these are long fast courses on closed public roads.

As with several of my independent ventures, the Miura was an obvious target for an *Auto Italia* feature. Restoration story apart, I wrote a piece on Miura misconceptions. The three basic models were quite different from each other. Too much to describe in this book, so for Miura geeks only, here are my dirty dozen on Miura misunderstandings.

Number One: They take off at speed.

Right and wrong. High-speed front-end lift happened on early cars if the rear springs had settled too much and the fuel tank (at the front) was empty. Any car with the wrong rake angle will lift. The situation disappeared with the SV as the rear ran higher, partly due to taller/wider rear tyres, revised suspension and better air management at the front.

Number Two: Early cars are faster.

Wrong. The power and the chassis evolved with the model: P400 Miura, 350bhp. Miura S, 375bhp. Miura SV, 385bhp. The first version P400 had chassis weaknesses. All models had A-posts that were too slender. Each model got progressively stiffer and progressively heavier. The SV was the fastest, especially in the braking and handling departments. The SV with its ventilated discs and revised rear suspension handles well, better than the earlier cars.

Number Three:
The occupants get cooked by the engine.

Wrong. Psychology plays a part because the V12 is visible through the glass screen right behind you. Provided the bulkhead is appropriately insulated, there is no cabin temperature problem from this area. The

21 – 23: Monza circuit. Flat-out exiting the Parabolica onto the start-finish straight.
22: Above the snowline on the Milano – Sanremo Rally.
24: Miura – a simple car to maintain. It really is...

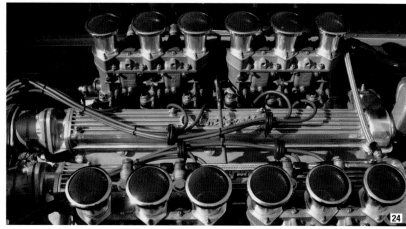

greatest heat source is the greenhouse effect of the large windscreen into a relatively small-volume cockpit. Late SVs had an option for air-con but there was a packaging problem. After-market air-con is available but I wouldn't go down the air-con route as it leads to complications. On a warm day, set the vent system to ambient/cold, partially open a window to ensure airflow and enjoy the V12 music.

Number Four: They are unreliable.

Wrong. This all depends on how well maintained they are. Once sorted, they are simple and reliable cars. It is essential that the carburettors are rebuilt along with the ignition system and everything else. Frequent oil changes are a good idea especially for the P400 and Miura S as the engine and gearbox share the same oil.

Number Five: They are expensive to maintain.

Wrong and right: Parts and labour prices are high, but a good example will need little of each. On the plus side, there is no cambelt to worry about. Servicing is simple. Plus, a clutch is cheap and can be changed in one hour.

Number Six: They catch fire.

Wrong. The main reason for a fire is that a carburettor may be faulty and collecting fuel into the air filter box, which is located above the engine – you can guess what happens next. With rebuilt carbs and new fuel lines, they don't catch fire. If you are a worry monster, there is plenty of room for an unobtrusive race car fire system. Better still is to run with no air filter box. Just have some fine mesh over the twelve trumpets. It is then simple to check for leaks. There can be no build-up of fuel, and most importantly of all, it looks fabulous.

Number Seven: They are noisy.

Wrong. This is another psychological problem due to being able to see the engine. The mechanical thrash from the engine is far quieter than that of a Ferrari. The exhaust system is efficient and well packaged at the far

rear end of the car. Miuras are not noisy.

Number Eight: They have issues with the sump.

Wrong. The split sump explained: the P400 and the Miura S had an oil system where the engine and gearbox shared the same oil, just like the old Minis. While this is not an ideal situation, modern oils and frequent oil changes solve the issues. The Miura SV had two separate compartments for engine oil and gearbox oil. This is the split sump. Do not confuse a split sump with a dry sump.

Number Nine: They need a limited slip differential.

Wrong. This is unnecessary as traction is excellent. Only a handful of late SVs had an LSD. Even race-spec Miuras hardly need them.

Number Ten: They suffer from oil surge.

Oil surge can be a problem. A Miura on a race circuit needs a dry sump, as was fitted to the precious few Jota versions. If you corner hard in a Miura without a dry sump, centrifugal forces will send the oil away from the pick-up pipe. The oil pressure gauge needle will plummet, and the oil light will illuminate. You then have one second to rectify the situation, either by a massive loss of speed or by straightening the steering.

Number Eleven: They have poor sitting positions.

Right but fixable. The steering wheel angle is all wrong and too far away. This can be improved by slotting the bracket holding the steering column and lower it. Then fit a spacer behind the steering wheel that will bring it closer for reach, and up away from your legs.

Number Twelve: They have poor torsional rigidity.

Right. The outer sills are merely alloy covers. The actual sills beneath are not strong enough, especially on the early cars because they were thinner and drilled for lightness. Any restoration should include much work to strengthen the sills. The windscreen pillars are too slender. The torsional rigidity is not as good as modern

25

cars, but as a classic car, it is good enough.

In 2005, our triple test featured one of each of the three Miura models: P400, P400S and SV. I don't think this had been done before or since. Word has it that 764 Miuras were made and that about 400 are known to exist. In 2005, at the time of our triple test, a Miura had a value of circa £150k. Today's (2021's) values range from £1 million for a barn find to over £2 million for a good one. It has been said many times that the Miura SV is the world's best-looking car.

OLD BILL IN ITALY

An invitation to spend time in Rome with the Italian Polizia Stradale and their Lamborghini Gallardo made a great story. Police forces worldwide are always keen to improve their relationship with the public. Getting people onside is a key factor to efficient policing. Italians are proud of their supercars, so the Italian police scored a positive publicity achievement with their striking blue and white Lamborghinis.

A second Gallardo joined the force and today they have a Lamborghini Huracán. Both cars are donations:

the first from the Lamborghini factory and the second from an independent donation. Before you dismiss this PR *coup d'état* as a media stunt, these patrols have teeth. The officers are the best of the best and go through a rigorous training schedule, while the cars are kitted out with the very latest high-tech equipment.

Despite having my collar felt by the Italian Police for speeding near Maranello in a Ferrari 360CS, I was more than happy to call a truce and visit the Rome HQ of the Polizia Stradale. You remember in the middle of the First World War when the British and the German troops put their guns down for a while so that they could play football in no-mans-land? Well, that is what it was like when Michael Ward and I entered the Polizia Stradale's compound. Instead of bomb-craters and football, we met a pair of the nicest chaps you could ever meet – two of the specially trained police officers qualified for the Lamborghinis: Massimiliano Finore and Giancarlo Bravo.

They talked us through the high-tech kit before we followed them out onto Rome's version of the M25 motorway. Traffic was heavy with lots of stop/start,

26

25: Michael Ward image that was adopted by the Polizia for publicity purposes.
26: Rome, for a story on the police Lamborghinis.

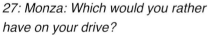

27: Monza: Which would you rather have on your drive?
28: Milano – Sanremo Rally. Getting to know my uniformed competitors.
29: The view of the Polizia from the Miura while entering Sanremo.

slow/fast traffic. Personal space in Latin countries is much closer than it is in Anglo-Saxon lands. This translates to close company on the road, which the Anglo-Saxon should not mistake for aggression. Driving styles are loose with a car's body-language being far more informative than indicators, which are a sign of weakness and rarely used. Our motorcycle outriders swooped and leaned intimately, hand-on-front wings of moving cars. This created an extra lane just wide enough for the Gallardo, complete with blue lights flashing and our camera car to carve our way through the traffic.

I interviewed the officers and we published a Q & A session. The story was much publicised in the Italian

media. After the interview, I was given a phone number should I ever need it. This was a get-out-of-jail-free card, that I have stupidly lost.

We entered the Milano – Sanremo Rally in the Miura SV and ran in close company with a police Gallardo.

Day one, Friday: 210 entrants arrive in the paddock at Monza. It was a pleasant surprise to see that our sizeable police escort of around 30 police motorcycles was to be fronted by my new best mates in the police Lamborghini Gallardo.

We sign on and scrutineer. Scrutineering in Italy means looking at documents, not the cars. This is to counteract litigation regarding mechanical condition, should there be an incident. Naturally, there is an amazing lunch and we are joined by Josie and Phil Ward who will be taking photos at Monza. In the afternoon, we have the Monza circuit at our disposal. The organisers demanded to see our race licences, which we never had, because we didn't think we needed them. We were ordered up to a room to get medical examinations and another room to receive race licences. At the medical, we were asked if we felt okay. We nodded and our card was stamped. Up to the next room to pay a modest fee and we both had our Italian race licences. The whole thing took less than five minutes. A Miura on a race circuit is a rare sight. The car performed superbly.

Days two and three and the rally is whatever you want it to be: a blast along the spectacular route, or a gentle drive. There is also a regularity competition if that is your thing. Hospitality is of the five-star variety. In several towns and mountain villages, there were welcome parties and goody bags passed through the side windows. The cockpit could take no more. Then Jane was handed a massive platter of cakes that blocked our vision. About a mile further on, I saw two pensioners. We stopped, handed them the giant platter and sped off. Many times on the rally, our Miura was in close company with the police Gallardo. The Lambo convoy was as quick as it was extrovert. The unwritten rule was no damage to any people or property. At last, we were in an event that suited the Miura perfectly. After 360km of roads that I did not know existed, we arrived in Sanremo. A party, an overnight and it was all over.

BACK HOME AND GREY

Editor Phil Ward and I are waiting in the cold. It's a grey unsilenced test day in a grey month at a grey Silverstone. A tow truck trundles away to excavate a beached racer from the Silverstone gravel. All is as quiet as a fall of snow. Time passes. We await the arrival by road of a Le Mans Daytona. "I can hear a Ferrari," says the Editor. The distant sound waves dance. The Le Mans Daytona is in two places at once:

minutes away in time and distance, but in spirit, it is already in the paddock. Eventually, it rumbles through the main gate, over the bridge into the paddock, breaking up the ambient monochrome, resplendent in its red, white and blue patina. It stops at our feet. Racer and engineer Gary Pearson switches off the 12 cylinders and creates that weird sensation that everyone who has been in a race paddock recognises. That shocking, bouncing silence you get when a 125db race engine suddenly cuts off. It is difficult to explain, but many will know what I mean.

The priceless 1971 Pozzi Daytona is another of Carlos Monteverde's cars. We had done our apprenticeship with Carlos and with Pearson, who would have debriefed Monteverde on our conduct. With the test session starting, Pearson gave me a briefing, "'That's the ignition switch and that's the starter button. Enjoy". Daytonas have been called fast trucks. The Pozzi race car has a 30% increase in the power to weight ratio. Still a truck but a quicker one. Feeling fulfilled, the Editor and I leave a Silverstone that somehow no longer seems so grey.

30 and *31: Big banger Le Mans Daytona at Silverstone. A world of V12 noise.*
33: Long race with a compulsory pit stop to check tyres pressures. etc or for optional driver change.
34: Maserati Corse, being a British GP support race, gave me two pit passes for the Ferrari F1 garage.
35: Silverstone GP support race. Maserati brings its own garage.

BAVARIA TO SILVERSTONE IMMEDIATELY

I was with German tuners Novitec lunching in Bavaria when a call came from Maserati, "Could you get to Silverstone immediately to drive one of our cars in two support races for the British Grand Prix?" I replied, "Er... yes, delighted." I had less than five hours to get on track at Silverstone and had already missed the morning's practice session. I badly needed a Harrier jump jet. Luckily, I had a return flight booked that would suffice. I phoned Jane to meet me at Heathrow with all my race kit and photo ID for GP passes, plus everything necessary for three days at the circuit. At the Silverstone's main gate, I could hear the Maseratis engaging in their late afternoon practice and qualifying sessions. Naturally, I had no entry tickets and at the main gate, I was refused entry. After a while, one of the Maserati mechanics arrived with two entry tickets. I signed on and only had time to complete the regulatory three laps needed to be able to race the car. This was my first race weekend racing with Maserati Corse, and it consisted of two races supporting the British GP. The

36

one hour race had the option of two drivers per car. A pit stop was compulsory, even for a sole driver like me. It was fantastic and the team was happy with my performance. They said that I could expect more drives.

CHOBHAM AND BUSINESS

The next job was to test one of the most butch cars in the world and a favourite, namely a 1965 Iso Grifo Bizzarrini A3/C – American muscle wearing Armani. I can't think of a more muscular historic GT. The venue was the Chobham test track.

The next stop was the Dunsfold track where we featured some companies that rent out supercars. This is where 'butch' turned to 'bunch'. P1 Performance Car Club gave us a bunch of fast cars to play with. Knowing how quick these cars are and how careful you must be not to damage them, I am surprised at the optimism of supercar rental companies. I am also amazed that they can make a profit. Letting anyone loose in these cars must create problems. These words, however, are an example of why I am not a businessman.

37

FERRARI AND HELICOPTERS
Day 1

My fairy-tale schedule was to sample some 360 Challenge cars at Monza plus some glittering add-ons. The journey began when I and 22 Fleet Street journalists boarded a private jet at Farnborough bound for Bologna. A fleet of big black Lancia Thesis limos with a police motorcycle escort whisked us through blanked-off road junctions and red lights. We lunched at Maranello's Montana restaurant. Our convoy then swept through the factory gates. A presentation was given by Ferrari personnel and we toured the factory.

Across the road from the factory is the Fiorano test track. A heavily disguised matt-black car is circulating in the rain. Although this future model is disguised, the soundtrack is unmistakably Ferrari. It was 5pm on day one and we needed to get to our night stop, which was near Monza and a good four hours away by car. But this is Ferrari, so a squadron of helicopters was

38

39

36: Is there a more muscular GT than a Bizzarrini A3/C?

37: Supercar hire. Suits you sir.

38: Michael Schumacher cooking.

39: No place to hide from the swiggly lines (data).

40: Like a G8 convoy, Fleet Street journalists (and me) sweep into the Ferrari factory.

41: And then darkness joined the rain.

42: Ex-F1 driver Enrico Bertaggia was running the show at Monza.

43: And then it really rained.

44: Monza – to the palace in a squadron of helicopters.

standing by. The weather was menacing, raining and deteriorating. Our eight whirlybirds made their exit carrying us up up and away. Well sort of, up to just 500ft for the low cloud ceiling and at 125 knots (144mph) and heading due north. We flew low over Milan's horrendous traffic to land like a swarm of bees in the grounds of a stunning palace – the Villa San Carlo Borromeo. It has history going back to the eighth century BC. Over dinner, Ferrari's Communications Director Al Clarke discussed all things Ferrari.

Day 2

Our fleet of black Lancias forced its way through the traffic to Monza. Like a G8 convoy we claimed priority at all road junctions. As we arrived at the historic track, it started to rain. Then it really rained. Then it bucketed

down. "It can't rain this hard for very long." I said. But it does. God was perfecting his biblical version of rain.

One or two cars splashed about on the flooded track, me included, but high-speed aquaplaning forced us back into the pits. We waited. We watched. We lunched. Then Enrico Bertaggia, our chief instructor and ex-F1 driver eighth announced, "You will all get your drives, rain or no rain – my responsibility." He thumped his chest.

In the late afternoon, darkness joined the show. We never got a dry run but at least some of the rivers and lakes across the Monza track had partially dispersed. With mostly non-motoring journalists present, many had neither driven on a racetrack, nor driven a Ferrari – let alone a competition version in these dark and flooded conditions. The bravest journalists were not scared of being labelled fearful and declined the drives. However, racer journalists are different. The Fiorano Ferrari instructors were chums and fellow UK ARDS instructors.

Our suit-wearing, shade-wearing chauffeurs with black Lancias were ready to take us to Bergamo Airport for our return flight. The Autostrada was flooded and blocked with crashed cars making us late for our flight. But when you have your own jet, lateness is not quite the same. We landed at Farnborough Airport a whisker before the late-night curfew. Like a royal jet, our Dornier taxied right up to our parked cars and 20 minutes later I was home. Air travel as it should be, and a taste of Ferrari's *dolce vita*.

COINCIDENCE OR WHAT?

Switzerland is an unusual place for a De Tomaso story, or is it? Let's start at the end. Alejandro de Tomaso died in 2003 and today the Modena factory is closed. Sounds terminal but it is not that simple. Alejandro's son, Santiago de Tomaso, was active in promoting the De Tomaso marque. A new owner is in the process of resurrecting the De Tomaso label.

Comparisons are often made with Colin Chapman. Both had motor racing in their blood, both had car factories, both utilised the backbone chassis, both had links with Ford and both had to be as hard as nails to survive.

We travelled to Dietikon in Switzerland to meet De Tomaso collector René Killer. The little yellow car is as low and as light as cars get – waist-high and at 695kg. It is a fraction of the weight of today's sports cars. Unlike Colin Chapman's Lotus Elan, the Vallelunga's steel backbone chassis has its motor mounted behind the driver. Chapman went on to do a similar thing with the mid-engined Lotus Europa in 1971. No surprises that de Tomaso and Chapman were seen spending a lot of time talking to each other at a 1962 Motor Show.

René and I went for a drive in the yellow jewel, which included a run up a new hillclimb course. Switzerland allows hillclimbs but banned motor racing after the 1957 Le Mans crash that killed 90 people. The light was fading for our photoshoot and in mountainous

45 – 47: A coincidence? Santiago de Tomaso just happened to be passing during our photoshoot of the De Tomaso Vallelunga on a quiet Swiss hill.
48: Think of the Vallelunga as an Italian Lotus Europa.

regions, the trick is to gain altitude to find light. We rocketed up the Mutschellen hillclimb course and continued up a road to nowhere to find a well-lit hilltop. Whilst photographing the De Tomaso on this deserted Swiss country road, a passing car stopped and somebody famous came over to us. We each thought that one of our group had somehow pre-arranged it. Out stepped none other than Santiago de Tomaso who just happened to be passing. You could have knocked us down with a yodel. Coincidences do happen.

THE REPUBLIC OF IRELAND

From the refinement of a Swiss hillclimb, I found myself at Mondello Park Circuit in the Republic of Ireland. Opened in 1968, Mondello Park is located 25 miles from Dublin. I had at my disposal the 2.25-mile full circuit, which was opened in 1998 by the then Dublin resident Damon Hill. The circuit is owned by the family of the late Martin Birrane (1935–2018), who started racing in England in 1967.

Thanks to Fiat, we had free reign of the Irish circuit where Fiat racing is exceedingly popular. It was like the olden days in England and a pleasant contrast to how bureaucratic, rule-bound, obstinate, daft and expensive things can be at some English circuits. Irish

49 and 50: Mondello Park. Budget racing with Fiat Unos and Puntos – and Irish hospitality.

hospitality and après-race are legendary. The 2.25-mile lap has many straights leading into tight turns, which, when racing, is a recipe for contact during late-braking/diving-up-the-inside manoeuvres. I tested the 1300 Uno of Gary Cunningham and the Punto Abarth of Barry Rabbitt.

This was my first trip to Ireland and I noted that the Irish speak very quickly. This prompted some research to find a global league table of fast speakers. The global leaders are the Japanese with 7.84 syllables per second (sps). Closely followed by the Spanish at 7.82sps, the French at 7.18sps, the Italians at 6.99sps and the British at 6.19. The slowest is Mandarin at 5.18sps. So, what about the Irish? Research mentions that the Irish speak English faster than the English, but I have no measure of the speed. I do know that Guinness is Irish and that the Guinness world record for speed speech is held by an American rapper, Ricky Raphel Brown, at 14.1sps. I digress. The Fiat racing scene in Ireland was healthy. I noted that in Ireland (like everywhere else) motor racing is meant to be a non-contact sport, but then so is ice hockey.

TURBO TALES

It was in 2005 when Italian motorsport industry bigwig

Claudio Berro told me that soon, virtually all petrol and diesel road cars would be turbocharged. And that electric or hydrogen cars would eventually take over. It sounded outlandish at the time, but he was right. Industry guys think a long way into the future.

Turbocharged production cars for Europeans arrived in 1972/3 with the BMW 2002 Turbo. In 1973, turbo efficiency gave me the idea to build a turbocharged wide-bodied Jaguar E-Type for racing in the Modsports Championship. The long-stroke engine was an ideal candidate for forced induction as it did not like high revs. I bought an American book on 'How to Turbocharge your Aeroplane' as this was the only book I could find on the subject. I bought an early 3.8 fixed head coupe and built the car at home. The garage door was a 1/4inch wider that the E-type's wide body and F1 tyres. Allegedly, I tested the slick-shod racing E-Type on the public roads late at night. Officially, the car broke cover testing at Brands Hatch. *Autosport* magazine reported on the car, whereupon the Modsports Association – fearing an arms race – banned turbocharging. Today, that turbo E-Type exists as a slot racer. But who knows..., maybe a resurrection is due?

History repeated itself (this time without a ban) when in 1999, I built a turbocharged Alfa Romeo GTA. The project was too complicated and too technical to explain in this book. Here is all you need to know: it looked like a 1960s wide-bodied GTA racer, but it had

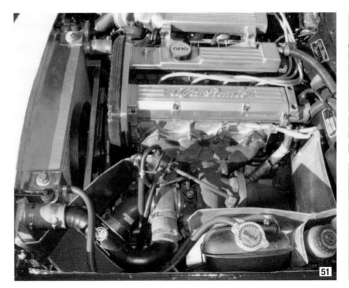

500bhp and weighed 790kg (640hp/ per tonne). I built the engine from an Alfa Romeo iron block 16-valve engine – same as a Lancia integrale. It was reliable, successful and a multiple race-winning car. The *Auto Italia* feature on the beast was written before the car was fully developed with much invisible under-body aerodynamic work. This was necessary to solve its high-speed wheelspin. Air resistance was trying to stop the car, while 500bhp was trying to do the opposite. It was fitted with MoTec engine management by the specialist technician Lee Penn (LAP Engineering Ltd). To help finance another project, the mad Alfa GTA Turbo ended up in the USA. If only I could have kept all the cars that passed through my hands.

51 – 56: Another cult car – the 500hp/ 790kg GTA turbo that I built in the late 1990s.
52 and 53: Testing at Snetterton with engineer Lee Penn.
54: Early 1970s and I built a new-fangled turbocharged E-Type. Modsports banned it.
55: A new slot-car version. Cult status achieved.

2006
London Evenings

The year started with a mid-winter evening party at HR Owen's Chelsea Ferrari/Maserati dealership. Top-end watch-maker Audemars Piguet was the new sponsor for the Maserati Trofeo Racing Championship. Andrea Antonnicola, managing director of Maserati GB and ex-F1 driver Johnny Herbert were on hand to describe the 2006 Trofeo Audemars Piguet Maserati Europe Championship. I chat, I do my best to promote the series, I hope for another invitation to race in the series and I leave. Job done.

It is now late winter and Kensington's Olympia Exhibition Hall has an Italian show of food, wine and the *dolce vita*. I spent much of my early years in Italy and have been commuting back and forth all my life. While I spent most of my time in the UK, I have always wondered whether I should live in Italy and gave it a try. When I said that I would move to Italy, my friend Carlo Caccaviello – who moved from Italy to the UK – told me that I would never stay in Italy. I tried and failed, Carlo was right. However, it gave me the opportunity to spend time in Italy. The wondering was over. For me, Italy is best enjoyed as a regular and well-connected visitor, and not as a resident.

MY FAMILY, MUSSOLINI AND A FIAT

This story was titled: *"Mussolini's Gift; Roberto Giordanelli Drives a Car That Once Belonged to His Father's Employer."* While I did drive Mussolini's Fiat 2800 Dual Cowl State Phaeton by Viotti of Turin, my father only drove his military vehicles. He was a law student when, at 19 years of age, found himself at several battles, including Tobruk and El Alemein. In 1943, what was left of the defeated Axis forces were cut-off on the Tunisian peninsula. They were surrounded by several Allied armies on land, at sea and in the air. The Italians had long since run out of supplies, equipment and munitions. They were never supplied much in the first place and so relied on foraging instead. The Italian military chose and ranked its officers by their social class and not by anything useful. My father became a prisoner of war (POW) and then Italy changed sides and joined the Allies. Contrary to the stereotype, German Field Marshall Erwin Rommel referred to the Italian infantry as "Lions lead by donkeys". My father ended up in the POW camp on Kempton Park Racecourse in Sunbury-on-Thames. Nearby, he met his future wife (my mother), who was also in the Italian military, but happened to be in the UK when war was declared. After the war, my father – who was proficient in Latin, Greek, French, English and of course Italian – was offered a position as a language teacher at a private school in Norfolk, which he declined. Instead, he worked for Fiat UK in Brentford, where he rose to become the Investments Control Manager. Retired and aged 87, he had a road accident whilst riding his bicycle. The injuries sustained led to his untimely death aged 88.

My father, who was a political liberal, never met Mussolini, although my mother did when she joined the Italian Intelligence Service *(Servizio Informazioni Militare)*. She could speak both languages without an accent. As she was in London during the war, she obviously kept all this secret. As in ancient Rome, the fascist government renamed the Mediterranean in the

1: London drive in the Fiat 2800 State Phaeton given to General Franco of Spain by Mussolini.
2: My mother chatting with General Graziani and later with Mussolini. In WW2 London, she avoided capture.
3: Teenage law student Paolo Giordanelli volunteers for WW2 and is flown to the desert war.

old Latin style of *Mare Nostrum* (our sea). Mussolini told my mother that it was no secret that the Mediterranean was Italy's prison, because the British controlled both ends: at Suez and Gibraltar. With much parental and grandparental wartime military activities, I noted an obvious 'risk-taking DNA' in the family.

Mussolini's car was chauffeur-driven in period by the racing driver Ercole Borrato and on, this day in London, by me. As part of the road test, I asked my father if he would like to drive his one-time employer's car in London, but he declined saying, "If it is like any of the army vehicles that we had in the North Africa campaign, it won't have any petrol." I took the fabulous Fiat on a jaunt around Hyde Park, the Mall, Knightsbridge Barracks and on roads typical of a state jamboree. Italy was not going to see its leaders in foreign limos, so it built its own. These Fiats were used by the likes of King Vittorio Emanuele II and Pope Pious XII, Benito Mussolini's mistress Claretta Petacci and Italian film director Roberto Rossellini. Mussolini loved fast cars and promoted Italian motorsport. After a while, he gave the Fiat 2800 to General Franco of Spain. An Italian friend of mine commented, "Trust Mussolini to give Franco a secondhand car." General Franco, who preferred Rolls Royces, subsequently gave the car to a Spanish marquis. It then had several Spanish owners until a French journalist from Toulouse bought the car in Spain. He drove it to his family farm in the Pyrenees. It changed hands once again to its current owner who had the car restored by one of France's finest restoration companies.

When looking at this large car, you should keep in mind that date: 1938. Its smooth curvy lines are more like those of an early 1950s car than a pre-war one. Fiat – who also built aircraft – was aware of developments in aerodynamics. You really need a human being in the picture to fully appreciate the Fiat's generous size. I drove the car down the Mall, Whitehall, Trafalgar Square, Knightsbridge and around Hyde Park. The test drive came to an end in Kensington when the car ran out of petrol, just as my father predicted. *"Te lo detto"* (told you) were his words.

SERGIO SCAGLIETTI AND BELGIUM

Ferrari UK handed us the keys. Phil and I had an appointment in Belgium and took the Ferrari 430 across the Channel. We were to represent the Brazilian collector and racer Carlos Monteverde at a party held by Jacques Swatter's Ecurie Francorchamps Ferrari dealership in Belgium. Jacques Swatter (1926–2010) was a racer, journalist, Ferrari main agent and head of the Belgian racing organisation Ecurie Nationale Belge.

One of the guests was Sergio Scaglietti. I introduced myself and we chatted. In 1951, his bodyshop in Maranello was opposite the Ferrari factory. He worked on countless Ferraris and became very close with Enzo and his son Dino. In 1970, Scaglietti sold his business to Ferrari. Although he continued in the business until the mid-1980s when at the age of 65, he retired. He was my father's age and a fellow military veteran, so I had a good idea how he thought. Sergio Scaglietti was 13 years old when his father – a brick layer – died of pneumonia. In 1940, Sergio joined the army. After WW2, he set up a vehicle bodyshop near Modena, where he and his two co-workers worked day and night – often sleeping on the workshop floor – to pay the bills.

Shaking his hand, I could tell by the hard skin that he was a hands-on worker. He told me how a designer would come into the workshop with some drawings. Scaglietti could see immediately if any changes were necessary. He then went his own way sculpting in aluminium or steel so that the design would work. He said that the designers could work quickly knowing that any errors in their designs would be ironed-out by Scaglietti. He was an engineer and an artist, who happened to work on car bodies. No art has superiority of any other form of art. I liked Scaglietti a lot.

BOLOGNA AND GETTING TO THE CHURCH ON TIME

The Bologna-San Luca hillclimb is a competitive Italian event and an absolute gem. Although most of the entrants were in Italian cars, I covered the story in a Lotus and sold the feature to several magazines. In 2006, my partner Jane owned the well-known ex-Ian Walker FIA spec 1965 Lotus Elan 26R (180bhp and 525kg). I loved that car. It was right up there with the

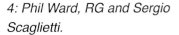

4: Phil Ward, RG and Sergio Scaglietti.
5: The Garage Francorchamps period truck.
6: Bologna to San Luca – the start. A serious and competitive hillclimb.
7: The steepest corner I have ever seen.
8: Receiving a trophy from the organisers.

best racing cars I have driven. The *Bologna to San Luca Gara di Velocitá in Salita per Auto Storico Trofeo 'Alessandro Ferretti'* was having its 50th anniversary. Superbly organised by Dottore Francesco Amante and his Scuderia Bologna team. The 50 gorgeous cars entered this year were almost all from Italian entrants, including cars from the Alfa Romeo Museum, but it is impossible to keep an extraordinary secret like this for very long. The event is timed with three practice runs on Saturday and three runs on Sunday.

The San Luca hill overlooks the city. Photographs can't capture gradients. On seeing the climb, the engineer in me thought, "Maximum load, minimum air speed. This needs a purpose-built hillclimb car, not a racing car."

The startline is in Bologna under the Meloncello Arch. Built in 1732 in a Baroque style, it is at the bottom of a staircase-steep hill that takes you to the hilltop Sanctuary of San Luca. The 550m (1,800ft) climb is just 2.2km (1.37miles) in length. It may be short by Italian standards but there is nothing like it in the whole world. In a city that can boast 40km of arcaded streets, it should be no surprise to learn that this hillclimb is lined

by a magnificent portico. The road even crosses into the structure in a couple of places. Spectating is free of charge as it is at all Italian hillclimbs. With bars and cafes at the bottom, blazing sun, or rain protection on the way up and more bars at the top, spectators can also take in the magnificent panoramic views of Bologna. Not only that but they are literally an arms-length from the action. One of the great things about this meeting is that, it takes place in a city. This means that if you have partners not interested in cars, they can be despatched to the bountiful attractions of beautiful Bologna. Founded in 1088, Bologna boasts the world's oldest university. It is also a shopper's paradise.

As for the driving…, take a deep breath. The average incline over the 2.2km is one in four and at one point one in two. The UK's steepest gradient is Porlock Hill in Devon which only claims one in four over a short piece at the bottom. Cars depart each 30 seconds. The starter's fingers gradually curl closed… 5, 4, 3, 2, 1. The traffic light turns to green. Engine screaming, off the clutch, sideways and disappear. Launching the car from under the Meloncello Arch, the horizontal road lasts a

9: Lotus takes the flag at Bologna San Luca.
10: Cool poster for a cool event.
11: Lamborghini Gallardos in Miami – one of my rare trips outside of Europe.

few metres before you hit the hill. Our Lotus scampers up the rise. Spectator arms, legs and heads hang out between each of the 666 arches that line the course. The devil is in the detail. Considering the standing start and two first-gear corners, my average speed of 75mph means that the little giant killer must have been travelling at well over 100mph in places – up a twisty one in four hill. Driving on racetracks rarely gives the driver a sense of speed. On this hill, with a portico arcade on one side and trees and concrete bollards on the other side, it felt more like 200mph. I can't remember being in such a hurry to get to a church. Quick lightweight car versus brick wall or concrete pillar could be career limiting. The Orfanelle turn included a brief incline of about one in two. Our time was only bettered by two of several sports prototypes. A class win and a third overall was good enough. Being Italy, the modest entry fees included four-star accommodation and gastronomic extravaganzas. For Jane and me, events like these are embedded in our memories, more so than 'just another race day'.

MIAMI AND LAMBORGHINI

Lamborghini jetted me to the Florida Keys to try out the new Gallardo Spyder. Fears that I would never get to exceed the 55mph limit vanished when those nice Lamborghini boys and girls pointed me in the direction of Florida's Homestead Miami Speedway. Apart from our multi-coloured supercars, this fabulous automotive superbowl was empty. I could only imagine the atmosphere when it is full. On the 1.5-mile oval, a Nascar can lap at an average speed of 170mph, while an Indycar average is 201mph. There is also a 2.21mile road course.

The test included some road driving and a dinner where I asked the question, "When will Lamborghini revert to rear-wheel drive?" I knew I had stumbled on a secret car when the mouths of the Lamborghini bosses opened and nothing came out. It is always the same when journalists quiz manufacturers. The manufacturer will only talk about the past and the present, while the motoring hack only wants to know about the future. It just so happens that my other job is in motor racing, where I have driven a Reiter Engineering FIA GT1

Murciélago where the 4WD has been ditched in favour of rear-wheel drive. I know what a Murciélago is like with rear-wheel drive. I know how much traction is available (a lot). With the arrival of smart traction control, the days of rear-wheel drive sports cars flying backwards off the road have gone. Ask Ferrari.

I also spent more time with Valentino Balboni, Lamborghini's celebrated test driver. He spoke of how the Lamborghini company had to fight for its existence in the post-Ferruccio, pre-Audi days. He said that the 'Indonesian' period was the worst. I told him that he had done well to go from the production line to ambassador and asked him which is better, 2006 or 1968? You don't need to know his exact reply but think about it… He was 21 with a dream job, in Italy, in 1968. As for the top-secret car – I deduced that Lamborghini will be making a lightweight two-wheel drive version of the Gallardo, to be launched in 2011. It would be called the 'LP 550-2 Valentino Balboni'. The man was to have a car named after him.

FORMULA ONE TECNO

In the olden days, all you needed to go Formula One racing was a small industrial unit, where you could rivet together an aluminium chassis. The rest of the parts were off-the-shelf items: a Ford Cosworth DFV motor, a Hewland gearbox, AP for the brakes and clutch, a few more bits and bobs and hey presto: Monaco, champagne, girls and helicopters, here we come. In the early '70s, BRM and Ferrari did it the hard way by making their own engines and transmissions. There was another F1 team that did not go down the 'big Formula Ford' route. That team was Tecno.

Here is a fairy-tale story. Once upon a time in 1962, two brothers – Luciano and Gianfranco Pederzani – founded the Tecno company in Bologna to build go-carts (now called karts). Their karts won the 1964/65 and 66 World Championships. The brothers progressed by building winning cars in F3 and F2. Only one way to go now and Tecno built their PA-123 F1 cars employing the drivers Nanni Galli, Derek Bell, Francoise Cevert and Chris Amon. However, F1 is a cruel business and while they competed in the 1972/3 F1 World Championships there were no wins, although they did score a sixth place. If you think that is irrelevant, perhaps you should build an F1 car and try to come sixth. In 1973, the fairy tale came to an end. But for this lowly test driver the fairy tale awoke when I drove the car at the Aeritalia track in Turin. I had done my test driver journalist apprenticeship to the point where I was becoming

12: Oval racing. More to it than meets the eye.
13: RG and Valentino Balboni at Homestead Miami.
14: F1 PA-123 Tecno drive at Aeritalia. Powered by a 440hp three-litre flat 12, similar to the Ferrari unit of the period.
15: Best F1 result was sixth. Not bad for a tiny organisation.
16: F1 Tecno in a rather nice trailer.

known in Italy. The late Lorenzo Prandina assisted by Landi Engineering brought this time-warp car to the track. The car had a very Italian flavour – chassis, engine, sponsor and even red paint.

Single-seaters are tailored to fit a young jockey perfectly, so naturally the car did not fit me. I think of the words of the writer Gore Vidal, "Never pass up the opportunity to have sex or appear on television." Surely, he should have included driving an F1 car in that statement. The Aeritalia runway and perimeter test track are long overdue a good sweeping. The V12 Tecno motor is rated at 450bhp at 12,000rpm in a car weighing only 590kg. Stones and grit shot-blast the pristine paint on the Tecno's flanks. I needed a proper race circuit for a full appraisal. But I got a taste for the car – a good one.

AMBITION AND A FERRARI P3 AT SPA

The opportunity to drive a Ferrari P3 at Spa is another example of how racing and test-driving worked to help each other. As a teenager, I knew that I wanted to spend my life motor racing. I had no idea how to achieve it. I knew that I would be no good at finding sponsorship. I also knew that I am no good at making money. I seriously considered abandoning my five-year engineering studies and apprenticeship to sweep the floor for a race team in the hope of gaining a test drive. Then what? Suppose I was good enough to get a race drive with a pro team. What would happen when I lost that drive? Would I find another? Would I become one of thousands of pro race drivers with a short career? Then what?

As a teenager in the 1960s – and by accident – I studied and became a qualified mechanical engineer, with a deliberate emphasis on the practical. This meant I could build and prepare my own racing cars. This gave me race experience. By combining that with race instructor work, I gained drives in other people's cars. I kept a race car of my own if/when other drives dried up. Nothing is forever – not even motoring journalism. All the above explains how in 2006, I was standing in a pit garage at Spa preparing to go on track in a Ferrari P3.

Officially called a P3/412P and sometimes a 330P3 or P3/4, in the interest of ink conservation, let's call it a P3. Chassis number 0844 was made in 1966 and is the first of only three. I was looking forward to comparing the P3 with preceding endurance Ferraris as well as those that followed: the 512S, 512M and 312P – all of which I had driven. One of the P3's race wins was right here at Spa-Francorchamps in the 1966 Spa 1000kms driven by Mike Parkes and Ludovico Scarfiotti.

The P3 was supplied by the ever-impressive Tim Samways Sporting and Historic Car Engineers who knew me from previous work. The track was courtesy of RMA Trackdays. The Samways team gave me no pre-drive briefing. It meant that they believed I didn't need one, which I quite liked. The solitary seat was positioned almost in the centre of the car. Typically, and like the Porsche 917, the P3 is right-hand drive since there is a weight advantage on right-hand race circuits. Most race circuits run clockwise. The world's most beautiful racing car and the world's most beautiful racetrack await. Weighing only 700kg and with 410bhp, the P3 munched up the Spa track.

THE CHILDREN'S ALFAS AND OTHERS

There were several road tests of new and used Alfa Romeos. At the time, my two sons, Dino and Niki ran a 166 2-litre and a GTV 3-litre. The 166 was okay, it did the job. The GTV 3-litre was a rocket ship and coped as well as practically possible with front drive. It was fast and could have been reliable had an Alfa Romeo designer not located an oil line in a ridiculously low location. It lightly grazed a nasty speed bump, lost its oil and destroyed the

17 and 18: Dream drive. Ferrari P3 at Spa. One of the cars involved in the famous Daytona 1-2-3 finish.
19 and 20: Sons Dino, a geologist in Pompeii and Niki enjoying Lamborghini hospitality.
21: The Maserati management team at Silverstone.
22: Two wet races. We did okay.
23: RG and Keith Wood.
24: The Maserati hands-on crew at Silverstone.

engine before any warning lights illuminated – a fine example of crap design. A good designer should be a pessimist. Only an optimist would place a vulnerable oil pipe at the lowest point on a car. Alfa replaced the GTV with the Alfa Brera and weirdly, simultaneously, with the Alfa GT. The Brera is famous for its lack of storage inside the cabin. Who designed the interior of the Brera? Does he or she still have a job?

The *Auto Italia* team then tested a new Alfa Romeo 159 Sportwagon, fully loaded on a road trip across Europe. It was great and looked good. I recently thought of buying a used one because they cost nothing. I was put off by hearing that some had terminal chassis problems with the GM designed floorpan. How can this be? What were the designers thinking? Everything they needed to know had been invented. Why didn't the designers Google "How to design a car's floorpan?"

MASERATI TROFEO AT SILVERSTONE AND DRUG ADDICTION

Telephones are like racing cars. They can devastate as easily as they can delight. This is a story about a delight. Ring ring…, "Would you like to drive the Toora-sponsored VIP Maserati GranSport in the Silverstone Trofeo race at the weekend supporting the FIA GTs?" I replied in the affirmative. Another works drive: whatever was in the diary for that weekend was cancelled. This is where a racer needs a partner or spouse who is prepared to live with a terminal risk-taking drug addict, which fortunately mine does. To employ a psychological term that UK team boss John Danby uses, "Racers must have the madness." By that he means total commitment and be fiercely competitive in all conditions.

The deal was for me and another magazine editor, Keith Wood, to share a car for two one-hour races. Keith was ex-Formula Ford and an ex-saloon car racer. In the first race, all was going well in torrential rain we were mid-pack when the red lights came on, ending the first race. Supermodel Jodie Kidd, whom I had instructed at Goodwood, was running 17th and whacked the wall on

the wet start-finish straight. This is a regular wet-weather booby trap at both of Silverstone's pit walls. The standard of racing at the sharp end was high. First and second-place men were FIA GT drivers Diego Alessi and Alberto Cerrai. Keith and I finished both wet races in the top half of the field. Just dropping into a one-make modern race series is never easy. Even F1 drivers like Johnny Herbert, Tiff Needell, Ivan Capelli, Ralph Firman and Jacques Laffite, who have all raced these cars, do not win. There were three cars driven by well-known racing journalists. Our goal was to beat them, which we did.

LAMBORGHINI MIURA JOTA

While the Jota looked like a modified Miura, it wasn't. It was so radical that the word 'modification' is inappropriate. It was a totally new structure in the approximate shape of a Miura. In 2006, I wrote a story about Piet Pulford's replica Jota. Lamborghini's original Jota was destroyed in a high-speed road accident. Pulford's donor car for the replica Jota needed everything. This made it a good project for a one-off Jota reproduction. In period, the story went like this:

1966 – The fast car world is turned upside down as the first supercar is born, enter the Miura.

1969 – Bob Wallace had been the Lamborghini test driver since 1963. Lamborghini let him make a wild Miura: the Jota (ch. no. 5084).

1969/70 – The Jota is used as a mobile testbed and as a tool to frighten journalists on Italian roads. Top speed: over 190mph. 0 –62mph: 3.6 seconds.

1970 – Lamborghini sells the one-off Jota.

1971 – Brescia dealer Enrico Pasolini sells the Jota on to an industrialist: Dr Belponer. Before delivering the Jota, Pasolini gives high-speed joyrides in the car. With a secretary in the passenger seat, the car goes out of control at 150mph. The Jota is destroyed and after a month in hospital the occupants survived.

The Jota's weight tells a tale. The standard Miura weighs 1,245kg. the factory Jota reputedly weighed 900kg, while Pulford's replica tipped the scales at 1,000kg. If faced with a Jota replica to judge, you will need a stopwatch to confirm a 3.6 seconds 0–60mph, some scales to check its weight, a racetrack to check its handling because its chassis and suspension is unlike that of a regular Miura. And of course, a test driver who

27 – 29. Police taking an interest at Silver Flag. Police always enter cars from their museum and always win a prize.

30: Jane talking tech with inquisitive chaps.

31: Lotus 26R. Dramatic wheelspin starts guaranteed.

25: A factory replica of the original Miura Jota.

26: Piet Pulford's Miura Jota replica.

knows the difference.

The Jotas you might see today are not to be confused with the half-hearted dressed-up Miura SVJs that were built for the Shah of Iran and others. The factory recently built a copy, but I don't know how accurate it is. You would have to get Valentino Balboni on his own and ask him. The original/real Jota was destroyed in 1971. Pulford told me, "You would have to be mad to build one." I like the link between Pulford's 2006 madness and the madness of the original in 1969. But then in 1969, you could do anything mad and it would be considered normal. You could even fly to the moon.

A HILLCLIMB, A BUS AND A TELLING OFF

The sun is almost directly overhead. It is the summer solstice and I am covering the story on another Italian hillclimb, that I nick-named 'an Italian Goodwood.' What better way to cover the story than from a driver's seat? This time it was in Jane's ex-works Lotus Elan 26R. The Vernasca Silver Flag startline has spectators almost at arm's length on one side, behind a barrier. While on the other side there are photographers in the death zone. The spectators express much enthusiasm with the quicker cars. Some cars wheelspin off the startline, a few take it easy. Our little Lotus is capable of dramatic starts, with wheelspin being the new clutch. The 350hp/tonne Lotus fish tails away. While the spectators punch the air, a new startline official is livid and later I receive a bollocking.

Later, I parked the Lotus in the mid-way town of Lugagnano to take some photos for magazine stories and enjoyed the café life. Inside said café, a policeman entered sheepishly asking if I am the driver of the yellow Lotus in a nearby parking area. He tells me that a bus had hit the parked Lotus. The bus vs Lotus Elan battle can never be a good one for the smaller vehicle. Exiting the café and expecting to see a crushed Lotus, the damage was a barely visible mark on the rear bumper.

The next day and it is time for the third and final run. The angry startline official is looking at me with one hand gently moving up and down to signify calmness.

With the spectators demanding a repeat performance, I duly obliged. At the prize-giving, the startline marshal who had previously screamed profanities at me looked at me shaking his head. Sometimes it is good to be bad.

MONACO

Monte Carlo used to be Italian… well, Genovese. In 1297, a crafty Francesco Grimaldi and his gang dressed as monks (*monaco* is the Italian word for monk) sneaked in one night and seized the monastery. The Grimaldis have ruled the billionaires' metropolis continuously ever since. The French annexed it in 1789 while they were revelling in their revolution. But let's not be too hard on the once-Italian Grimaldis or the French, as they give us the showbiz extravaganza that is the Monaco Grand Prix. I walked the circuit and once again was amazed how TV fails to reveal the inclines, cambers and tightness of the world's slowest racetrack. Who said that the Monaco GP is like hosting a bicycle race in your kitchen?

Up the hill from the startline I drift (on foot) past the Hotel de Paris and into Casino Square. You know when you have made it because you never have to park a car. Despite a huge parking space, a fat-cat driver abandoned his supercar in the middle of the road with its V12 purring unsupervised. He then strolled into the hotel. Out came the doorman to park the outrageous machine amongst the cocktail of supercars.

If you are a yacht watcher, Monaco is the place. The port is constantly being enlarged to cope, as the superyachts grow in number and in size. An on-board submarine and a helicopter on the poop deck are normal. The only type of poop you will ever see in Monte Carlo.

SOUTH AFRICA

From the glitz of Monaco, I return to the UK and soon find myself boarding a night flight with photographer Andrew Brown for my red-eye airlift, bound for Johannesburg. You don't need a time machine to travel back in time. Just choose your location carefully and hey presto. Like most countries, South Africa has its good and bad bits, but more so. Andrew had organised a two-week trip to test over a dozen cars at Kyalami GP Circuit and Zwartkops Circuit.

After a sleepless night flight in cattle class we arrived at about 6am and went straight to Kyalami. Ten cars on test included racing cars and trackday cars of various makes. When they told me that I would be driving at a Kyalami trackday, I was still thinking in English. You get the picture: no lap timing, ask permission to overtake, indicator on, wave a car by, "After you old chap. No no no, after you." A UK trackday starts with a doom and gloom briefing, evolves into a bollocking and finishes

32: Monaco. There is nowhere else like it.
33: Kyalami GP Circuit and the natives are friendly.
34: Well, what do you think? Er... Ok, but I can't turn the steering wheel.
35: Super-ightweight 750kg Alfa GTV Twin Spark.
36: Kyalami – snapper Andrew Brown who organised the South Africa trip.
37: Zwartkops circuit South Africa and the Carabinieri get everywhere.
38: Ultima powered by 3.5-litre Alfa V6. It was quick.

with threats of being sent home. It does work as I can remember UK trackdays in the early 1980s, when accident rates were massive. A South African trackday relives those olden times and takes them further by making the event competitive. A trackday at Kyalami is an all-out competitive event. Every car is fitted with a transponder. All laps are timed. All results are posted on the wall and prizes are given to each class. We had a briefing, which went like this, "No short sleeves or shorts, and try not to take anyone out." It is racing by another name, except no licence or experience is necessary. A new Mini Cooper S followed me into a fast turn and rolled itself into a ball of scrap metal.

After a sleepless aircraft night flight, followed by a scorchingly hot day competing for nine hours in ten different cars at Kyalami without a break, I was exhausted, dehydrated and ready for bed. Our accommodation was kindly provided at the fortified ranch house of Alfa Romeo specialist Dawie de Villiers. Its four-metre-high perimeter wall had a two-metre-high electrified razor wire barrier. There was also a well-stocked gun rack in the hall and private security vehicles patrolling the perimeter. Welcome to SA.

Upon arrival at the house, I presented Dawie with a bottle of finest single malt scotch whisky. While all I wanted after an uncomfortable long-haul night-flight and gruelling day was several glasses of water and a bed, Dawie had other ideas. He insisted that present company get stuck into the whisky. I have only ever been a lightweight when it comes to alcohol consumption, but it would be rude to refuse. Late at night and drunk, Andrew and a couple of SA Touring Car racers then took me to a night club. Dying of thirst and in a daze, many tall glasses of fruit juice were brought to me. These turned out to be strong cocktails, but I was too far gone to notice. When I eventually went to bed, it was in a fully clothed, shoes-on, unconscious state. It took me two days to recover and since then, my alcohol consumption is effectively zero.

Once recovered, we visited various car owners and road-tested some classics. We also spent much time at

Dawie's 'Glenwood' Alfa Romeo workshop. From the mid-1970s to the mid-80s, Alfa Romeo used to make cars here, so enthusiasts have a strong connection with the brand. Dawie was modifying many V6 Alfa engines with considerably enlarged capacity, like a 3.7-litre 24v capable of up to 400bhp in race trim.

A trip to Zwartkops Circuit was great and included a test drive in Patrick Gearing's racing Alfa Romeo Giulia Super dressed up in Italian Carabinieri livery. Then a tale of two Alfetta GTVs: a Glenwood 3.7-litre V6 racer weighing 1,200kg, and a super-lightweight (750kg) GTV2000.

BMW race boss, Hennie van der Linde, then offered me a BMW works Castrol-liveried BMW 330i Touring Car. It had the heaviest steering of any car that I had ever driven. It was a matter of applying whatever steering lock that my muscles could muster. Whoever drove that car should enter the arm-wrestling Olympics. A trackday in 2006 at Zwartkops costs £18 (£26 in today's money). The circuit café served everything you

need at very low prices. What a change from the UK where bottled water costs more than petrol. The atmosphere is laid-back and the whole day had a friendly, family feel.

The motorsport people in South Africa are a first-rate bunch. Compared with Europe, South African motorsport has a power fetish. It is a bit like the USA, where nimble lightweight cars are not for real men. What is considered more important here is horsepower. After two weeks in South Africa, I learnt a lot. I know one or two people in the UK who tell me how they would love to live in SA. While I met great people there and revelled in SA motorsport, I could never live there.

P1 OFFSHORE POWERBOAT RACING

It was time to do another silly thing. In 2006 Class 1 Offshore Powerboat Racing there was an average death rate of one or two competitors per year. When you learn that this applies to about 40 people, the stats reminded me of Russian roulette. I was pondering how death by

39

39: P1 Class 1 Kerakoll.
My flying boat.
40: My crew and championship leaders Mario Invernizzi and Giovanni Carpitella.
41: RG ready for action.
42: TV crews in chase helicopters.
43: Girl power. The P1 Corporate Club.

drowning is one of my least favourite ways to die. This is a story about violence. Brutality in the form of a wild ride in a 160mph, 2,000hp powerboat. Photographer Michael Ward and I jetted to Milan to pick-up an internal flight to Bari in Puglia at the heel of the Italian boot. The Mediterranean Grand Prix was our target. A ride in a top P1 Class 1 World Championship Offshore powerboat is one of those times when you consider the risk/reward formula and ignore it. The lure of Italy overwhelmed the dread of a powerboat ride.

I thought about famous racing drivers who have tragically lost their lives or been injured, doing risky things outside motor racing. Simply from memory I thought about lives lost: David Purley aerobatics; Graham Hill and Tony Brise, light aircraft. David Lesley, Cessna jet; Colin McRae helicopter; Alessandro Nannini, helicopter; Davey Allison, USA, helicopter. Then there are the serious injuries: Alex Zanardi, both legs amputated in Indycar, after which he was again nearly killed and this time left with brain damage after a

crash on his handbike; F1 driver Robert Kubica, badly smashed rallying in his spare time; Michael Schumacher, when a camera helmet-mount penetrated his brain whilst skiing slowly (I have seen the footage). Most poignant of all, I thought about ex-Ferrari F1 driver Didier Pironi. At the 1982 German Grand Prix, Pironi had a horrendous crash that smashed his legs ending his motor racing career. Pironi switched to powerboat racing and in 1987, Pironi was then killed in a disaster at the Needles Trophy Race near the Isle of Wight, that also took the life of his two crew members: journalist Bernard Giroux and his friend Jean-Claude Guénard. Their boat, Colibri 4, rode over the wash of a distant ship, sending Pironi's powerboat into a high-speed overturn. Then there are the incalculable number of non-famous driver casualties of which the media do not make us aware.

I considered a recent snapshot of my life. I was motorcycling and motor racing in several cars. I had been in an ancient aircraft performing aerobatics. I had been on a racing motorcycle sidecar outfit. I was testing racing cars and carrying out other high-speed tests. I was race instructing. I was hands-on in a dangerous workshop. A dragster ride at Santa Pod. I was up ladders on the roof of my house and I had been horse riding. In other words, if I wasn't asleep, I was in danger. Today, that danger list has been halved, although the next story upped the risks.

This powerboat report also concerned a one-hundred-year-old luxury car maker turned top marine engine manufacturer. In the early 1900s, Isotta Fraschini made sumptuous cars to rival Rolls Royce: Today, they make huge marine engines. The CEO gave us a factory tour and presented us with beautiful two Isotta Fraschini wrist watches. Still at the Isotta Fraschini Motori factory, the powerboat Kerakoll was sitting on its transporter like a missile at a Red Square military show. Two 1,000hp Isotta Fraschini engines are fitted to Kerakoll, the name on the record-breaking boat that was leading the P1 Powerboat Championship. The next day I was sentenced to be

strapped to this missile, which has more power than two Formula One cars. Isotta Fraschini marine engines start at 11-litre and go up to 62-litre.

The P1 World Championship is the aquatic equivalent to Formula One Grand Prix motor racing but without safety. It is the morning of the practice day and high in my hotel room, I look down on the 19 boats that will soon be fighting it out. The venue is the Mediterranean Grand Prix round of the P1 World Championship in Gallipoli. There are two Gallipolis: Gallipoli in Turkey where in 1915 there was a proper battle that cost the lives of 300,000 Turks and 250,000 Allied troops. And the Gallipoli in the Puglia region of Southern Italy, where everyone has a great time. We are in the latter. I used the opportunity for other features, like a Puglia travel story, a factory story on Isotta Fraschini, plus visits to local car collections hosted by the local car club. How about a motorbike fitted with an engine from a Fiat 127? A great example of making the most of what is close at hand in this economically poor south of Italy. Today, the terminology is called upcycling, as if this ancient practice is new.

In the Gallipoli marina, my boat is warming up with a deep rumble. The sea at the aft end gently boils.

44: Engine room – 2,000 horses and a man's head.
45: Mario Invernizzi introduces RG to Kerrakoll.
46: P1 powerboats spend a lot of time in the air.

Kerakoll is a regular race winner and record breaker. It is longer than a London bus and there is just enough space for four people. The racing regulations permit a maximum crew of three. The shape of the lightweight hull can withstand the shock of high-speed impacts with water that has taken on the characteristics of granite. Nestling under the rear deck, the power of 2,000 horses. With the boat spending a lot of time flying, cooling water for the engines and intercoolers enters the craft via the bottom of the hollow rudder.

At full power, the Kerakoll-liveried boat consumes diesel at a rate of 8.3 litres per minute. P1 powerboat racing reminds me of F1 motor racing in the 1960s, as the teams spend time socialising instead of being whisked away in corporate aircraft the minute they get out of the cockpit. In the interest of research, this writer and photographer joined the teams and organisers in the buzzing Gallipoli nightlife. In the harbour-side restaurant, there was an in-depth technical discussion on whether spaghetti vongole should use linguini.

It was time to get ready. I am to ride in the back seat behind Captain Mario Invernizzi (steering) and Giovanni Carpitella, throttle. On with orange P1 race overalls and my white crash helmet. Then a long wait in the hot sun.' A Dutch official approaches. 'You can't use a white helmet. The rules stipulate orange only.' The thought of a 3,000-mile, four-flight, five-day trip without a ride or a story loomed. Radios crackle up the line of command till the buck stops. I hear the words 'Journalist, white helmet, visibility, helicopter rescue, rules, blah, blah…' Here was my get-out-of-jail card. Saved from being smashed and drowned by not having an orange helmet. I was not going to die that day. But we are in Italy where if they want something to happen, it does. And if they don't, you meet an impenetrable Soviet-style Iron Curtain. I get the nod, white helmet it is, bugger. Another delay as one of the rescue boats breaks. It hits unlisted fishing nets on the course. Finally, we get a green flag. Manoeuvring Kerakoll between the gin-palaces is tricky. With no bow thrusters, a stiffish breeze and a lightweight boat, we gently pinball between the yachties.

Captain Mario Invernizzi – the steerer – had been screaming down his mobile phone at someone for about ten minutes. His arteries and veins are popping out of his red face. He is throwing things around, yelling and is beyond livid with whomever is on the other end of the phone. I was thinking how you would never get near a racing car in that condition. Fortunately, Giovanni Carpitella, the throttle man, was the king of cool.

Tales from other pilots of frequent spine-crushing impacts sprung to mind. There was also mention of how powerboat racers get progressively shorter in height. Even if you don't crash, P1 powerboat racing is dangerous. There is no briefing, although I was told about the monster G-forces that I must endure. Knowing the laws of physics, I think to myself: "Keep your jaw closed if you like your teeth". "Never stand bolt upright unless you like wheelchairs". "Use the handrail to reduce the load on your spinal column". "Don't push your tongue forwards unless you want to see it on the floor."

Slowly, we rumble out to the open sea with pitching of rodeo-riding proportions. The sea is choppy which is bad, but the captain is no longer on the phone, which is good. The general harshness is reminiscent of a racing car cockpit. Noise builds. Speed rises and then the horrendous high-G slamming begins. My pilots are connected by intercom, while my ears are assaulted by man-made mechanical madness. The throttle man gives full power if the prop is in the water and shuts the throttle whilst flying.

If you are a mile away from Kerakoll on full chat, you know something big is happening. It's a bit like hearing, or rather feeling, a distant column of armoured tanks speeding through a city, like in a war zone, or Paris on Bastille Day when fast-moving armoured tanks shake the whole capital. At close quarters, the sound makes the hairs on the back of your neck twitch. With the two engines millimetres from my feet, the noise and the feeling of power is surreal. While the rest of the world hears the deep hair-raising rumble of 2,000hp, interior decibels are dominated by the high-pitched whine of four giant turbos and wind noise. I knew that if I shouted

47: The Lamborghini-powered boat explodes when we hurtled past the crew in the rough sea.
48: A regulation orange helmet.
49 and 50: The instruments in the boat are melted.
51: The burnt-out hull is lifted from the water.

at the top of my voice, it would go unheard. We hurtle across the sea at aeronautical speeds. The laws of physics appear to be broken. Sea water has become steel. The propellers have become 2,000hp gear wheels biting into the sea of metal like a mad rack and pinion. These two 11-litre straight sixes make 1,000hp each at 2,800rpm. Turbo diesels always have high torque. Measured in Newton metres (Nm), the figure here would be several thousand Nms. Drive and propulsion feel as positive as in a racing car. At 30mph, water is not water as we know it. Just as in aeronautics, air becomes semi-solid at supersonic speeds, so at 100mph, water evolves into a new rock-solid element.

The waves on the sea become irregular. They combine with considerable wash from other boats, one of which (no. 76) explodes and is well ablaze. The awesome-sounding 1,600hp, petrol-powered, Lamborghini-engined boat of ex-tennis champion Adriano Panatta becomes a casualty. It is a huge fireball. What is left of the carbon-fibre boat melts under a huge column of smoke. We flash past the stricken craft, its three-man crew are thrown clear, with just their orange helmets visible in the rough water. Now I understand how white helmets would be invisible amongst the white foam in a choppy sea. While boat 76 sends smoke and flames into the sky, Kerakoll (no. 66) sends a huge plume of water skywards. They say that the feeling of speed doubles on water. I had no idea of our speed other than it felt insanely out of control.

The impacts on Kerakoll's hull build to shocking levels. Interspersed with the smooth heaven of flight. High-speed bellyflops are bad enough. Worse is the brutality that involves yaw, roll and corkscrewing. When landing at an angle, the hull presents a keel-free flatter surface. It skids across the surface of sea until it crashes into an unyielding wave sending it who knows where. Back-breaking impacts of 6G are commonplace with peaks to 9G. The pilots will tell you that the G-forces are no trouble for the boat; it is the people inside that are the problem. As for accidents, they say that

danger comes with top speed in a light swell that hides a rogue wave. Boats can roll, spin, nose-dive deep underwater or back-flip. The throttle man reads the waves hundreds of metres ahead of the speeding boat. Gallipoli blurs into the distance as I try to think of a comparison for readers to understand. In 1967, I was returning home from the Marcos factory as I had an ambitious plan to build a Mini Marcos for the Le Mans 24-hour race. On the way home in my 'Wimbledon Stadium' Ford Anglia, I had an enormous high-speed car crash that involved two huge impacts, a considerable period of silent flight, followed by multiple rolls and more heavy impacts. So, if you want to know what P1 powerboating is like, it is like having a serious high-speed car crash that goes on for an hour.

It was time to leave. I had parked our hire car in a place that incurred someone's displeasure. I replaced the stabbed tyre with the spare wheel. At Bari airport, our flight to Milan had a two-hour delayed take-off time. We landed at Milan in time to miss our connecting flight to London. The flights were on different airlines, we had no help. All the desks at Milan were closed. We were stuck. I had just enough battery in my phone to call Jane in the UK who booked us two new tickets Milan – London for the next day. We slept in the airport. Compared with a P1 Offshore Powerboat ride, a ceramic bed in the form of an airport floor was the height of luxury. The adventure continued when we landed at Stansted Airport. The baggage on the carousel circulated. Everyone picked up their bags and departed – except me. At the baggage desk, I filled in the lost baggage form, including my address for eventual delivery. I headed home bagless. Many days later, I was outside my home in Surrey and presumed that someone about 50m away was going on holiday because they had a wheelie bag. Said person then left the bag on the pavement and drove off in a van. A 50m stroll and an investigation of the abandoned bag and all was well. It was my bag with my race kit, powerboat notes and camera. The powerboat story could finally be put to rest.

2007
Bologna Motor Show

Winter 2006/2007 and it is showtime. A trip to the Bologna Motor Show was Italy's premier automotive showcase. It differed from UK shows by being less technical, louder and assisted by numerous showgirls. All the manufacturers were there with current and concept cars. It was good to see the *Polizia Stradale* with a stand. The Abarth stand was very popular as it had the most showgirls, although I suspect that today, I should not have written that.

The motorsport hall was a bit like *Autosport* meets *Max Power*. It had too many sound systems – each blasting out different pop music – competing at ear-bleeding volume. There was plenty of show but not enough go. Unlike the UK's Autosport Show, Italian race car builders don't go to motor shows to find components. It was such a relief on the ears to exit the raucous motorsport hall destroyed by din. Outside the many halls was an off-road course complete with towering roller-coaster rides in untethered Land Rovers. This was scary to witness, let alone ride.

ALFA ROMEO AND MUSSOLINI AGAIN

I keep metaphorically bumping into the Italian dictator Benito Mussolini. *Auto Italia* has put me into two of his cars. This time in a rather sporting 1935 Alfa Romeo 6C 2300 Pescara Touring Cabriolet belonging to Dottore Ugo Isgrò. Last year, the car won a prize at the Pebble Beach Concours d'Elegance and was first at the New York Concours. *Auto Italia*'s Simon Park (writer, composer, chart topper, orchestra leader and my doorman) also drove it. The car is so elegant. But there is more to the dashing Alfa than good looks. This car is a road-going

version of a state-of-the-art 1930s racing car. The driver can also control the stiffness of the rear dampers via a dash-mounted knob, an advanced feature for 1935.

From Alfa's foundation in 1910 up to the Second World War (1940), the company was in the business of making racing cars and top-end bespoke vehicles. Mass-production cars were not on the agenda. Winning races, especially against the Germans, was seen as a way of improving Italy's world image as well as generating national pride. When Benito Mussolini seized power in 1922, he backed Italian engineering, be it for land, sea or air records. In 1933, Alfa Romeo came under state control – a situation that was to remain until the Fiat takeover in 1986.

Mussolini's personal chauffeur for 20 years was Ercole Boratto (1886–1970), who was also quite handy as a racing driver. Boratto's duties also included those of a bodyguard and personal assistant. In the 1936 Mille Miglia, Boratto took this actual car in our story to 13th place out of 70 starters and third in class. In 1957, the Mille Miglia ended after too many deaths. However, road racing continued in Italy's colonies. Boratto won the Tobruk to Tripoli 300-mile race at an average speed of nearly 90mph in another of Mussolini's Alfas.

NURBURGRING AND TWO PRECIOUS FERRARIS

The editor was on his mobile phone to *Auto Italia*'s insurers, "Yes. Two Ferraris. Yes. Millions of pounds. And yes, on the Nürburgring Nordschleife" First to test was a 250 California Spyder, followed by a rare alloy-bodied 275 GTB/4 Longnose, both loaned to us by Dr Hartmut

1: Mussolini's Alfa Romeo 6C 2300.
2: 'Hot Wheels' ramp at Bologna.
3: The noisy Bologna Motor Show. Fiats within Fiats.
4: Abarth stand promo girl.

Ibing, who was happy for us to give the priceless machines a run round the Ring. In 2021, a California Spyder would cost you about $20 million.

The Ferrari 250 series was the first time that the prancing horse was tethered to anything that resembled a production line. Hollywood stars lined up to buy them. Time to feast my eyes on an alloy-bodied 275GTB/4 Longnose. With regards to styling, few 1960s GT cars have stood the test of time better than the 275GTB. It is a masterpiece. So many of its styling and design features are visible on contemporary GT cars. Whoever it was at Pininfarina who penned this Scaglietti-built car, had da Vinci-esque future vision.

The 21km Nürburgring Nordschleife may be no place for such a boulevardier as a California Spyder or a lightweight 275GTB/4 but taking them on this tortuous trip demonstrated just how effective they are.

Here were two cars I could happily have spent all day waltzing around the Nordschleife, then driven over the Alps to gently cruise on Mediterranean coast roads.

AUSTRIA, A GERMAN AND SOME LAMBORGHINIS

Reiter Engineering had hired the Austrian Salzburgring track for exclusive use. They brought along five racing Lamborghinis and we were there to drive them. Exclusive use at this circuit had options: marshals or no marshals, with ambulance or without ambulance. The winter track was icy and we had no marshals. None, but we did have an ambulance standing by. In 2007, exclusive use of the circuit cost €3,000, which is less than a tenth of the price for a UK track.

I first saw the Murciélago R-GT two years ago, testing at Spa. The noise it sent ricocheting around the Ardennes Forest was so menacing that when the car returned to the pits, I was too scared to look at it. Now I must drive the thing on ice and at an unfamiliar circuit. We had the perfect ingredients for a career-ending monumental shunt but the bravest man at the circuit was not me or the team's chisel-jawed racing hero Peter Kox, but race team boss Hans Reiter for trusting anyone

5: Ferrari 275GTB/4 and 250 California Spyder at rest.
6: Expensive cars at play.
7: Monster Murciélago R-GT.
8: A smiling, trusting Hans Reiter.
9: Hot car, cold track.

7

with his monster Murciélago R-GT, or his 'baby', as he calls this GT1 Class racing car. Some baby, compared with a regular Lamborghini Murciélago, the Reiter Engineering R-GT packs half-as-much-again in the power-to-weight department. This is one rock-hard mother of an angry rodeo bull. Now imagine that bovine bolide on a tricky track surface that is icy, wet and dry all on the same lap. The Salzburging is in a valley bottom, which at the time of the year saw little direct sunlight.

Fast, furious and unforgiving, no gentleman drivers were allowed to race in GT1. It was for professional drivers only and with one German eyebrow raised, team boss Reiter says, "Even zen, zer are professionals und professionals."

8

9

In 2007, Reiter Engineering competed in FIA GT1 and the Le Mans 24-hour race. But what about the private teams? Manufacturers don't like supporting privateers. This is because they have little control over the team and are terrified that a loose cannon privateer may do something silly that could damage the manufacturer's brand, however Reiter Engineering has some limited factory help.

The Murciélago R-GT before me was in Le Mans specification. This means low drag bodywork. Downforce is still there but reduced to give more straight-line speed. If religion is the opium of the people, then downforce is the opium of the tyres. The rules for GT1 were rather free. This meant that to be competitive you did not modify a road car. Instead, you started with a blank sheet of paper and built a prototype in the shape of the original car. The cost was so vast that there were relatively few GT1 cars. Therefore, GT1 was always under threat, eventually being banned in 2011.

The GT1 rules in 2007 tried to limit engine power. Naturally, engineers found a way around the restrictions. The original power curve, where power rises to a peak and tails off, is gone. This car quickly attains its max power. Here 'max' comes early and stays with you. Hans draws a flat line in mid-air with his finger to describe the torque curve.

Hans also reduced the weight from 1,650kg to 1,050kg and then added ballast in the form of strength to meet the 1,125kg regulation weight. A standard road going Murciélago weighs 1,650kg. The power-to-weight ratio was now 47% higher than the road car at 533hp/tonne.

Be scared when you read this. Hold a cushion or something. Racing cars are like horses, wasps and angle grinders. They know if you are frightened. If they sense your fear, they bite you. Reiter's GT1 is intimidating to look at, intimidating to sit in and intimidating to drive. GT driver Peter Kox gives me a ten-second briefing as I strap myself to the raging bull. He tells me four things: "When you change gear, really mean it. The brakes feel light, but you must trust them.

10

The car weaves at high speed on the straight. And finally, you need lots of time in this car, which you don't have."

Before driving the GT1 Murciélago, I learn the circuit in a stealthy Reiter Engineering, modified Gallardo. I think I am going quickly in my Gallardo when the wailing Murc R-GT hurtles past like a meteorite in a ball of freezing spray. My immediate thoughts are, "That car is a god and so is whoever is driving it." That god was Peter Kox who had editor Phil Ward in the passenger seat. At a massively high speed on a straightish section of the valley bottom – and with no run-off area – the GT1 had a monumental high-speed spin. Fortunately, no damage was done and Phil certainly had a day to remember. Meanwhile, I returned the Gallardo to the pits. Hans Reiter would make a great poker player. I am about to snatch his 'baby' and he is as cool as a cucumber. I clunk the GT1's sequential gear lever into first gear. The clutch pedal is only used to move off from rest. A shudder and a gear-indicator light on the dash confirms the action. No matter how scary, you must show a car (and an angle grinder) who is boss.

On the track, I may be in charge of the car, but the track is now in charge of me. Overnight ice is reluctant

10: Reiter Engineering big wing Gallardo GT3 'Stealth Bomber' produced 520bhp at 8,000rpm.

11: Retired Lamborghini Diablo GTR kept by Reiter to play with and frighten their guests.

to melt at 3 degrees Centigrade. Now I am on track in the Murciélago hurtling past the Gallardo. Now I am God. But unlike God, the Pope, or experts on social media, I am not infallible. This GT1 racer takes no prisoners. If I make a mistake, there is no cushy torture chamber for me, just a hyper-speed career-destroying appointment with the cold steel of the armco barrier. Slippery cornering moments are bad enough, but more worrying is loss of control in sixth gear. You must be super-quick to catch a slide. You need to anticipate loss of grip to correct it. Then you must instantly undo the corrective input before the car reacts or you will get into a terminal tank-slapper.

There is no four-wheel drive and no ABS in the GT1. Without traction control, power must be fed in just so. Too slow and you are nowhere, too fast and ditto. A corner approaches and there is no simple mashing of the middle pedal. No, with the Lambo, you need a delicate touch while all hell is going on around you. Brake too early and you get swamped by the opposition. Too late and you flat spot £3,000 worth of tyres in a nanosecond. Definitely pro drivers only.

The commotion that is going on violates all senses and feels more intimidating than with the GT cars of old.

Visibility is very poor. No centre mirror due to the solid bulkhead. Just a pair of wobbly door mirrors angled at the trees and the sky. The Reiter team has given the car some toe out, at the front to help turn in, but it makes the car spooky on the straights. The light controls make it a bit of a video game. But unlike a video game, there is no 'resume' button if you get it wrong.

Then there is the noise. Oh, the noise. Observers hear the hair-raising Doppler scream from the mental six-litre V12 – perfectly apt as Mr Doppler used to live in Salzburg. To bystanders it is the *"Sound of Music"*, yes, that film was shot here too. You would swear that the motor is running close to the 18,000rpm of current Formula One engines, but you would be wrong. Reiter says that in this case the motor's 7,000rpm sounds like 18,000rpm because of the mods to the engine and the harmonics of the special exhaust system. We tested Reiter's cars into the night. The test drive was over. I fought the bull, but who won? Let's call it a draw. An eye-to-eye stand-off with another of Lamborghini's furious machines. I quit while I was ahead and went to look for a cushion.

THE DEVIL'S CAR

Every time I get into a Lamborghini Diablo, something illegal or mad happens. There was the time that I already mentioned when Valentino Balboni and I went for a wild ride in an experimental Jota version of a Diablo. It was like being in a video game but if it went wrong, I would be meeting El Diablo in person. Then there was the time at Spa in 1996 when, allegedly, I was sneaked into a Diablo SVR race car in the pouring rain on a race day. Then there was the Diablo drive on the Salzburgring on an icy day and cold dark night. Then at RAF Cottesmore, I had a drag race against an Italian Air Force Tornado jet fighter. I was briefly ahead, then the Tornado blasted ahead. I could feel the radiation from the reheat and it was gone. Fortunately, the Diablo's windscreen didn't melt. I learnt to tease the Diablo. It is like ringing the Devil's doorbell and running away. He really hates that.

LOLA IN ITALY

Time for a meaty racing car, namely a 1972 three-litre Lola T29 Tecno sports prototype and at Franciacorta Circuit. The Lola was a clever English chassis mated to substantial Italian power; a marriage between the two is certain to work. Isn't it? The ex-Jo Bonnier 650kg Lola (ch. no. HU4) has a 440hp Formula One Tecno engine, resulting in 677hp/tonne. Originally it was red and came with a 2.0 Cosworth FVC motor making 275hp.

After 108 Formula One Grand Prix races with many wins in F1 and sports car racing, Jo Bonnier was killed at Le Mans when his car (another Lola-Cosworth, a T280) was in collision with the Ferrari Daytona of the Swiss driver Florian Vetsch. In 1975, the Lola went to Italy. Its owner, Signor Paganucci and Signor Landi of Landi Motors, fitted the Tecno engine (number 14) and painted the car yellow. I first saw this Lola Tecno at an

Italian Hillclimb where it broke one of its driveshafts. Game over, had it been a German team, but not for an Italian team. A local road sign was commandeered, dismantled and its steel scaffold pole was cut and welded onto the car's driveshaft flanges. It did the job for the weekend and has since been replaced by a proper driveshaft.

We can all understand the attraction of fitting monster power to a car. Substituting a 275bhp engine with a 440bhp engine must make the car quicker, right? Well, not necessarily. A racing car is simply an object that changes speed and direction. Let us break that down into its three functions: acceleration, deceleration and cornering. Each of the three functions is equally important. A power increase can only assist one of those tasks. If it does this at the expense of the other two, i.e. via extra weight, the result can be a slower car,

12 – 15: Lola T290 Tecno.
The age of the wing-car begins.
16: Ferrari 312B3 Spazzaneve.

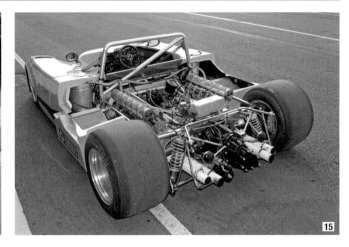

not a faster one. However, the Brits had been putting Formula One Cosworth DFV engines into small prototypes with success. The French did similar, squeezing F1 three-litre V12s into the Matra 620. The big power increases worked amazingly well. I know, I have raced against them.

Climbing in and settling down is the easy bit, especially in the commodious interior of the Lola. A bit too laid back, as I am straining my neck to see the track rather than the sky. I can't find any crutch straps, which means that at this near-horizontal posture, the four-point belts would offer minimal restraint as I would 'submarine' under them. The Landi crew presses all the right buttons and the unsilenced flat-12 barks to attention. So responsive is the motor that one millimetre of throttle movement slams crash helmet onto the rear bulkhead. I soon work out why. The Lola Tecno has hillclimb gearing, i.e. very short. This makes the car very responsive to throttle inputs. It is pure period 1970s sports prototype and a bit more. The four open pipes emit decibels like nothing else. The combination of huge power, fat sticky rubber and low gearing makes the car enormously quick in a straight line. Finally, to address the question – is the Lola Tecno quicker with its three-litre F1 engine? The answer is, yes and no. Yes, if developed well. No, if not. But in this case, lap times are not really the point of the exercise. If it still had its 275bhp Cosworth engine it would not be the celebrity it is today. The marriage of this English chassis and Italian engine will not need divorce lawyers. Little did I know in 2007, that in 2018/9 I would be racing a 300bhp Lola T298 sports prototype.

FORMULA ONE FERRARI 312 B3

Question: How do you get a drive in a Formula One car? The answer is complex as there are a few options. First, you need to differentiate between driving and racing an F1 car. I have driven six but raced none. Being silly with global statistics, the odds for being an F1 Grand Prix racer are one in 400 million. This is calculated as eight billion global population divided by 20, the number of

modern F1 drivers. The lottery odds are 14 million to one. This means that you will win the lottery 28 times before you can become a current F1 racer.

To reach the top of that pyramid, there are thousands of great drivers who have spent fortunes and failed. Today, there is a tsunami of parentally funded teenagers pursuing Junior Formulae with a hope of reaching the top. Routes to the top exist, but which top? There is the modern F1 World Championship and Historic F1. Via my test driver job, I managed to drive six F1 cars with the most modern from the 1990s. The 1972 Formula One 312B3 Spazzaneve (Snowplough) was Ferrari's development car, a test mule, bridging the gap between the 312Bs and the 312Ts. Landi Motors of Lucca were on hand to put me in the car at the Autodromo di Franciacorta.

The 312B3 also bridges the gap between cigar-shaped mechanical grip cars and the downforce cars to come. When it was shown to the press at Monza in August 1972, it created quite a stir. Jacky Ickx tested it and, apart from returning to the pits with a dead rabbit in one of the front NACA ducts, did not like it. He has since signed his name on the paintwork. Arturo Merzario was the principal test driver and was also unimpressed. He complained to its designer Mauro Forghieri that it was too nervous due to its short wheelbase. The nose presented too much aer-drag with little downforce. The big rear wing was shifted back to try to improve the aerodynamics but to no avail. Much was learnt from the 312B3 Spazzaneve and the forthcoming 312T benefitted from the experiment. While the Spazzaneve served its development purpose admirably, it never raced and is therefore devoid of decals and roundels. Parked on the empty pit-lane tarmac it was a time-warp scene. Surreal with just red paint, aluminium and Ferrari badges, we half expected the Commendatore to stroll along the pit lane.

F1 cars since the 1970s had bespoke foam seats that simply lifted out. Each driver would have his own tailor-made seat. The removable seat was made for Arturo Merzario who is tiny. For me, the foam 'seat' simply lifts

out as it has no fasteners or structural function. Even blindfold, you can tell which decade your perch is from. Cockpits once roomy enough for swinging cats and flailing arms gradually shrank. By the 1970s, they were cosy with just enough room to operate controls, while G-forces gently rattled the drivers. During the 1980s and 90s, G-forces increased and cockpits became very narrow. Cars that fitted one driver were useless for another. The Spazzaneve is beautifully made and fits me very well.

I have always been amazed how road and racing Ferraris were so different. From the mid-1960s to 1990, Ferrari road cars were ergonomically challenged. Whereas the racing cars from the same period were

17: The world's fastest snowplough on test at Franciacorta.
18: Post track test contemplation in the pit garage and getting the words down for the feature.

19: Better a head injury than to be seen wearing a full-face helmet...
20: A tricky driving selfie with a Canon SLR camera.
21: Does the Maserati's chassis plate look original?

not. Why didn't anyone at Ferrari notice this?

To get from standstill to moving in the pitlane, you feel for the bite point on the clutch and hold it at the bite-point until the car is travelling at about 15mph. Nothing reassures a pit crew more than a new driver who can master an on/off racing clutch and move off gently. The Spazzaneve has a very short wheelbase (2,300mm); great for hillclimbs or tight circuits like Monaco but decidedly twitchy at Monza and most GP circuits. As a comparison, a 2022 Mercedes F1 has a wheelbase of 3698mm, i.e. a massive 1.4metres (4ft 8in) longer wheelbase.

The Franciacorta circuit really suits the Spazzaneve. Weighing just 540kg and with 480bhp, the car has a power-to-weight ratio of nearly 900bhp per tonne – an enormous figure and virtually useless unless it can be applied to the track efficiently. With the giant Avons warmed up, the F1 Ferrari attacks the tight turns go-kart style. Cars of this era still had suspension travel and therefore plenty of 'feel'. The more modern the F1 car, the more 'video game' the feel.

Downforce escalates with speed. Double the speed

delivers four times the downforce. In the slow (sub-60mph) corners, this short wheelbase lightweight F1 car has ample grip. On the fast turns, its aerodynamics cannot be relied upon and while the red car doesn't lift its nose like a '60s F1 car, it doesn't suck itself to the track either.

MASERATI A6GCS, OR IS IT?

The Coys transporter unloaded the Maserati A6GCS race car at our test track. It was due to be sold at their auction sale in Monaco for an estimated £1 million. I never followed up the sale results, so I don't know how well it sold. When I wrote up the test drive, I had no idea regarding its originality or authenticity. Later at the Monaco auction, a German expert accosted me, shouting that the car was a fake and that I had misrepresented it. I replied that my job was to drive the machine and report on its performance, which I did. There was a separate column published with the track test regarding history that was supplied by Coys, which – at my instruction – the magazine clearly titled 'History supplied by Coys'. I wrote that because I did not know the facts and did not trust Coys. If you want to know about a car's provenance, I am the last person you should ask.

The historic racing car scene is awash with fakes. It is a minefield where you can tread carefully and buy well, only to find out later that there is another car on the same chassis number. Some wealthy racers own a rare and priceless racing car and have an exact copy made for them to race.

As a test driver, you should pack the right kit before going off to the test track. For this car, I chose period race clothing, i.e. a Harris Tweed jacket, cloth cap, goggles and brown brogues, which were only for day use, as it has been said that gentlemen never wear brown shoes after 6pm. I was enjoying a gentle drive in the car when health and safety officials noticed what is going on, "You can't drive that car without a crash helmet." I said nothing and thought about the 1953 Maserati drivers Fangio, Moss, Behra, Villoresi and Musso who raced wearing linen caps.

GERMANY AND TECH SPEC
Whenever I read a vehicle test, I expect/demand to see a tech spec sidebar in the feature that lists all the essential numbers at a glance. A sidebar is jargon for box listing technical information. Having the tech data scattered amongst the text, or indeed missing, is most annoying and unprofessional. I had to fight for *Auto Italia* to adopt a tech spec sidebar, as the magazine designers prioritised photos over words. A typical example of such tech spec necessity was when I went to Novitec's HQ in Germany to test-drive a supercharged F430. Ploughing through 1,500 words to find torque figures or comparison figures with an original car is frustrating, time-wasting and sloppy. Upon mentioning the need for a tech spec box in the features, which I always supply, I am told to stick to the driving.

Whilst in Germany, I thought it would be disrespectful not to visit the Nürburgring Nordschleife. It just so happened that Ron Simons' race school had an ex-works Group A Alfa Romeo GTV6 Touring Car for me to

22

23

road and track test. The police near the Ring take no notice if they see race cars on slicks. It goes with the territory, unless there is an incident and then there is big trouble.

FOREIGN EVENT REPORTS AND MONEY
During 2007, I was racing several cars in the UK and Europe. Some of those events were not races but road rallies, hillclimbs or regularity competitions. It was an opportunity to syndicate the reports accordingly for the requirements of other magazines. "Yes, we would love some event reports, please send them in," came the replies. Many reports were duly published in the most prestigious car magazines. However, getting paid by

22: Hotter Novitec Ferrari F430.
23: Group A Alfetta GTV6.
24: Top man Claudio Berro knows everyone at the top of motorsport.
25: A good thrash in a one-off at an italian race circuit.

them was always a battle. Countless requests and time-wasting delays were normal. I might have to wait three months to get paid. My choice was persistence or non-payment. Not being that hungry and too busy doing other things, I eventually refused to supply the slow payers and stuck with one or two quicker payers.

Whilst in Sanremo, a mutual friend, Nuccio Magliocchetti, invited me to lunch with his friend Claudio Berro. Claudio lives near Sanremo in an eco-house with a helipad, located on top of a hill overlooking Monaco. If you are looking for a James Bond location, this is it. Down at the beach restaurant we chatted and I learnt that Claudio has been a top executive with several motorsport companies including Team Manager Ferrari F1, Maserati Corse, Abarth, Lotus and Caterham F1. From 1979 to 1984, he competed in rallies with Peugeot and Alfa Romeo. The list goes on… He is a big fish in the motorsport corporate world. I used the opportunity for a magazine biography story. Enough of that, let's discuss food. The restaurants in Bordighera and Sanremo have mini angle grinders that they use to cut the hard shells of lobsters carefully and invisibly, so that when the dish arrives on your table, the seemingly impenetrable creature falls apart with the lightest touch.

THE UNIQUE AGUZZOLI AND ORIGINALITY

In 1963, father and son Giovanni and Sergio Aguzzoli decided to have a go at making and racing their own GT car – the Condor Aguzzoli. As for the name 'Condor', I am afraid that sex must rear its ugly head here. It is rumoured that the name Condor is related to one of the founders who circled his female prey, condor-style, before striking. The condor is a vulture with a 10ft wingspan, about twice the width of this car. Nowadays, the car is simply known as the Aguzzoli. The Italians had noticed that the British were winning races with their new-fangled racing cars that had the engines located behind the driver.

The Aguzzoli family had an Alfa Romeo dealership in Parma and they gathered a team of engineers to build this rear-engined sports car. Autodelta boss Carlo Chiti

kept a watchful eye on the project and helped with GTA/TZ motors. Think of the Aguzzoli as a rear-engined TZ. Their first car, the Mk1 was a learning process. It was dismantled and the Mk2 was at Franciacorta Circuit for me to test-drive with 170bhp and weighing 560kg. At 304bhp per tonne, it could be reasonably quick, provided the rest is engineered well.

Sitting – or should that be lying down – in the Aguzzoli, I had a good view of the underside of the roof. My legs were splayed and a distant steering wheel was crushing my knees. Now, I have been to every corner of Italy for more years than you need to know and I have never seen any creature whose body shape would fit this car. I suggested that the appalling ergonomics were fixable. Looks of horror from the team, "But it would not be original". I sigh and say nothing. A great car spoilt by an impossible sitting position. I suggest a compromise of fitting a spacer behind the original wheel, "Not original" came the predictable reply.

The car has never had any mirrors or seat belts fitted. "Original", they said before I could speak. In the UK, I have witnessed a steady increase in the pursuit of originality. This is nothing compared with the Italians' obsession with originality. Anyway, the Aguzzoli was a noble effort.

HOW TO DRIVE OLD RACING CARS AND PHOTOGRAPHY

Question: What is it that makes a historic racing car successful?

Answer: Lots of things, but the one I favour most is the ability to push (and hold) a car at the limit – and beyond – with impunity. I don't mean little wiggles but huge, long drifts that go on and on, before the car comes back into line, without fishtailing or spinning. A good balance with an absence of understeer is vital and difficult to achieve. Race regulations state that these cars must run on grip-free Dunlop historic crossply tyres. The tyres match the historic period. Fitting modern tyres to an historic car would introduce many problems, like chassis and suspension failures, as well as danger. Running on Dunlops designed 70 years ago is okay unless you are buying them. Depending on the car, they can wear out in one race and they cost around £300 each. A little bird told me that – allegedly – they are made in Portugal and cost £15 each to produce. Racers can live with tyres that lack grip. However, the short lifespan, the monopoly, and the excessive cost of the tyres needs addressing.

The first time you drive a race car on Dunlop historics, beware that when you arrive at turn-1, you might have a heart attack. At first, you feel that there is no grip. This is

26: The Aguzzoli GT was a fine effort that was never developed.
27: The designer of the ergonomics overlooked the shape of a human being.
28: Ferrari 500 TRC at speed.

because there is no grip. If you have come from a modern or slick tyre race series, you will be in for a culture shock. The trick to driving these cars is to always have them 'loose'. Well, okay, maybe not on long straights. Where going sideways on trackday tyres or slicks might be a risky experience, on Dunlop historic racing tyres, you build up to a situation where you 'float'. It is a bit like waterskiing or getting a speed boat 'on the plane'. The difference between straight line speeds and cornering speeds are higher with a historic racer. It's all part of the fun, provided the brakes work. Of course, they don't work like modern brakes. Historic brakes fade, they pull, the brake fluid boils and the pedal sinks to the floor. F1 driver Martin Brundle summed it up, "The brake pedal on a historic car is somewhere to rest your foot while you are having a crash." In 1961, Graham Hill summed up the brand-new small disc brakes on a racing Jaguar E-Type as, "Lethal". From 1961, E-Type

racers quickly fitted the larger versions fitted to the 1959 Jaguar Mk9 saloon. As for the 1957 Ferrari 500TRC, there were no new-fangled disc brakes, just ancient drum brakes. Jaguar was ahead of the game with the D-Type equipped with four good-sized disc brakes. Ferrari always waited to see if British innovation, like rear engines and disc brakes, worked before adopting them.

Top race car preparers DK Engineering brought along such a Dunlop-equipped car to our test track. To bring the TRC down to basics, it has 190bhp and 720kg equating to a power-to-weight ratio of 264bhp/tonne. In 1957, when road cars were built from wood and stone, this was an astronomical figure. Let's compare the Ferrari's 264bhp/tonne with a typical 1957 sports car and a 1957 family saloon. A sporting Alfa Romeo Giulietta Spider made 74bhp/tonne, while an Austin Cambridge produced 48bhp/tonne.

Auto Italia photographers at the time included Phil

29: Sideways testing.

30: Lancia 037 Stradale driven all the way from Wimbledon.

31: Mike Kason's Alfa Corsa-engined Fiat X1/9.

32: Tony Berni's Abarth 1300 OT.

33: Ex-Tony Castle-Miller 1000 TCR.

Ward, Michael Ward, Peter Collins and Andrew Brown. They each had their own photo style. Phil (ex-RAF and BBC) held the traditional ground, with perfect RAF focus to spot Russian spies. Michael also had convention but with added emphasis on composition and action photography. Peter was all action, with frequent into-the-light atmosphere shots, as was Andrew, although being artistic meant that Andrew was sometimes unreliable with deadlines.

Photographing the Ferrari 500TRC was a routine event; in this case it was Michael Ward. The Dunlop-shod Ferrari was east to drift for a customary oversteering shot. It could be carried out at relatively low speed and close to the photographer. Risk for photographers is always present. Apart from taking snaps in the death zone (i.e. facing an oncoming car that is sliding), a photographer also hangs out of a moving camera car – usually untethered – for car-to-car photography.

ABARTHS ON TRACK AND A FORGOTTEN F1 CAR

The *Autodromo di Franciacorta* was the venue for this annual event. There were historic Abarths as far as the eye could see. This was an opportunity not to be missed. I must have tested a dozen cars that day for future features. There were single seaters, sports prototypes, sports cars and saloon cars. The day was a reminder of just how many cars Abarth produced. Then there were the modified Fiats that had borrowed the Abarth name.

Although titled as a trackday, it is run to what in the UK would call a racing test day, i.e. no rules on overtaking, timing allowed and an open pit-lane. And unlike the UK, it included a proper Italian four-course lunch in the circuit's classy air-conditioned white-table-clothed, waiter-serviced restaurant. In Italy, lunch and dinner times are cast in stone. Star guest's included Anneliese Abarth, Carlo Abarth's wife and – for a while

– a creditable contributor to *Auto Italia*; and Dottore Renzo Avidano, the Abarth works team manager in the 1950s, '60s and '70s and 'number two' only to Carlo Abarth. I asked Avidano what he thought of the renaissance of Abarth by Fiat. After a long pause for thought, and a short sigh, he called it "A purely commercial venture. Not in the spirit of true Abarth." He is right; 'old Abarth' existed for the sake of the cars and for racing. Yes, it had to make money, but only so that it could develop the road and racing cars. Avidano commented on how race wins sold more cars. Whoever coined the 1960s phrase, "Win on Sunday; sell on Monday," got it right, and research shows that it still works today.

On arrival at the circuit, the sight of a crumpled 1000TC was sad. While some cars like the 1000TC are capable of a 'grip roll', i.e. rolling over without having hit anything, this roll-over was due to a mechanical malfunction. A rear hub had failed, detaching the wheel and brake assembly, pitching Marco Gnutti's 1000TC into a multiple roll. In good old-fashioned style, the vehicle had no seat belts, the doors burst open and the driver was thrown out of the car – a reminder of what racing used to involve. He was unhurt. No other incidents took place.

Robert Wadsworth deserves a mention because he drove his 1982 Lancia 037 Stradale all the way from Wimbledon to lap the Franciacorta Circuit. The French Police stopped him simply because one of the cops was an enthusiast and wanted to have a look. Then there was Mike Kason's Fiat X1/9, which must be the world's most developed X1/9. After race preparation that cost well into six figures (UK pounds), the 320bhp/700kg X1/9 deserved a good test whereupon it received much praise. I wondered if it was an example of how feeling can flout finance. Test drives in Tony Berni's superb and super-rare 1300OT, followed by an Abarth X1/9 Prototipo and Tony Castle Miller's 1000TCR ended the track work. This successful day ended with some short speeches, before devouring a work of art: a one-metre-square liqueur-laced Abarth gourmet cake washed down with finest pink prosecco.

The next day, I found a forgotten Formula One car. I never drove the Serenissima M1 AF, but I did write the story. As Shakespeare said, "Life is not all ale and cakes." Here are 15 words to sum up that 1,500-word history: Rich kid inherits a fortune. Goes F1 racing. He was unsuccessful but the car survived.

34 and 35: Serenissima M1 AF at the Silver Flag hillclimb.
36: Alfa 159 JTS Q4 at the Ring.
37: Posing with Alfa 75 school cars.

RETURN TO THE NORDSCHLEIFE

A trip to Germany to gather stories, comprising of four of the team and a mountain of kit. Winter is approaching, so what car should we take? Alfa Romeo gives us a 159 Q4 3.2 JTS. This is late 2007 so the flood of buyers for SUVs has yet to swell compared with today. Current UK Government advice to switch to smaller cars is being ignored. If you have ever driven a large, modern, luxury SUV, you will understand why. Writing this today and as a long-time convert to the SUV, using a saloon car for a transcontinental trip feels old-fashioned.

As usual, I do all the continental and UK driving regardless of time or distance. I know my place. In any case, unless a car is driven well and moving slowly, I don't like being a passenger. Arriving at the English Channel, there is a choice: boat or underwater train. I have used both countless times and prefer the boat, provided it includes the P&O first-class Club Lounge. We whizz through France and Belgium and find ourselves in Germany at the Nürburgring Nordschleife. We join an RMA Trackday at the world's most dangerous and world's best race circuit. Uniquely, RMA permits overtaking on either side, which places it at the top of my list for trackdays.

Our day was devoid of grip. Think – ice hockey puck on a virgin rink, rather than rubber tyre on tarmac. It looks damp, but Mr Grip is having a day off. Sheet ice would have been easier as you know where you stand. At RMA trackdays, drivers receive a necessarily stern briefing. Like World War One infantry preparing to walk slowly towards machine-gun fire, we are told in no uncertain terms that some of us are going to have a bad day. A Caterham slams into the armco on the slow follow-my-leader-look-see-lap. RMA boss Graham Clarke calls a re-brief. "Any more bad driving and I shall cancel the meeting without a refund and you can all f*** off home". This did the trick in reducing casualties. The two-day trackday went ahead with some more bent metal but no injuries.

Our red Alfa 159 Q4 joins the session proper. Wearing my instructor hat, I spend a lap instructing one of our party. An Audi A4 Quattro is following us. The Audi's body language suggests that it would like to overtake. I instruct my man to slow slightly to help the Audi. It creeps by, spins and is destroyed against the barrier. I knew that we were travelling as fast as the slippery conditions would allow. Audi-man paid the price. Having a press car for more than five minutes was a rare treat and enabled me to write what real world ownership would be like.

2008
Lamborghini Jarama and Rock and Roll

I have a soft spot for pre-1974 Lamborghinis. Lambo spotters will link the date with the introduction of the Countach. Post-1974, for me, the house of the raging bull lost its appeal. Of course, for most supercar enthusiasts, 1974 would be the beginning of their interest in the marque. With age comes the questioning of the purpose of the supercar. Lacking supercar passion, my writing would default to facts. To make the story authoritative, I would 'dial up' some passion and hope that no one notices. I am not alone and know that this is how some other road testers write about supercars.

The Jarama is one of the more restrained cars from Lamborghini. Like the Islero, the 350GT and 400GT, the Jarama is a gentleman's Lamborghini. The Jarama is named after an area outside Madrid famous for breeding fighting bulls. The Jarama name was also adopted for Madrid's race circuit. I have fond memories of spending two weeks at Jarama Circuit mucking about with race cars and dining out in nearby workers' restaurants – the best way to appreciate real/magnificent Spanish/Madrileño cuisine. I remember working at the circuit very late one night when a couple of Formula Ford drivers decided to go testing in the dark and obviously with no lights. I love that kind of free thinking.

My first of many Jarama drives was way back in the 1970s when I was looking after the cars of the Mungo Jerry Band. Roger Earl is the brother of Mungo Jerry co-founder Colin Earl. Roger was based in the USA with his own band, Foghat. However, for a while, he kept his Jarama GTS in the UK. In the 1970s, Roger and Colin left me the car to sort out a few minor issues, while they went off to the USA. Roger Earl's brother Colin (Mungo Jerry keyboard player) also had a string of supercars. The lead singer, Ray Dorset, drove an Aston Martin DB5 Vantage. For a while in the 1980s, Colin was also my business partner at Rossi Engineering, where we restored yet another Jarama. Having hands-on experience with any car helps enormously when writing about it or racing it.

The Jarama's short-stroke V12 screamer is what these cars are all about. You must remember that in this period, big four-litre screamers were cutting-edge technology. During the 1960s and '70s, the Jaguar E-Type was the yardstick by which fast cars were measured: 150mph and 0–60mph in six seconds, and one third the price of the exotics. The long-stroke Jaguar motor was big on torque but soon ran out of puff at the top end. Consequently, changing gear at approximately 5,000rpm was good enough. I soon worked out that 5,000rpm is where a Lamborghini engine woke up. The Lambos come alive between 5,000rpm and 8,000rpm. To get the best from any Lamborghini, it needs to be on-tune, on-song and on the red line. The Jarama had similar performance to an E-Type but only if you were at high rpm making a colossal noise. It was in the 1970s that I understood the Lamborghini breed.

My last Jarama test was in 2008. Resplendent in

1: To get the best from the Jarama it needs to be on-tune, on-song and on the red line.

Kermit-the-Frog green, the test car (ch. no. 10384) delivered to our track was the property of Lamborghini Club UK's member David Price. Another day done and another story to write. More rock 'n' roll happened when I looked after the cars of Perry Bamonte of The Cure.

NOT DRIVING, GLADIATORS AND G-FORCES

While a Maserati MC12 is a racing car and therefore up my street, writing about one without driving it is not my speciality. However, a job is a job and it needed to be done. I spent two days at Adria and the Bologna Show to report on the technical, the race history and a works driver profile of Andrea Bertolini.

The MC12 is as ugly as sin and just as desirable. It is wider than a Hummer, longer than a minibus, has no rear window, no luggage space, no ground clearance, and most of them only have one seat. They were so successful in racing that the FIA had to rewrite the rule book. At the Adria Raceway, I interviewed Bertolini and went on to lap the circuit with an MC12 GT1. I am using the preposition 'with' rather than 'in', as I was driving a Lamborghini Murciélago R-GT/GT1 race car at the time, shadowing and marvelling at the MC12's blinding pace and the sheets of flame from the tail-pipes.

After a day with the MC12 and Bertolini at Adria, Maserati invited me to Bologna where Bertolini demonstrated the MC12 in front of an enthusiastic Motor Show crowd. My job was to go along for the ride. Welcome to carbon fibre world, the super-light black stuff was everywhere. During our brief off-stage wait, I could see the big crowd in the amphitheatre that surrounded the track. Visions of the Roman Colosseum sprang to mind. The MC12 is massive on the outside and miniscule on the inside. We waited for the nod. The V12 exploded into life, those nearby jumped out of their skins. Whang, whang, whang it blipped; if it had a conventional rev counter, the needle would never have kept up. Here everything was digital and electronic although the paddle shift was gone. Bertolini clunked the sequential lever in first gear and, like modern-day

gladiators, we blasted out of the building and into the arena laying smoke and rubber. A thousand fists punched the air. Bertolini kept the car loose flicking the tail out on every turn, occasionally choosing a section of crowd to entertain with a doughnut and burning tyres before continuing the lap. No one was under any illusions that this was a show, a bit of fun – the world's poshest sports car brand having a tyre-smoking end-of-term bash.

Bertolini brought the MC12 back to the indoor paddock to waiting film crews and more interviews. I shook his hand and drove away in a loaned Maserati GranTurismo. In the silence of the GranTurismo I considered all the different forms of racing cars. If you had to divide them into two categories, it would be with or without downforce. If your car is struggling to corner at 100mph, try 150mph. It takes a racer time to develop

2: Fiery exhausts on the fabulous Maserati MC12 GT1.
3: Passenger with Andrea Bertolini at the Bologna Show.
4: Rear wing writing table for signing your life away.

Evans and Roger Clark, 'Don't worry Roberto. Provided we are not looking through the rear windscreen, we will be alright.' said Roger. This time I was in the Zero Car at the Sanremo Rally. The purpose of the Zero Car is to open each stage. It also doubles as a 'safety car'. It is equipped with flashing lights and a siren. It also needs to go fast. This tells the marshals and spectators who are lining the route Italian-style, that the next car will be travelling at lunatic speeds. The principal driver of the Zero Car (a Fiat Grande Punto Abarth) was a friend and local rally hero, Nuccio Magliocchetti. Nuccio let me drive, but we both knew that I wasn't going quick enough on the blind narrow mountain roads with unprotected precipices. I know my place and soon swapped seats. We were connected to Rally Control HQ via a two-way radio. Helicopters were also giving chase through the mountains. Ex-Ferrari and ex-Maserati, ex-Peugeot and ex-Lotus sporting boss Claudio Berro was then the Abarth sporting boss. A reminder of how the fast-moving corporate world is very different from my world.

When the FIA Intercontinental Rally Challenge (IRC) came to Sanremo, Abarth was the talk (and sound) of the town. Abarth even brought a high-tech aircraft-hangar-sized road-show exhibition centre. The Sanremo locals are happy that for a whole week, unsilenced rally car will be blasting through the streets on the wrong side of the road, ignoring all road rules with everyday traffic. The rally paddock is on the seafront, and the stages are in the mountains. The police at Italian motorsport events are on side, and rather than set up speed traps, they help the competition cars. Sanremo (pop 60,000) is always grid-locked with traffic. The rally cars are exempt from all traffic laws on the many journeys to and from the stages, from seafront to mountains. Almost every weekend, Sanremo hosts a festival or sporting event. For three days, hundreds of local men volunteer to marshal hundreds of kilometres of mountain road day and night, in all weather and in many cases at high altitude. Countless ambulances, fire engines, breakdown trucks and rescue helicopters are

5: Nuccio Magliocchetti driving the Sanremo Rally 'Zero Car'.
6: Punto Abarth 'Zero Car'.
7: A glorious Stratos – part of the historic element.

trust in downforce. A good sporting road car can reach 1G lateral or braking. A purely mechanical grip race car on slicks might approach 1.5G. The world of downforce sees anything from 2G up to 5G depending on many factors. Plus, these G-forces relentlessly attack the driver, coming and going constantly from every direction, be they from speed changes up or down or directional changes left and right, or a combination of the aforementioned. Moreover, these multiple changes happen constantly and in split seconds, giving the driver nanoseconds to react to the fast-unfolding scene.

SANREMO RALLY AND MORE MADNESS

This was my first experience at a modern FIA IRC rally. Previously and for another magazine, I had been in three works Fords on forest stages piloted by three legendary drivers including Malcolm Wilson, Gwyndaf

on hand. Being Sanremo, the residents are also on side, even those in the remote mountain towns who endure the inconvenience of road closures.

The breath-taking roads of the Maritime Alps on the Sanremo Rally make the Nürburgring Nordschleife look like a walk in the park. From our Zero Safety Car, we see it all, narrow mountain roads, scary unguarded precipices, crashed cars, broken cars and a burnt-out one. Tragically, late at night, a well-loved local driver, Ivano Benza, died when he suffered a heart attack at the wheel of his Renault Clio rally car. Fifty years old Benza was the Vice President of the Automobile Club of Sanremo and everyone here knew him. With satellite monitoring, an ambulance reached him immediately. He lost his struggle for life just before reaching the hospital.

Some glorious ex-works historic rally cars use the stages for their parallel historic rally. Watching, hearing and feeling the Alitalia and Pirelli Stratos – lamps ablaze – power-sliding through the mountain-top towns of Apricale and Baiardo (altitude 900m, 3,000ft) is etched in my retina. Add plenty of pukka works cars like Martini

Lancia Delta integrales and Audi Quattros and the appetite is suitably whetted for the rally proper.

I now know why rally spectators trek to remote locations. The mountains are alive with a party atmosphere. There is a camaraderie amongst the spectators that is absent from circuit racing. The average spacing between rally cars is one minute, but the arrival of each car varies. The 'shout' goes down the line as a car approaches. The stillness shatters as a fired-up driver and navigator fling their state-of-the-art machine at outrageous speeds down roads designed for donkeys. A car howls by, your head spins, a rush of dust, some spectators dash along the roads to new positions, diving for cover as the next 'shout' goes up. Trying to control the spectators is like trying to herd cats. I try to think of a simile and bingo: this rally is the automotive version of the Pamplona Bull-Run.

A TIME BOMB, A SPIN AND A FIRE

Reiter Engineering arrived at Adria Circuit from Germany with a troop of Lamborghini race cars. Reiter

9: Tired, end of season engine.

10: No smoke without fire.

11: Pilot and pit crew – but no car!

8: Hot laps at Adria in the Reiter Lamborghini Murciélago GT1.
9: Tired, end of season engine.
10: No smoke without fire.
11: Pilot and pit crew – but no car!

suggested the orange/grey Murciélago R-GT1 would be mine for testing. I had driven it previously at the Salzburgring in slippery conditions, so a dry run at Adria would complete the test. It was out on track with a smoky exhaust that no one seemed bothered about. This was a lightweight rear-wheel drive Murciélago R-GT1 race car that is infinitely quicker than a road-going version. I suspected that this was going to be a hard car to master. A pre-brief from works driver Peter Kox confirmed it, "In GT1, you have to work a lot harder for minute gain. It is not worth the effort, but that is how it is." were his experienced words.

I get the usual five-second briefing from Peter Kox while I am trying to fathom out the unfamiliar controls. I look about. There are three pedals, but not as we know them. "Oh..., and only use the clutch pedal on down-shifts, not up-shifts." says the flying Dutchman. A big sequential lever has a hardly perceptible wobbly top. This wobble cuts the ignition only on up-changes, to ease the gearshift. It creates deafening gunfire from the exhaust system on every gearshift, as unburnt fuel ignites. It also has a cooling effect on the combustion chamber. What else? A dash read-out tells you what gear you are in.

The smoky exhaust was getting worse. Racing cars are time bombs. It is not if they explode, it is when they explode. My turn to drive and I trundle out of the pits in the machine that for the entire morning has been

shrieking, howling and banging the air, as well as shaking the ground. Now it is my turn. Corner exit traction is amazing and huge speeds are quickly achieved. I notice that the smoky exhaust is getting worse. There is smoke in the cockpit and after a few laps I decided to return to the pits. Being a naturally aspirated engine, I deduced that a damaged piston was allowing the crankcase oil to be burning in the combustion chamber. On my in-lap the time bomb exploded. There is a car-shaking clunk and vibration. A broken piston had sent its conrod through the block. I switched off the motor and thought I could coast silently back to the pits. However, escaping engine oil had collected on the undertray. On the last turn before the pits and at low speed, engine oil spewed off the undertray onto the rear wheels and spun the slow-moving car to a stop. The oil from the undertray also found the hot exhaust and the car burst into flames. Marshals were soon on the scene and extinguished the flames. The time bomb exploded while I was handling it. While I was devastated by the blow-up, Reiter was surprisingly calm, saying "It needed a rebuild anyway."

Reiter could have sued me into bankruptcy. Being a freelancer, I would have been abandoned by everyone to face a court case and ruin. I have already mentioned how an unnamed owner of a historic Le Mans car

bankrupted an innocent freelancer who also had a time bomb explode in his tenure. Freelancers are impoverished people compared with the wealthy owners of expensive cars who usually have no hesitation in sending in their lawyers. Indeed, this attitude is often why they are wealthy. Thank you, Hans Reiter, if ever you are lying wounded in no man's land under heavy gunfire, you are another one who I would crawl out and save.

Reiter then sent me out on track in some other GT race cars. A normal motoring journo would never get near to driving such vehicles. You need plenty of race experience before any responsible editor would entrust the magazine's integrity to a lowly writer. You also need to serve your apprenticeship with the race team boss to get a drive. Any negative signs: inexperience, nerves, joyriding, unprofessional race clothing, etc. will be picked up and you will be shown the door. Likewise, being too keen and giving a feeling that you are going to show the team what a great driver you are will also result in a boot up backside.

MUGELLO ROAD RACE

In 2008 and 2009, Jane and I entered her Lotus 26R in the Mugello Road Race which took place in the sunny Tuscan hills in and around the modern GP circuit. I love

12: Reiter also provided a GT3 Gallardo to play with at Adria.
13: Unique, ex-Salvadori Cooper-Maserati at Silverstone.

road trips, so transporting the 26R across Europe was part of the fun. As I was selling the story, perhaps I should say that it was all part of the job. Steeped in history, the old 66km Mugello lap is three times longer than the old Nürburgring Nordschleife. This two-day event has something for everyone. Cars entered are FIA spec from 1914–1975. Entrants can choose from one of three categories: Rally (i.e. competitive and against the clock), Regularity (i.e. with target times) and demonstration (non-competitive). Sections of public road are closed for the competitors and part of the event also takes place on the modern Mugello GP Circuit.

Sixty beautifully prepared historic race and rally cars entered the 'rally proper', plus 31 cars for the 'regularity' competition, with a further 35 cars electing to race un-timed.

Ex-works drivers Nino Vaccarella, Teodoro Zuccoli, Nanni Galli and Sandro Munari were following the action organised by Scuderia Clemente Biondetti and the ACI (Automobile Club Italia). Previous result sheets of this demanding Targa-Florio-style road race read like a who's who in the history of motor racing. The list is endless, but here are a few names: Merzario, van Lennep, Zuccoli, Munari, de Adamich, Vaccarella, Hezemans, Siffert, Elford, Stommelen, Giunti, Borzacchini, Ascari, Maserati, Ferrari, Pierpoint, Piper, Scarfiotti, Schetty, Widdows, Brambilla, de Filippis, Edwards, Konig, Kinnunen, Ligier and Nuvolari. The Mugello Stradale is certainly one of those 'only-in-Italy' events.

COOPER-MASERATI AND ONLY ONE PEDAL

It is 1963 and wedding bells sound for another international marriage: a state-of-the-art English chassis mated with an advanced Italian racing engine. What could possibly go wrong? The one-off Cooper-Maserati 5-litre Sports Racing Car, is also known as a Cooper Type T61P Monaco Mk5, or simply as the CM. In 1964, it was raced by the great Roy Salvadori (1922–2012). The CM has emerged from decades of hibernation. At

14

the 2007 Goodwood Revival, Salvadori at 86 years of age had a long chat with the current owner, Michael O'Shea. According to Salvadori, 'There was no time to go testing. No set-up was achieved, and the CM was a real handful.' Could this brutish car ever be tamed? This is where I became involved not only for a magazine track test but also as a handling consultant and race instructor.

Time warp original except for some cosmetics: here was a car that missed out on testing and development. That task – together with some endurance racing – was carried out in 2008 by a team including, its valiant owner and Maserati Club Chairman Michael O'Shea, renowned historic motorsport engineer Steve Hart and me.

Dropping in a 5.0-litre, 455hp V8 racing Maserati Le Mans engine sounds like an easy way to go faster but race engineers know that what you then have is another car. A car that will need a complete rethink if it is to go faster than it did with its original lighter motor.

My first drive is a brief one. The task at Silverstone was to find a dry set-up. As the rain arrived, so the test session was red-flagged due to several cars beached in gravel traps. Then it really rained. Game over. All I noted

was oversteer on turn-in, oversteer mid-corner and power oversteer on exit. I also noted much lift-off oversteer. Even more nerve-racking was its craving to oversteer at top speed on the Hangar Straight.

My first race sharing the car with owner Michael O'Shea was at the Brands Hatch GP Circuit. With the car not sorted and another deluge of biblical proportions I aquaplaned and splashed around the flooded Kent circuit before handing over to Michael who did well to finish the race in one piece: Michael – being an ex-powerboat racer – revelled in the rain.

Our next attempt testing was at Silverstone but was cut short when, at 120mph, an ancient magnesium wheel disintegrated, sending the three-wheeler on a wild ride. Nobody died and the car was okay. With the car still not sorted, it was time for the next race at the Silverstone Classic. In the paddock, a gentleman of some years told me that he drove this actual car along the A3 Surbiton, Surrey, one night in 1963 when he worked for John Cooper. "It was how we tested them before delivery," were his words. Michael started the Silverstone 90-min night race, but it was all over at the

14: Oversteer city.
15: Le Mans-spec 5-litre, 455hp Maserati V8.
16: Keeping the car straight for the car-to-car pictures.

15

driver change due to an unstoppable oil leak. Long faces, wild handling, off the pace and wondering if the car could ever be tamed, we really needed a proper test session – something the CM had never benefitted from in its entire 45 years.

The day came when CKL Developments hired Goodwood Circuit; and it was dry. Maserati guru Steve Hart Racing was there to make adjustments, while I spent the day behind the wheel planning the next change in set-up after every two laps. By the end of a demanding day's testing, the CM was spot on and ready for Michael's judgment. With shadows lengthening, after six laps, he returned to the pits, beaming. Job done. We had the monster under control. With time quickly running out and a P&O Dover-Calais ferry to catch, the Cooper-Maserati went straight from Goodwood to Magny Cours in France for the next race in the prestigious Masters Racing Series. In the one-hour Sports Racing Masters race, the CM shone and was right up there with the best. Quickest of the Coopers, it ran amuck amongst the more modern GT40s and was not a million miles behind the later Lola T70s. With a muscular power-to-weight ratio of 636bhp per tonne and its low frontal area, acceleration was relentless, delivering colossal straight-line speeds.

At the chequered flag, we were happy with our second-place class trophies.

At the 2008 Goodwood Revival Meeting, Michael went on to finish seventh overall against the world's best, most of which were more modern. In 2010 at Silverstone, we finished first in class and second overall in the Italian Historic Cup, beaten only by a more modern Osella PA1 Sports Prototype. On the last lap, the CM was out of fuel and a brake pipe had broken, rendering two of the three foot pedals ineffective. After the chequered flag and I silently nursed it freewheeling into the paddock. I warned Sid Hoole pit crew whom were running the car that (a) it would not start, and (b) when they push it, it will not stop. Somehow with only a clutch pedal and steering wheel operative, we made it onto the podium. The magazine feature included a history story of the car written by Peter Collins.

After the Anglo-Italian Cooper-Maserati, it was time for some proper Britishness at Mallory Park in the form of three Jaguar XJS racing cars in various forms. I went on to race Stewert Lyddall's V12 version of the XJS with success. Racing a British car in the UK has many advantages with plentiful and affordable parts, and abundant specialists.

16

2009

The Sanremo Grand Prix or Not

Tucked away in Northwest Italy near the French border, Sanremo used to have its own F1 Grand Prix from 1937–1951, excluding four war years. Initially, the GP took place in the centre of Sanremo, thereby blocking the coast road. After a while, the GP moved to the neighbouring suburb of Ospedaletti where a very fast street circuit left coastal traffic uninterrupted. Local restaurants still display photos of Grand Prix greats like Nuvolari, Fangio, Ascari, Varzi and Villoresi. Today, the 2.1-mile long Ospedaletti Circuit hosts a motorcycle GP revival event every two years. It was good to see the legend that is Giacomo Agostini still doing his stuff. A kart race also takes place. The circuit is wide and fast, although being in a town presents its challenges. Its long palm tree-lined sea front would see cars and bikes reach huge speeds.

I had a cunning plan. As I knew one or two influential contacts in Sanremo, I thought about the possibility of a Sanremo Historic Grand Prix Revival to be held – like the nearby bi-annual Monaco Historique – on alternate years, i.e. one year Monaco, the next year Sanremo GP, etc. Via my contacts, I arranged a meeting in the Ospedaletti Town Hall with the Mayor. He said, "Yes, great idea but you would have to clear it with the ACI the Italian Motorsport governing body." I arranged a meeting with the local ACI president Sergio Maiga. As *Auto Italia's* Peter Collins was in town, he joined the meeting. I put the same question, "How about a GP revival race meeting?" The reply was unsurprising, "Too

dangerous unless you invest heavily in safety standards." Knowing that it takes Monaco three months of work and vast sums to transform the Principality into a race circuit, I knew that this would be unlikely for Sanremo. Then, reflecting on the existing motorbike GP demonstrations, I asked the ACI boss, "What about historic racing car demonstration laps with 30-second start intervals, plus a concours, top auction house sale, historic festival, car clubs, etc, etc.?" From his body language and the tone of his answer, I could see that this would be acceptable. "How much interest could you drum up?" asked the mayor.

There it is. The locals are motorsport-friendly, all that is needed is an organiser. I went away and thought about it. Organising a Festival of Speed type event would be beyond my abilities. If there are any Dukes or big names out there who would be prepared to add a global event on the Riviera to their portfolio, it is there for the taking.

LAMBORGHINI WORKS TEAM, SILVERSTONE AND A DUEL

Lamborghini was late to motor racing because the founder, Ferruccio Lamborghini, was against it. He was too busy building the business to go racing. In the late 1970s he retired and the company fought on with financial problems and several owners. Racing involvement arrived in 1989 with supplying engines to F1 and for Offshore Powerboat racing. In 1995/6, the

company built racing versions of the Diablo for their one-make series (1996–99), after which privateers campaigned them in other championships. Under Audi management, the company could see, and more importantly, afford to advance Lamborghini's racing heritage. The Super Trofeo began in 2009 with the world's fastest one-make championship. It continues today, while Lamborghini is also having much success in international GT racing.

The call came, "Would you like to drive in three 40-minute races in the Super Trofeo Race Series?" *Auto Italia* would have a prestigious story to publish and Lamborghini would receive positive publicity. Plus, as was the way with the Maserati race series, Lamborghini presented me with an extra bonus in the form of works team race overalls.

I shall always remember this weekend at Silverstone because my father passed away as I was packing my kit to head to the circuit. At 88 years of age, he died due to complications following an accident whilst cycling. My choice was to stay home and feel desolate or be at Silverstone – joined by two close family members – and still feel desolate. I chose the latter, although the desolation did not go away. The Lamborghini enclosure at Silverstone was like the Italian Embassy in London in that it became part of Italy. Lamborghini even brought their own Italian restaurant. I had previously been testing with the team at Misano and at Adria. I gave the team my feedback and no doubt this influenced their decision to invite me to race in the Super Trofeo.

The weekend's format was one 30-minute free practice session, one 30-minute qualifying and three 40-minute races over a three-day weekend. This round of the Lamborghini Championship was on the same bill as the British GT and British F3 Championships. Interestingly, the lap times for the highly modified GT cars were virtually the same as the Lamborghini Super Trofeo LP560-4 cars – demonstrating just how fast these Swiss watch sponsored Lamborghinis can go. The Lamborghini Blancpain Championship is a one-make series with some freedom. While engines and

transmissions are sealed, suspension set-up is not. Several professional race teams were running the Super Trofeos, including Reiter Engineering who have close links to Lamborghini. The factory brought along two guest cars: Number 1 was a black car, which I shared with teammate, Lamborghini's own race driver/test driver, Mario Fasanetto. The other guest car was the white car of Le Mans, Sebring, and Daytona winner Andy Wallace, sharing with *Evo* magazine's tester and racer Roger Green. Never mind the other cars in the races, the weekend was sizing up to be an *Auto Italia* versus *Evo* competition.

Arriving at the circuit for the early morning briefing and practice session, my entry tickets were inside the circuit and the outside ticket counter was closed. No option but to employ the age-old trick of evading unbending security guards by hiding in the back of a car that did have passes. Lamborghini then organised entry tickets for Jane and my son Niki who were at the main gate. After practice and qualifying, I could see that our lap times were off the pace. The set-up had too much understeer, which is a killer of lap times.

It was obvious that the quick teams had better set-ups than our off-the-shelf 'guest' car. At best the 'journo cars' scraped into mid-field position. Even pro racer Andy Wallace was well off the pace. As this was a race weekend, we could not afford the luxury of the countless adjustments that are typical of a test day. There are literally billions of set-up permutations.

Information is power and I looked at some interesting data. We over-lapped my lap data with that of championship leader Fabio Babini. While I was carrying more mid-corner speed than anyone else, I was late on applying power coming out of all the corners. Teammate Mario Fasanetto was having the same problem. Take Luffield Corner for example. This is the vital right-hander before Silverstone's original start-finish straight. Data showed that our car was virtually on the straight before we could apply full throttle. We had excessive understeer and both of us found that the early application of power was impossible as it pushed the

nose ever-wider. This alone destroys lap times like nothing else. The fastest cars were already on full power half-way round this turn carrying much extra speed all along the next straight. I didn't need the data, as I followed a couple of quicker cars through Luffield. I could see that their front wheels had a 'neutral' attitude, while mine had excessive steering angles. We made some minor changes, but the time-sapping understeer remained.

I drove fast but without risking body damage and witnessed some of the quicker cars hurtling into gravel traps, only to see Land Rover-esque escapes from these bunkers thanks to the Super Trofeo's four-wheel drive systems. With a podium place implausible, our realistic target for the three races was to beat the *Evo* magazine's white car. The final result was 2-1 to *Auto Italia*. My teammate Mario and I missed a 3-0 victory by finishing our last race one second behind our rival's car. This showed two things: 1. Every split second on track or in the compulsory driver-change pit-stop counts. And 2. *Auto Italia* is a faster magazine than *Evo*.

LUCIANO PAVAROTTI AND NICOLETTA

This press launch of the GranTurismo GTS Automatic had the usual ingredients: impoverished writers thrust into the luxury and VIP opulence. Humans are predictable creatures. For instance, by spotting the word, 'Automatic' in the title of this Maserati GranTurismo GTS, some of you – me included – had already fixed our opinions before reading about the car or driving it. My job includes understanding the engineering and the dynamics and then explain them in ways that can be understood by a normal-ish person. Electronics and associated technologies have vastly improved how automatic transmission functions.

Writing about cars should get to the point with the least number of words. On press launches, the company usually has one of their chief engineers on hand. It is always a good idea to chat with an engineer. You will undoubtedly learn something that is not included in the press pack.

Our test route included mild Modenese traffic, a sprint along the A1 autostrada followed by many hours of demanding Apennine mountain roads. There are faster production cars on the market but if 0–60mph in five seconds and a top speed of 185mph is not fast enough for you, then you may want to consider counselling or motorsport.

Then came a special occasion just outside Modena. This launch included a dinner party for a handful of press at the house of Luciano Pavarotti (1935–2007). Pavarotti had recently died of pancreatic cancer. Our host was the great man's second wife Nicoletta Mantovani. She and her six-year-old daughter Alice welcomed the guests. Pavarotti was a footballer, a painter, a Juventus supporter and a Maserati man. His first Maserati was a Sebring with several Quattroportes following. This was an evening of gastronomy and music, with one of the great man's students performing three operatic renditions. While Pavarotti selected his students carefully, he never charged them. I learnt that 35-year-old Nicoletta Mantovani was Pavarotti's former personal assistant and second wife. She was 39 years younger than Pavarotti. They were recently married, and Alice was their child. Pavarotti had been married twice. He

was married to his first wife Adua Veroni from 1961 to 2000 and they had three daughters. At the dinner, there were about a dozen dinner guests. Later in the evening, I chatted with Nicoletta when she asked me if I would like a tour of the house. The tour included the upper floor. In their bedroom I asked what it had been like being married to a global star. She replied saying that as she had been at the great man's side for many years, she was used to it and enjoyed every minute, especially having the time to watch her daughter, Alice, growing up. Born in 1935, Pavarotti's professional career began in 1961. He rose to worldwide celebrity status well beyond the world of opera. He died at home in his bed, aged 71.

ROME, MASERATI AND THE CIRCUS MAXIMUS

Five international racer journalists joined the Maserati Race Team at Rome's Vallelunga Circuit. The objective of the exercise was to test GT4 and Trofeo race versions of the GranTurismo MC with works drivers Andrea Bertolini, Michael Bartels, Thomas Cremonini, and Ivan Capelli. One of my fellow racer journalists was Derek Hill, the son of the 1961 F1 world champion Phil Hill (1927–2008) who raced for Ferrari. Looking back on

5: Fast Maserati – mountain roads.
6: Test drive selfie while cornering.
7: The unique Life F1, an exotic-engined enigma.

events, it is easy to see mistakes. An opportunity was missed in that I could have interviewed Derek about life as the son of an F1 world champion.

It was a good day mucking about with the Maserati team at an almost exclusive test day. I say, almost, because Ferrari was there testing a race car. As it wailed into the distance, Maserati's amiable press officer Andrea Cittadini quipped, "That is Modena's second-best marque." The comment made me smile.

Rome's 2,000-year-old Circus Maximus was the largest space for chariot racing in the Roman Empire. It could seat 270,000 spectators and is still there. The lap length was about one mile. Chariot racing has since given way to motor racing at Rome's 4.1km Vallelunga race circuit, which was opened in 1951. Its ten corners are tricky to learn as most are blind. I had the track to myself except for Bertolini testing the other GT4 and the Ferrari team who were testing a race car.

The team was always keen to hear my feedback, some of which was adopted, some not, depending on various logistical factors. An overpowerful servo and no ABS apart, the set-up was perfect for the job intended and very safe, although I reckoned that if you put a super-quick pro in the car and he would request a stiffer rear, with resultantly pointier nose and a more nervous animal. At the coffee machine, I put this to Capelli and Bertolini and we all agreed that the current Trofeo set-up is the best compromise. By the way, it takes 50 coffee beans to make one espresso. If one bean is bad, the coffee will suffer.

My time at Vallelunga was running out fast and I still had several laps to complete. This was the first time that I drove quickly on a race circuit to save some 'tenths' to catch a plane. Out of the race car, into a waiting taxi, I changed into civvies en route to Rome's Leonardo da Vinci Airport wondering what a Roman chariot racer or race mechanic from the Circus Maximus would have thought of Vallelunga and racing cars.

FORMULA ONE AND LIFE

How many F1 fans can remember the 1990 Formula One Life? Its W12 engine was a cunning plan. In the days before a computer could tell you that you were wasting your time, great ideas were designed on the back of a napkin whilst dining with like-minded friends. A bit like having the crazy idea of launching a magazine

confined to Italian cars, except that the magazine notion worked and would have proved the computer wrong.

The 1990 one-off W12-engined Life Formula One car was a failure. It was so slow and unreliable that its talented drivers Gary Brabham and Bruno Giacomelli failed to qualify the car for a single Grand Prix during that 1990 season. With the 1,500cc turbo era at an end, race teams needed 3.5-litre naturally aspirated engines with c700bhp. The 1970s Ferrari engineer – and designer of Ferrari's 308 engine – Franco Rocchi had been toiling away on the design of a compact 3.5-litre W12. The design included siamesed conrods to reduce the length of the crankshaft and engine block. A W12 is a good packaging exercise.

Enzo Ferrari was not interested and Rocchi left Ferrari in 1980. But Rocchi was a man on a mission and by early 1989, his W12 was built and ready for marketing; unfortunately, there were no takers. Then along came entrepreneur Ernesto Vita who bought the rights to the W12 hoping to make some money. Again, there was no interest, so Vita (which in English means Life) decided to build a Grand Prix car for the coming 1990 season using the W12. Vita had a Russian wife and through her contacts managed to find some sponsorship from a company that worked on satellites – hence the Russian logo on the car.

The Life Racing Engines team was based in Modena. The Life F190 was ready to rock 'n' roll, but Gary Brabham failed to qualify the car for the first two races and left the team. In came veteran Bruno Giacomelli who did no better in the next 12 races. Not only were there constant and serious engine problems but even when the motor did run, it only produced 450bhp when the opposition had 700bhp. Furthermore, the car was so overweight that its lap times were not even up to F3000 standard.

We went to the Autodromo di Franciacorta to carry out a track test on this unique machine. The car had been rebuilt by Preparazioni Montanari of Reggio Emilia. Chief engineer Marco Montanari talked me through the car. The engine started via a crew-operated remote starter motor. Cranking over with the turbine-like hum of a V12, the W12 exploded into er... life. On the move, the motor was silky smooth and, thanks to re-profiled cams, was very torquey. Its three banks of four cylinders made a noise that was initially painful before aspiring to torture. Naturally I forgot my earplugs.

Life has its problems, and the alternator was not working correctly. With voltage in mind, I drove the car hard in the hope that the alternator would satisfy the fuel pump and spark plugs, but I too became one of Life's victims and rolled to a silent halt free of any form of electricity. With aeroplanes to catch and time running out, sadly our photography was of the static variety. But

8: Bird's-eye view of an engineering indulgence.
9: The generous and trusting Lorenzo Prandina supervises the driver handover.

10: Just 250 examples of the RWD Gallardo Balboni were released.
11: The plaque is inscribed with the great test driver's signature.

I did drive it – honest. I complimented the inadequate track test with some technical stuff. I also mentioned that the W-engine has been with us since the dawn of the internal combustion engine. Indeed, in 1909, it was with one such motor that the magnificent man, Louis Blériot, in his flying machine, made the first flight across the English Channel.

TWO LIGHTWEIGHTS AND ONE HAS A NAME

I love it when the badge on the car is the name of a person, especially that of a living individual. And I love it when a manufacturer makes a lightweight version of a production car. Enter the Gallardo LP550-2 Valentino Balboni Edizione Limitata (only 250 made). The car was named after the renowned Lamborghini test driver. At 50kg lighter, it is 'new' Lamborghini's first departure from 4WD to RWD for the Gallardo.

The RWD Gallardo Balboni is more fun to drive than the 4WD version. However, the big win will be in the Balboni's long term financial investment. The car not the man. Although the man will never starve.

Lamborghini followed up the rear-wheel drive Balboni lightweight trend with the four-wheel drive Gallardo LP570-4 Superleggera (Super lightweight). Weighing in at 1,340kg, it was lighter and more powerful than the RWD LP 550-2 Balboni. I tested both. Over dinner, I also chatted with Lamborghini's chief of research and development Maurizio Reggiani who is super keen on weight reduction. However, unlike Colin Chapman, Reggiani is constricted by far stricter regulations and type approval. On a napkin, he drew a graph of the weights of Lamborghinis. Decades ago, they hovered around 1,200kg until the end of the Miura years. Then the line went off the napkin onto the tablecloth, only returning to the napkin in the Gallardo years. Looking me in the eye, he said, "This is a very different car."

The new car – the four-wheel drive Gallardo LP570-4 Superleggera – was posing on a plinth in front of the magnificent Hotel Alfonso XIII in Seville's smartest square. The dense doughnut of excited kids surrounding it was how I knew the Superleggera was there – a seemingly insignificant observation, but one that links Lamborghini with a copper-bottomed future.

Andalucía is often referred to as the Land of the Bull, so what better place to strap yourself to a mechanical bull. After the road test came the track test. The sparkling new Monteblanco Circuit was on hand with over eight different track configurations. Verdict: on paper, technically and dynamically, the newer LP570-4 Superleggera is better than the LP550-2 Balboni. Which would I choose? I would go for the Balboni. It is purer. It is a limited edition and I like a car with a person's name.

ABARTH, WAR AND A POKE IN THE EYE

I was really looking forward to this track test of an Abarth 2000SP (Sports Prototype). In my teens, I was always fascinated by the cars with the scorpion badge that won 11 world championships. The nearest I came to owning one was with that gloriously chaotic book that is the Faza Abarth 'King of Small Cars' bible. The company appealed as valiant underdogs and giant killers. Abarth is Italian but with a foreign name. How can that be?

Here is a history lesson as my family has a wartime connection with the subject: Karl Abarth was born in Vienna in 1908. His astrological birth sign was Scorpio. His father was from Merano in the German-speaking Alto Adige corner of northern Italy and his mother was Austrian. The Italo-Austrian border had shifted. Originally at the Alpine water-divide, which is a natural mountain-top border where water from the high peaks that flows north was in Austria, while south flowing areas were in Italy. However, Austrians had moved this old Kingdom of Italy border south into the Italian Alto-Adige region, bringing their people and German language with them. World War One (1914–18) and my paternal grandfather, the Cavalry Officer Pasquale Giordanelli – aided by five million soldiers – returned the border back to its original and natural location at the

water divide. A few million deaths later and all is peaceful. Today, the Alto Adige region of Italy is like Belgium in that it has two separate communities speaking in two different languages.

After leaving school at 17 years of age, Karl Abarth went to Italy for two years to work for Carrozzeria Castagna in Milan. He then returned to Austria to work for a motorcycle factory where he rose to test rider and racer, winning his first race in 1928. He became European Champion five times, but his racing career ended when he had a serious racing accident in Linz that required two years of convalescing. In the early 1930s, he moved permanently to Italy to join his father. His father's Italian nationality made it easy for his son to assume Italian citizenship: Karl Abarth became Carlo Abarth. Abarth founded his own company Abarth and Co in Bologna in 1949, moving two years later to Turin. The factory was adjacent to the Aeritalia test track that we regularly used.

On test at the Autodromo di Franciacorta is a 1970 Abarth 2000SP belonging to Abarth specialist Tony Berni. The 2000SP has a neat purposeful look about it. Studying its components, I cannot help thinking about the mountain that Abarth had to climb to be competitive against the Porsches, Lolas and Chevrons. The Porsche 908 was instantly competitive, while the quick

12: Franciacorta circuit and the rapid Abarth 2000SP.
13: A spot of high speed car-to-car photography.

Brits could concentrate on chassis and suspension design. Lola and Chevron never had to worry about engines or gearboxes. Power units could be cherry-picked from the best engine sources and Hewland supplied lightweight, reliable off-the-shelf transmissions. Abarth on the other hand did everything in-house.

Removing the covers, we can see that the 2000SP has a conventional tubular steel space frame with fibre-glass body and aluminium floor and bulkheads. In true prototype fashion, it is right-hand-drive, which gives a corner-weight advantage on race circuits as most corners turn right. Technical numbers which stand out are 250bhp and 530kg equating to 472bhp/tonne. Some years before testing this car, the ex-Abarth man 'Beppe' Volta, told me how they would test the prototypes on the roads outside Turin in the dead of night. "But what about lights?" I asked. Beppe said that the police didn't mind, as long as the race cars had a torch, hand-held or taped to the cars.

However, what leaps out and pokes you in the eye is the engine location. Where Lola and Chevron and just about every racing car manufacturer, placed the engine ahead of the gearbox, Abarth (and Porsche) did the opposite. Contrary to engineering principles, the

bespoke Abarth motor pokes out the rear, well-aft of the rear axle line. Abarth called it *fuoribordo*, which is Italian for 'outboard'. In period, the story goes that Arturo Merzario wanted a mid-engined car. Abarth tried back-to-back tests with conventional mid-engined layouts and also with rear-engined configurations. And guess what? The rear-engined layout was quicker. I do not know how or where the tests were carried out, but with the benefit of history and experience, two things spring to mind. Firstly, that in 60 years, little has changed, the mid-engined location for racing cars is virtually universal. The second observation is how Porsche 911s work so well with their engines overhanging the rear axle line, 'outboard' Abarth-style.

Carlo Abarth's private life was eventful. He was married three times. He was first married in Vienna. He married his second wife, Nadina Abarth, in 1949. They lived together in northern Italy until 1966 and divorced in 1979. The same year, about six weeks before his death, Abarth married his third wife, Anneliese Abarth, whom I interviewed at Franciacorta Circuit. She continues to head the Carlo Abarth Foundation and in 2010, wrote one of his biographies. Carlo Abarth retired to Vienna where he died young in 1979 aged 70.

14: *Seeing-in crew, owner and Abarth guru Tony Berni.*
15: *Engineering art by Abarth.*

Ferrari F1 and the Greasy Totem Pole of Success

I was sitting on top of the greasy totem pole of success. Driving a Formula One Ferrari F126 C4 1,000bhp turbo car saw the peak of my test-driving career for magazines. However, I felt a disturbance in the force. Things were changing. In the early days of *Auto Italia*, I wrote many articles for each issue and was regularly commuting to Italy. It was good fun but time consuming. By 2009, my motor racing work and other activities, all of which put me in a healthier financial place were increasing as my frequency in *Auto Italia* was diminishing. I was also still writing as an EU correspondent for another magazine. When you are on top of the greasy totem pole, your next direction will not be upwards. Let's look at that Ferrari F1 drive.

From 1966 to 1986, the F1 rules stated that engine size must be 3-litre or 1.5-litre turbocharged. That last 1.5-litre bit was an add-on because the blazer brigade did not believe that a 1.5 turbo could produce more power than a 700bhp 3-litre atmo engine. Technology always moves faster than rules and laws. The 1.5-litre turbos made 1,000bhp in race trim and up to 1,500bhp in qualifying mode.

This F1 Ferrari 126C4 campaigned the 1984 F1 season in the hands of the late Michele Alboreto (1956–2001). Alboreto won the 1984 Belgium Grand Prix in a 126C4. In April 2001 there was a tragedy. Alboreto was performing straight-line speed tests in an Audi R8 at the Lausitzring in Germany. A tyre blow-out caused his car to crash into a wall, killing the unfortunate Alboreto. After

the Ferrari's 1984 F1 race season, the 126C4 was sold and eventually ended up in the hands of the late Lorenzo Prandina who also perished, but at the hands of the 2020 global pandemic. Prandina was a fine chap and used the Ferrari purely for demonstration runs. My track test included the car's history and its evolution thanks in part to being redesigned by Ferrari's Englishman Dr Harvey Postlethwaite. I added my technical appraisal and a description of the drive.

Describing what an F1 car is like to drive is never straightforward. The following words are a touch techy but an F1 car deserves some explanation. This is my sixth F1 test. No supercar gets close to the power-to-weight ratio of an F1 car. Let's ignore the 1,500bhp (2,600hp/tonne) qualifying setting and look at its regular 1,000bhp and its 540kg weight. This equates to 1,852hp/tonne, which is more than a current F1 car at c1,500bhp/tonne. However, for countless reasons, a 2022/23 F1 car can achieve faster lap times. Another comparison is a bedroom poster 1,500bhp Bugatti Chiron with a feeble 750hp/tonne. For a real-world comparison, the Fiat Punto that I drove to Franciacorta Circuit had 64bhp/tonne. Driving an F1 car is not easy to describe. How about 0–100mph and back to stationary in five seconds? Welcome to the brutal world of F1. More complicated to describe is what happens when cornering.

To drive an F1 car, you need to do your apprenticeship in lesser cars and work up to this kind of ferocity. We take some static snaps. Then the team

1: Sitting where Michele Alboreto won the 1984 Belgian Grand Prix.
2: Leaning in the left-hander at Franciacorta circuit.

swaps the wets –used for transportation – for slicks. The cockpit feels right. Instrumentation and switch gear could not be more minimal. Like a 312 F1 Ferrari previously tested, the 126C4 has a homely feel, weird. This 1984 F1 car is from an 'analogue' period where the driver did everything; unlike today's 'digital' cars where banks of boffins are monitoring countless parameters on remote computer screens.

The Ferrari starts easily via the external starter and even idles smoothly at 1,500rpm thanks to a good ECU map. Before me, a 2.5km circuit of hot black-top. The burning hot day would help the tyres quickly reach their operating temperatures. I pull the grey wooden-topped lever left and back into first gear, up gently on the clutch and away…, very user-friendly so far. An easy change into second gear and still on a feather-light throttle, I am impressed with how easy the car is to drive. The brake pedal is brick-hard and its use is futile until the pads warm up. With some heat in the rubber, it is time to feel what is going on. With most cars, information is delivered via suspension movement. As an F1 car has precious little suspension movement, feel comes from the tyres. The steering weight informs me of front slip angles, while my eyes, backside and vestibular system decodes what is going on aft. I slice across the kerbs and the dog-tooth ridges naturally cause the whole chassis to flutter. I treat the kerbs with caution as they can 'tip' the car, instantly diminishing the tyres' flat contact patches; fine if travelling in a straight line, like in the middle of a chicane, but chaotic if there is some lateral force.

Time to wake up the horses. I increase the rpm to 6,000 and get that calm-before-the-storm feeling that a surfer has as he/she is drawn up to the top of a Pacific roller. Then at 7,000rpm comes full boost, pinned to the bulkhead, it takes me to over 11,000rpm before the power tails off. Provided there is just over 7,000rpm on the tachometer, there is guaranteed, lag-free rocket-ship acceleration. You can feel the rear tyres bite and the transmission note changes – yes, with this much torque, gears have their own unmistakeable sound system. To cope with the massive torque, the transmission is as big

3: The 1.5-litre turbos made 1,000bhp in race trim and 1,500bhp in qualifying mode.
4: Driving postilion is well forward of the power unit.
5: Fast tracking shot from the camera car.

as the engine. Provided I am in a straight line, with hot tyres, a dry track and a perfectly flat surface, then there is enough elasticity in the power delivery for tyres to cope. As for the noise, an F1 car somehow leaves this behind for Mr Doppler and the spectators to appreciate. Inside the car you simply hear a hard but rising monotone rhythm – bizarre.

Power comes in with a friendly gunpowder whoosh rather than a dynamite bang. At full throttle between 7-11,000rpm, there is an overwhelming tsunami of power. I can feel the whole mass of the car sit on its massive rear tyres. Direction feels governed by this rear road-roller effect making me reluctant to add excessive steering inputs as sooner or later the nose will dip, grip and dart. A fast aero turn would help keep the nose down. On full boost, my head is pinned to the headrest, making chassis vibrations wobble my vision. So far, I could have been describing a dragster but what about the corners? This is where I employ an engine dynamometer map in my head. This way I can balance power delivery to match lateral G-forces. I also need an aero-map in my head as, at sub-100mph, the invisible hand of downforce clamping car to track is largely

absent. The F1 drag coefficient (c_d) is high to create downforce and typically varies between $0.7c_d$ and $1.2c_d$ depending on set-up. Most road cars are about $0.3c_d$. In Franciacorta's tight turns, an F1 becomes a mere car. A fast turn arrives. I brake and as soon as I have finished trail-braking into the apex, I instantly apply a light throttle opening before the apex to balance the car and spool up the turbo. This means that as I exit the apex, there will be no turbo lag. This is standard style of cornering for a turbo car.

My time was up, and I thought I would be glad to get out of this projectile, but I wanted to stay in it to discover more. Finding that optimum miniscule slip angle for cornering, braking and acceleration with these hard-core F1 turbo cars is not easy. The hardest thing of all is coming to terms with the massive speed that can be carried into fast/aero corners. A low-speed corner will generate a maximum of 1.5 2G lateral. A high-speed aero turn could see 4G lateral. Here is when you need a neck that is as wide as a birthday cake. This F1 Ferrari would be a fantastic car for the Masters Historic Formula One Championship. With the testing done, it was painful to return the car to the owner. What a great car.

FROM F1 TO A PIP-SQUEAK

Unless you are an Italian car aficionado, you will not have heard of this delightful little car of which 1.3 million rolled off the production line. The Autobianchi A112 (1969–1986) was Italy's Mini. The A112 was made in several models including an 80hp Abarth version. In 2010, I track-tested two versions in Italy. They still are regulars on the Italian motorsport scene.

In the 1980s, I kept a UK-registered A112 at a family property in Cetraro, Calabria. Then in 1992, for reasons best sidestepped, I needed to make a quick getaway from Calabria with my two sons aged 17 and 9 years. With no time to arrange an alternative, the A112 was the only option. The car had been there for some years. It had obviously outstayed its six-months legal welcome, so bringing it back to the UK was no bad thing. It was, however, never serviced and rusty thanks to living outside a beach house. Amazingly, it made the 1,500-mile journey without any mechanical or authoritarian problems. Once back at the Rossi Engineering mothership, I restored it. You don't need big horsepower to have fun. Like an old Mini, or better still an A112, will bring a smile to your face.

MASERATI, MUGELLO AND JOHNNY HERBERT

There was pretty much an exclusive invitation for *Auto Italia* to join the Maserati Corse team at the beautiful

Mugello Circuit. Maserati even put Phil into a race suit. The company had launched a hot-rod road-going version of their GranTurismo, the MC Stradale. This solitary car had come straight to Mugello from the Paris Motor Show. Maserati also had a GT4 racing version on hand. The MC Stradale is a street-legal version aimed at buyers who would like a teeny taste of a race car without going racing.

With one solitary Paris Motor Show MC Stradale on hand, you may be thinking: what if some ham-fisted hack smacks it into the wall? Maserati's insurance was to put an F1 star in their reassuringly expensive car. Johnny Herbert is a Grand Prix winner, a Le Mans winner, a Sebring winner and a current historic racer whenever he receives an offer. His job on this day was to drive hot laps, chauffeuring our select group. My job was to test the current works GranTurismo MC race cars: both Trofeo and GT4 versions.

Despite the overall increase in cabin noise compared with a regular GranTurismo GTS, conversation inside the MC Stradale was no problem. "You can even talk in here," were my words to Johnny Herbert as he praised the balance and the way the Stradale's throttle pedal was virtually part of the steering, saying, "Very easy to drive. Great gearbox. A superb ride that is hard yet soft at the same time. Mugello is a temptress: beautiful yet complex. An aggressive circuit," Mugello's track length is 5.245km (3.259miles) and includes one of the

6: Sharing a joke with former F1 driver Johnny Herbert.
7: Roadcar meets racecar at the superb Mugello circuit.
8: Chauffeur ready for passengers.

longest modern straights in the world at 1.141km (0.709miles). In 2022 I raced a Chevron B26 at this fabulous circuit.

Johnny deserves a good mention here because of his determination, strength and courage. He had a remarkable racing career. He climbed the typical single-seater ladder via Formula Ford to become a Formula 3 champion. The next step was Formula 3000. In August 1988 at top speed on the Brands Hatch's GP straight, he was hit in the rear three-quarter by Gregor Foitek who had a reputation for aggressive driving. Foitek sent Herbert into the concrete bridge parapet, front-first and smashing his legs. This caused a multiple pile-up involving over a dozen cars, during which Herbert suffered more horrendous injuries. James Hunt, who was then coaching Jean Alesi, visited the crash site and returned shaking his head.

Herbert was badly concussed and his mangled legs were hanging out of the front of the car. The threat of amputation loomed. Thankfully, after multiple surgeries and months of physiotherapy, amputation was avoided, although the extent of Herbert's injuries would permanently hinder his mobility, leaving him unable to run and forcing him to change his driving style. Despite his immobility, quite amazingly, Herbert returned to racing at the beginning of 1989 in Formula One, scoring points on his debut at the Brazilian GP driving for the Benetton team. He then drove for the Sauber team and the Stewart F1 team where he regularly out-qualified his team-mate Rubens Barrichello. He also raced with Lotus F1. Indeed, I was at Claridge's Hotel in London for the launch party, where I interviewed the Lotus F1 team-mates Johnny Herbert and Alessandro Zanardi. After F1, Herbert made several appearances at Goodwood and moved into GT racing plus an appearance in the BTCC. In 2021, he was back racing a Formula One car at the Silverstone Classic. Today he is a Formula One TV commentator for Sky Sports. Our Mugello mission was a great low-stress trip. Onwards and upwards…

8

2011
Ancient Rome – Modern Car

Lamborghini chose Rome and the Vallelunga Race Circuit for the Aventador press launch. The party started at the Campidoglio (Capitoline Hill). Coinciding with Italy's 150th unification birthday party, the Aventador was presented to the Mayor at the City Hall for the celebrations of Rome's new title – *'Roma Capitale'* – and to promote 'Made in Italy'. A temporary Lamborghini museum was housed in the nearby Bramante Cloister. Then ten V12 Lamborghinis dating back to the 1964 350 GT paraded through the Eternal City. The company's technical director, Maurizio Reggiani, told me a long time ago that power-to-weight ratio would become a priority – and the Aventador is the proof.

You might have thought that the 150th birthday of the Italian state would have the whole country celebrating. The only time Italians wave the tricolore is for an international football match or if a red car wins a Grand Prix. Many Italians regard the Italian state as the enemy. Their home town and family are more important than nationalism. Italy is a stage, a film set and a theatre – wonderful to visit but not so easy in which to live. Style and the *dolce vita* are there, but so are problems too complex to describe here.

You may wonder what happened to the people that created the Roman Empire: an organised civilisation that covered the known world and lasted over 1,000 years. It's a little-known detail that when the Barbarians were at the gate, many Romans emigrated to Germany. Perhaps this is why – despite Germany's problems from 1914 to 1945 – it has not stopped Germany becoming Europe's leading nation. Don't worry about a handful of Germans in the Lamborghini factory – think of them as Romans. Even Stephan Winkelmann, the Berlin-born CEO, was brought up and educated in Rome.

The Autodromo di Vallelunga is just north of Rome. Black, white and orange Aventadors were in the pit lane rumbling on idle. Like a bee, I made a beeline for an orange car. Photographers dislike black or white cars as they rarely look good in a magazine. Zero to 100km/h in 2.9 seconds – the first proper car to break the three second barrier. It is also one of the first production cars with a carbon-fibre monocoque. Powered by a 700bhp motor and driving through a superb seven-speed transmission, you also enjoy 4WD, F1-style pushrod suspension and more. Audi investment has enabled Lamborghini to take an enormous leap forward – "a two-generation leap" were the words of CEO Stephan Winkelmann.

Everyone knows that the Aventador will be driven mostly at low speeds on fashionable boulevards by drivers who have average skills. We all know this: you, me, the engineers, the designers, the test drivers, the onlookers, the buyers, everyone. It matters not. Just as you don't pull 1G cornering or 1G braking in your everyday family car, so the Aventador will creep about with just the briefest bursts of show-off acceleration. Its 220mph top speed is superfluous. Similarly, you don't need an atomic wristwatch studded with diamonds, but if that is what turns you on, then why not.

I drove for countless laps, then Lamborghini's CEO Stephan Winkelmann quizzed me. My words to him were, "Great car. I wouldn't change a thing." When the dust settled and upon reflection, I might ask technical

1: Drifting the 700bhp, 220mph Lamborghini Aventador at Autodromo di Vallelunga.

director Maurizio Reggiani to tone down that spine-thumping 50-millisecond gear shift when the driver selects Race Mode.

BARCELONA TO PARIS ROAD TRIP

A suitable analysis to determine what kind of traveller you are might be as follows. Choice number 1: Club Class flight from Barcelona to Paris. Or choice number 2: Drive a Maserati from Barcelona to Paris. As a lover of road trips, you can guess my preference.

Seven hundred miles lay ahead, three Maseratis were warmed up, fuelled up and pointing north-east, with a night stop at a French chateau. Let's hit the highway and see what happens. Long lonely journeys are perfect for putting the world to rights. Reorganising the world is easy; ask any taxi driver. However, driving three Maseratis on my own would be difficult. Thankfully there were three drivers: photo editor Michael Ward (now also *Auto Italia's* MD), Silvia Pini (Maserati's press officer), and me (a general factotum).

I had three cars to assess: a wealthy boy racer's GranTurismo S MC Sportline (GTS), a sensible person's GranTurismo S Automatic (GTSA) and a look-at-me GranCabrio. Hmmm… it might appear that I have already summed up the cars before the test drive. But then anyone reading this may already have drawn the same conclusion. Barcelona and the startline – I can hear Freddie Mercury singing it now, inspired by the 1992 Summer Olympics. With a population of five million, it is the capital of Catalonia and Spain's second city after Madrid. It has a politically left-leaning tendency and a separatist movement, all of which are left-overs from the 1936–39 Civil War. Founded 2,000 years ago by the Romans, like so many Mediterranean regions, it has been occupied by numerous invaders. Now a world heritage site, it is a cultural centre with works by Antoni Gaudí and his chaotic cathedral. The bonkers basilica is an enormous tourist attraction.

It was appealing to divert from my usual UK to Italy commute. Instead of negotiating the Alps, I had the Pyrenees between me and my destination. The

2: Two of the three-car Maserati convoy posing for pictures.
3: Pit stop with Maserati PR girls.
4: Lost in France?
5: Growling GranTurismo.
6: Straight line steering test.
7: Sat nav route Spain to France.

Schengen Treaty has rendered most European borders obsolete. Thankfully there are still rigid demarcations when it comes to culture. For instance, at the French-Italian border near Monte Carlo, on one side of the line they speak French, shrug their shoulders and eat croissants. Take one step over the border and you speak Italian, celebrate the chaos and have brioches with jam inside. There is no overlap. Breakfast at the Pyrenean border and *torrijas* change to croissants.

While Europe is in danger of becoming an over-populated museum of bureaucracy and in fighting, nothing beats the cultural and gastronomic diversity of the Europeans. We stop in Carcassonne for lunch and take some snaps. The enormous walled city being an apt backdrop. I knew the area with affection as I had previously had a great time at a country house there with friends: the sculptor Andrew Dumont, Jane Eady and Marion Dumont. First settlements date back to 3,500 BC with the Romans constructing the first substantial buildings in 100 BC.

I have always noticed that the French are sensible.

They were early adopters of diesel-powered family barges painted grey – perhaps something to do with the proletariat guillotining the aristocracy. While Germany has no speed limit on its autobahns, speeding in France is met with draconian punishment. Successful speeding is an art form that requires knowledge, cunning, experience and common sense. To admit to driving at 184mph in a GTS on a French road could be professional suicide, so here is a hypothetical case. Just supposing I had driven at 184mph, I might have found that the nose gently ran ever wider in the tightening turns. This, I might have judged as reasonable handling – better than having the tail end misbehaving. Most probably it might have been due to some front-end aero lift, as the hypothetical speed was so high. I might have made sure that the undulations in the curve did not affect my outstretched arms and consequently apply disastrous unnecessary steering inputs. I might have decided that the deteriorating topography could cause me to abort a 187mph goal and settle for 184mph.

I might have made sure that I lifted the throttle ultra-gently to maintain equilibrium. A mistake at this speed might have been of plane crash proportions. Speeding in safe places – like quiet, wide-open main roads and autoroutes – is dangerous, as this is where Le Plod lie in wait. Gentlemanly speeding should inconvenience no one and should be invisible. Break this rule and you are a menace.

A Maserati is so *dolce vita*. But my opinions mean little, so let us consider the opinion of a well-wadded UK friend, as his perception may be archetypal. He has owned countless executive toys and expensive cars. He has an apartment in Westminster and lives on a country estate (and I don't mean housing estate). He used to regard the Maserati brand as a no-go area, quirky cars for eccentric people. Today he has warmed to the thriving Maserati marque, simply by the fact that you can't move in Kensington and Chelsea for Maseratis. But as he is not a car fanatic, his everyday vehicles are German, but now with an eye for the Trident.

After 425 miles, our trio arrived at our night stop at the Chateau La Chapelle Saint Martin, near Limoges. I looked forward to a very French evening and that is exactly what this delightful hotel delivered. One of the best things about travelling is enjoying the local gastronomy. This connects motoring culture to food culture and restaurant culture. Italian restaurant culture – like Spanish restaurant culture – has nothing to do with decor, furniture, lighting, service, nouvelle cuisine, fashion, chefs, gimmicks or location. It is all about the taste; local recipes that have evolved over millennia take precedence. Except that with the Spanish, it happens at 1am.

French fine-dining restaurant culture is a little like aspirational British fine-dining restaurant culture, in that the ambiance of a restaurant, the look of the food and the standard of service have priority. However, the best French food, like the best British food, is traditional basic cooking found in civilised homes, cafes and pubs. Above a certain financial boundary, I believe that in the UK, the more you spend and the more you go for 'fine

dining', the more I laugh at the offerings. I understand that my opinions conflict with the top-end UK restaurant culture, so I expect a kicking from high-end UK foodies.

Seven hundred miles and we arrived at our destination as sharp as we started. The Motor Village on the Champs Elysée saw a display of Italian cars and merchandising. Central Paris is beautiful and captivating, not the case with some of its suburbs, however this is no time to write a guidebook. Time for a taxi to Charles de Gaulle Airport.

MILLE MIGLIA MADNESS

One hundred and fifty Ferraris racing past the Pope's front door in St Peter's Square, tyres screeching round the Colosseum, the police doing everything possible to add to our pace – it was surreal. You had to be there. Describing four days of Mille Miglia madness won't be easy.

From 1927 to 1957, the real Mille Miglia was a 1,000 mile race on public roads lined with spectators. It was also a round of the World Sports Car Championship. The roads were one step up from narrow dirt tracks. I still can't believe how in 1955, Stirling Moss won the race at an average speed of nearly 100mph. The route passed though countless towns, cities and mountains. It

was dangerous. Approximately 56 deaths and counting... Then in 1957, Alfonso de Portago's Ferrari crashed killing another nine people, five of whom were children.

The race was banned; and from 1958, the format was a rally where speed limits had to be observed, but in 1961, the rally faded away. In 1977, it was revived and renamed, Mille Miglia Storica. This was now a regularity rally for pre-1957 cars which still presented some danger and casualties.

Since 2010, the Mille Miglia Storica has been joined by the Mille Miglia Ferrari Tribute, which is open to post-1957 Ferraris. I was invited to join Drummond Bone in his Ferrari 599. Drummond is one of the UK's leading academics, ex Master of Balliol, Maserati UK Club President and much more... More importantly, he is an ex-racer and always a racer at heart but don't tell anyone. The two Mille Miglias run on the same three days. Yes, we take three days to do what Stirling Moss did in 10 hours on narrow roads. First to leave the start line were the 150 cars of the 'Ferrari Tribute to the Mille Miglia'. The old cars start after the Ferraris have departed. Famous names in our group included F1 world champion Mika Hakkinen and Rowan Atkinson. The 150 Ferraris attracted 46 different models from 26 countries, including twelve 599GTOs and seven F40s.

Naturally the old car brigade loathes the arrogant Johnny-come-latelys in their ghastly Ferraris – especially those in new Ferraris. There was a faint whiff of Gumball from one or two Ferrari entrants – something that needs extermination if credibility is to be maintained.

This was Drummond's bash and he drove the entire gruelling event at around 14 to 18 hours per day. My job was navigation, controlling the timing gear and re-acquainting myself with the breath taking capabilities of the 599. With no regularity experience, I was on a steep learning curve. While the pros had all manner of high-tech electronic wizardry, we did it the old-fashioned way, with a pair of the most handsome clockwork stopwatches that were a gift to Drummond from Maserati. The regularity pros took the event as seriously as I would take a motor race. Watching the pros in action was eye-opening. I needed to focus, or the ever-competitive Drummond would shout at me.

Wednesday and Thursday – Brescia to Imola
Plenty of time for signing-on and scrutineering. In Italy, scrutineering means looking at documents and collecting goody bags. Thursday afternoon was for

8: Mille Miglia startline in Brescia.
9: Out in the country.
10: Typical public town welcome.

parading and getting into the party mood; Brescia was buzzing, its centre taken over by the Mille Miglia roadshow. The start of our MM was on Thursday evening at 6pm and the first day finished at midnight in Imola. Then came a late-night dinner and bed at about 3am. For someone whose normal bedtime is 10pm, so far, the MM was horrendous.

On the way from Brescia to Imola, there were time checks for average speed and many control points where a stamp was required to check that we were using the correct route. Officials fitted transponders for ID and timing. All cars were also fitted with GPS for position reports, emergency aid and speed monitoring. This info was also broadcast live on the internet. During the whole event, there were 54 regularity stages, including some at Vallelunga Race Circuit and on the Ferrari test track of Fiorano.

Friday – Imola to Rome

Four hours sleep, then up at 7am and away by 8am. The route was varied and included country roads and mountain roads. The target average speeds for each day looked easy. However, the route also included visiting 150 historic town centres, each of which puts on a show and a traffic jam. The approaches to the towns were always blocked solid, so our required average speed plummeted. This necessitated driving like a maniac whenever the road was clear. The route took us through San Marino and up over the snow line of the Apennines.

The police turned a blind eye to mad-driving MM competitors and the spectators' body language clearly demanded the highest speeds possible. While you might expect teenagers to punch the air and press imaginary accelerator pedals, little old ladies were just as enthusiastic. Parents brought their children and lifted their babies closer to the action, thereby rightly indoctrinating the next generation.

Common sense tells you that there is a limit on how fast you should drive down a narrow street lined with people. And herein lies the problem: we all draw the line in different places. Some drivers took it easy, while others really were flat out. The worst culprits were those who overtook on the wrong side of the road on blind bends. Egos abounded amongst these clandestine road racers. Just as the old MM was banned, so too could this modern version be stopped.

We arrived in Rome at dusk and gathered at Castel Sant' Angelo, the Emperor Hadrian's marvellous mausoleum. Then the incredible event that will stay with me forever, the police held back Rome's traffic and blocked all the junctions in our favour. 150 Ferraris sprinted as fast as they could lapping Rome's iconic sights. I wanted a magic wand to be able to beam certain people into the passenger seat of the 599. I would have begun with ancient Roman charioteers and

their race mechanics and ended with trying to put a smile on the face of an eco-activist, or a Puritan. An early night: we arrived at our posh hotel at 10.00pm. We dined and went to our beds at 1.00am.

Saturday – Rome to Brescia

After three and half hours of sleep, we were up at 4.30am and wheels rolling by 6am. We felt wretched and excited at the same time – bizarre. As a sports coach, this behaviour is the opposite of what I insist upon for my motor racing students. First stop – Vallelunga Circuit in a thick pea soup of early morning fog. Visibility in places was down to three metres. Generous target times were given – or so I thought. We underestimated the speed required as sneaky temporary chicanes loomed out of the super-dense fog to slow our lap time. Then more city drive-throughs, more traffic jams, more street parties, more regularity stages, more mountain passes and more high-speed driving. Then a shocking disaster. We had often been in close company with a very fast car that was always

11: En route visiting 150 towns.
12: Check point traffic jam.
13: 1000 miles on Italian B roads.

being driven dangerously. I guess it was this driver's belief that this was his opportunity to show that he was the world's best racing driver, when in fact he was just a thoughtless menace. He constantly overtook cars at crazy speeds on blind bends on the wrong side of the road. Every time he did this, it made me wince. He was just ahead of us on the way up to the Futa Pass. He was speeding flat out on a blind bend on the wrong side of the road. The inevitable happened. He collided head-on with an innocent motorcyclist. The biker was minding his own business on the correct side of the road and now, tragically, he lay smashed and motionless.

Eventually we rolled into the motor city that is Modena. Drummond put in a hot lap of Ferrari's Fiorano test track, having recently been coached there by the racing god that is Fernando Alonso. Our route took us – open-mouthed – right through some of the buildings of the Ferrari factory in Maranello and the Maserati factory in Modena. Then another myriad of city centres, all dressed up for the festivity.

Drummond was now exhausted and incapable of receiving any verbal directions but determined to continue. When we entered a roundabout with lots of exits, I would place my outstretched arm with finger constantly pointing in the direction of travel required. This would be directly in front of Drummond, and it was the only communication with which he could cope. Decades earlier, I learnt from Stirling Moss at the RAC Pall Mall that on the real MM, under extreme conditions, he too could only receive instructions from his navigator Dennis Jenkinson via hand signals. It worked. Moss also told me that when the spectators progressively narrowed the road to get a better view leaving no room for his car, he would wobble the steering to make the car appear out of control. This had the effect of instantly widening the road.

A thousand miles of enthusiastic and passionate spectators and finally, at 11pm, the finish line in Brescia. On the final day, Drummond had been at the wheel driving hard for 18.5 hours. He was wrecked, and I don't mean a bit tired. I can't think of an appropriate word for his level of exhaustion and commitment. Another posh hotel on Lake Garda, dinner and retire late. Despite the exhaustion, elation and relief – adrenalin granted us some late-night celebration time.

Sunday in the Villa Cortine on Lake Garda was for the prize-giving and lunch. The MM was well organised. Its arduous timetable and punishing route brought on a sense of satisfaction as much as it did camaraderie. Would I do it again? My answer would be rhetorical. Would you climb Mount Everest or swim the English Channel more than once? I guess some people have. As for us, despite having an amateur navigator, we managed sixth in class and 54th out of 150 overall. It was a bit like running a marathon or a 24-hour motor race – finishing was like winning.

A GOOD YEAR AND MORE RACING

For 40 years my personal life had been chaotic, albeit with a 14-year period of stability during the mid-1980s/90s. However, 2011 was the year when permanent stability arrived. Jane and I were married in Chelsea Town Hall, with a luncheon reception at the Bluebird and afternoon tea at the Lanesborough. It was a perfect day. Our Kings Road getaway car was Lofty England's personal Jaguar E-Type. Lofty was the Jaguar Racing Team manager when Jaguar won the Le Mans 24-hour race five times. I bought the car to convert it into a racer but couldn't bring myself to destroy its originality. I sold it and of course regretted the decision. To link E-Types with Italian cars, here is a quote from Enzo Ferrari when he saw the E-Type at the 1961 Geneva Motor Show, "The most beautiful car in the world. It is the car we should have made."

During 2011, I was picking up numerous drives in historic racing, thanks to my work as a race coach and handling consultant. It was also another year of racing in the Maserati Trofeo series with the team's new GranTurismo MCs. I had had four years (eight races) of such treats, so thank you Maserati. The venue this time was Donington Park with qualifying and two 40-

14: 2011. Chelsea Town Hall wedding. Getaway car is the Lofty England E-Type

15: An eventful two-part race in the Maserati MC Corse at Donington Park led to a respectable mid-field result.

minute races. Whilst testing with Maserati Corse in Italy, I pointed out several areas for improvement most of which were heeded. Mirrors and cockpit ventilation are often overlooked by race engineers. It was good to see that since testing in Italy, both issues had been addressed. Unaddressed however, was the super powerful brake servo that removed any sense of feel from the braking making a lock-up too easy. The penalty for flat-spotting a tyre in qualifying is to start the race from the back row.

Qualifying, and on the exit of Coppice, an important fast turn leading onto a long straight, the car immediately ahead of me loses control and is sideways on to me. The car behind me is on my bumper and also loses control. In a chaotic racing sandwich, I duck, dive and brake lock the inside rear tyre and just miss a multiple collision. The team checks my car and discovers that there is too much rear brake pressure. However, my punishment for a flat-spotted tyre is to start the races from the back row, despite attaining grid position in the top third. Rules are rules.

Race 1. On a damp track and running on slicks, there are plenty of incidents. Then a two-car crash: the accident was the usual thing – an over-optimistic driver going for a closing gap. This accident, plus slicks on what is now a wet track, spooked the officials into stopping the race early.

Race 2. Another back row start and the first lap was unusual. We were all tightly bunched going into turn 1 Redgate Corner. I quickly wriggle up to mid-field. Then I discover why. On every turn-in, a car ahead of me poured a sea of fuel from an open filler cap. Fuel on tarmac is slippery. This divided the field into pre- and post- fuel-spill cars. All around the track, the spilt fuel was a real problem. The gap between the two groups widened. Unlike an oil spill, fuel on the track is almost invisible. A mid-field race result was okay. The objective of the exercise was to avoid causing any damage and to write a story on the race, plus the series and the technical intricacies of the cars. Mission accomplished.

2012
Work or Pleasure?

I have an attack of blasé in 2012. At the Surrey test track are a pair of superbly modified Ferrari 458s: one is a tarted-up and power-enhanced road car, the other is a race car. Both are great jobs, well done by Evolution 2 with CEO Geoffrey Finlay and chief engineer Chris Warne. In my youth, the opportunity to play with such cars would have been a dream-come-true. After more than 20 years of motoring journalism, it felt like a dull day. It felt like work rather than pleasure. The solution was diversity. A little less writing and a little more motorsport perked me up.

BRANDS HATCH AND MORE CHANGE

In 2012, when the call came to report to Brands Hatch to track-test a Ferrari 456GT that had been converted for racing by Foskers, I felt at home. My first time on the Kent circuit was in 1967 at the Motor Racing Stables driving a Lotus Formula Ford. After a lifetime of driving round Brands Hatch, I wondered if I could perform it blindfolded. There is a test that sports coaches use. It is to ask your student to close his or her eyes and visualise a lap of say Brands Hatch. The visualiser says, "Start" and is then timed as he virtually

1: If it's fast, make it faster.
Re-engineered Ferraris on test.
2: Ferrari 456GT at Brands Hatch.

drives and ends a virtual flying lap. Crossing the virtual finish line with eyes still closed, he/she shouts, "Stop". The visualised lap should be within one or two seconds of a real lap.

Since 2001 my motorsport coaching delivered many race drives. The pay was okay and come 5pm, I had finished work. Writing work is never finished, as I would continually return to my words, research, rethink and make changes. Similarly, a fine artist can never finish a painting. The painter reaches a point where he/she 'abandons' the masterpiece to the market. Similarly, I am not far away from 'abandoning' this book. Race instructing had expanded to having private clients on a one-to-one basis at any circuit. This included being paid to share clients' cars in long-distance races. My job was to make the driver faster and safer via coaching and mentoring and make the car quicker via set-up consultancy and related technicalities. The private client work had a daily rate, three or four times more than I could earn at a race school. I could now earn in one day what I could earn in one month as a writer. While

I enjoyed the writing work, motorsport gave me more time, more diversity and more income. I also studied and qualified as a sports coach to add to my ARDS qualification. This meant having two occupations whilst running my own racing car and other activities.

AN OLD ADVERSARY RETURNS

A beautifully restored blue De Tomaso Mangusta started life as a red road car, was then converted into quick multi-coloured race car. It was now at our Surrey test track having been returned to being a fabulous road car. During its stint as a racing car driven by Freddie Moss in the busy *Auto Italia* Championship, it was alarmingly quick. A shark in a fishpond with zero opposition. I used the opportunity of the Mangusta test to include a few sidebars. There was a brief history of Alejandro de Tomaso and his cars. I wrote about the Mangusta's configuration, handling, and its American muscle. I included a piece about powerful American V8 engines that de Tomaso used to great advantage. I also incorporated my 'previous' with this car.

3: Foskers-prepared 456GT.
4: The Freddie Moss De Tomaso Mangusta dominated the Auto Italia *Championship*.
5: The Mangusta was later converted back to a road car.

During the late 1980s, I raced a Group A Maserati Biturbo against this Mangusta. I could not compare the Mangusta with the Biturbo as the Mangusta instantly disappeared into the distance. However, one day in the late 1980s, at Castle Combe Circuit, Phil and I were involved in making a promotional video for Sony. Three cars with multiple camera set-ups had to spend all day messing about, pretending to be racing. Those present were me in the Maserati, a Ferrari 308 and fast Freddie in the Mangusta. Rather than disappear into the distance, Freddie was alongside and we regularly ducked and dived swapping places like Hollywood heroes. Every so often, Freddie would get bored and roar off across the Wiltshire Plains. Even though we were filming side-by-side at over 100mph, the Mangusta's disappearing acts were spectacular.

2013
Big Race – Small Car

I had a racing client whom I was coaching who owned several cars, one of which was the ex-Hezemans van Lennep Dutch works Alfa Romeo GTA. It belonged to international award-winning architect Robert Clarke and he wanted me to race at the Silverstone Classic with a co-driver of my choosing. I used the opportunity for a story in *Auto Italia* magazine. My co-driver for the day was another driver training client, BP oil explorer, Geordie, historic sports car racer and Italophile Karl Wetherell. We were going to be in good company; I noticed some pro drivers and two Formula One names in our race: Arturo Merzario and Jackie Oliver.

The GTA had been looked after by Simon Whiting at Gran Turismo Engineering. It then moved to John Danby Racing (JDR). When I write the words, "looked after", these companies had little input in the overall competitiveness of the GTA. The budget for a ground-up restoration to full race spec was absent. The orders were merely to maintain what was already there. This meant that the GTA was still in classic car condition, albeit with some regulatory safety equipment. It was too original to be competitive against contemporary highly prepared built-from-scratch historic race cars.

A rolling start in the middle of a 60-car grid pleases spectators and race organisers. This is the balancing act with which organisers grapple. Close racing brings crowd-pleasing battles and, inevitably, contact. All very well unless you are the one paying the repair bills in this non-contact sport. The drivers' briefing is always the same: "For the rolling start, you must maintain the two-by-two formation until you cross the startline." In reality, at the corner preceding the start-finish straight, it's

pedal to the metal and the race is already clandestinely under way.

The July Silverstone Classic is the world's largest historic race meeting. A three-day spectacular with 100,000 spectators, 800 racing cars, 1,000 drivers, 7,000 classic cars on display, 20 races and countless side shows. The U2TC series is the International Under two-litre Touring Car Race run by Carol Spagg. It is for pre-66 Touring Cars conforming to FIA appendix K. Best described as cunningly upgraded versions of homologation specials. The best racing components for GTAs demand bespoke engineering, while the best racing kit for Lotus Cortinas are available from your local supermarket. This is partly why eleven of the first 15 finishers in the race were Lotus Cortinas.

Due to various problems, we qualified in 44th position on the 60-car grid. In the race we had five pit stops. Yes, five pit-stops. Three pitstops to adjust a slipping clutch, another to solve a three-cylinder issue caused by a badly designed foam air filter sock being ingested into a carburettor and an incredible fifth pit stop during Karl's stint to straighten a rear wheel arch rubbing on a tyre, thanks to a kamikaze Lotus Cortina. The problems were rapidly fixed by the slick JDR crew.

In another race, a Mustang they were running had a front-end smash, its bonnet at a crazy angle. The damage was assessed as it hurtled past the pits, the crew ordered it in on the next lap. Much tank tape was torn into strips in preparation. Hammers and levers were ready. The wounded Mustang pitted. In record time, the JDR crew had straightened the mangled bonnet, front wing and front panel and taped it all up. It re-entered the

1 – 3: Ex-works Alfa Romeo GTA entered in the under two-litre race at the 2013 Silverstone Classic.

race losing only some seconds rather than minutes. As for our GTA, without the JDR crew, we would have had a very short race and retired. Instead, at the chequered flag, somehow we made it to 40th out of 60.

TESTING WITH THE TEAM AT MISANO

I spent a weekend with the Maserati Corse works team at Misano Circuit on Italy's Adriatic coast test-driving next year's version (2013) of the GranTurismo MC producing nearly 500hp. I was the only journalist invited. The tech spec sits somewhere between FIA GT3 and GT4. These are the race cars used in the Trofeo World Series. The Trofeo World Series includes six triple-header rounds, which take place in France, Germany, England, the USA and China, with the grand finale in December in the UAE. 84 drivers from 24 countries competed. Arrive-and-drive heaven for those who can afford it and for this fortunate racer/writer. Entrants need a minimum of an international grade C race licence to be eligible.

The drivers are fiercely competitive and want to slug it out on a level playing field. When competitive GT pros or self-made men seek combat, you'd better watch out. Trofeo tussles have always been tough. At the time in its tenth year and with an average of 24 cars on the grid, this type of one-make racing can be intimate. There are plenty of video clips on the web. Cars are insured for damage, but drivers are responsible for the

4

first £10,000 of damage per incident, regardless of blame. Maserati kindly waived this punishment for me, should I be involved in contact. For their thoughtfulness, my priority with the team has always been to avoid any contact.

Maserati's technical director for the Trofeo World Series, Fabio Tosi, talked me through the 2013 version of the car. Conscious of my experience, the Maserati team are always interested in my feedback. They have their own test drivers and they also listen to the series' race drivers. As we know, information is power. The more feedback they receive, the more they can compare it and make appropriate decisions. The feather-light power steering tricks you into thinking that this is a flyweight racer. However, attack a low-speed / no-downforce corner too quickly and the laws of physics will tell you otherwise. I had previously mentioned to the team that previous GranTurismo MC race cars had an over-sensitive servo and no feel; it used to be so easy to flat-spot the sticky Pirelli slicks. Now however, my feedback was heeded and a new pedal-box with a conventional twin master cylinder set-up, and no servo, has perfected the braking system.

I drove for five laps, came in for a chat and then did five more. Each outing required a couple of laps to heat the slicks, as cold slicks don't work. At each pit-stop, technical director Fabio Tosi welcomed my feedback. I have driven countless racing cars and invariably return

4 – 8: Gloriously noisy Maserati MC Corse at Misano testing. RG's input helped perfect the car.

to the pits with a mental list of improvements that could be made. This time I had nothing to say. The 2013 GranTurismo MC was fit for purpose; it needed nothing.

For the story, I included a circuit guide to Misano. For example, here are a few words on the fastest turn. The *Curvone* (Big Curve) is as daunting as Blanchimont at Spa. The first time into this fast unfamiliar turn, I braked and downshifted sixth to fifth. I slowed too much. Gradually I trusted the aerodynamics, to the point where I was flat out in sixth gear. At very high speed, the downforce was so well balanced fore and aft that the once daunting *Curvone* could be taken flat. My lap times reduced and matched the quick guys. Maserati Corse was satisfied that they had a good car for the coming season.

RACING WITH THE TEAM AT SILVERSTONE

My work for *Auto Italia* was largely being confined to racing, which suited me. Once again, I was invited to Silverstone to run in three races, this time sharing the car with Spanish writer/racer Jaime Hernandez. My team-mate also had several Trofeo races under his belt with a fourth place and several top ten finishes. Despite being a nice bloke, your team mate is always your worst enemy. Team mates in any race series are never equally quick. Lap times reveal all and excuses are difficult to conjure up. The 'Racing Drivers' Book of Excuses' lacks a chapter on why you are slower than your team-mate.

The weekend consisted of 2x45 minutes of shared free practice on Friday, 2x20 minutes shared qualifying, 2x30 minutes solo races (one each) and one 50 minute two-driver race. As for the Gentleman Drivers label, I counted one, maybe two, but that was it. Due to economic cutbacks in GT racing and the like, young hot-shot pro drivers had migrated to the more affordable Trofeo. This has undoubtedly upped the pace. Drivers are now quick or very quick. I had to be restrained from strangling the commentator at Silverstone who was as out of touch with the 2013 Trofeo as it was possible to

9, 10 and 13: Auto Italia 'sponsored' Maserati MC Corse at Silverstone.

11 and 12: RG's team mate having an 'off' resulting in another mid-field finish.

be. His discourteous references to Gentleman Drivers (meaning slow) were as inaccurate as they were irrelevant.

2013 was when track limits (no corner cutting) were introduced to UK racing. However, the EU/FIA regs still permit it. Corner cutting makes a difference of about four seconds per lap at Silverstone. This equates to around 160m per lap advantage. Those four seconds would have put me at the front. But I was being a good boy and not corner cutting as I didn't want a penalty. I heard later that everyone else (all non-UK drivers) were corner cutting but excused, as the organisers decided to run on EU/FIA rules (i.e., corner cutting is ok).

I was doing okay and in the top ten just before the pit stop. My team-mate who was three seconds per lap slower, took over. We lost a few places in the pit stop due to a malfunctioning pit lane speed limiter (it cut the motor). My team mate then visited a gravel trap and brought the car home below mid-field but first in class because classes are split on drivers' age. I like that.

From someone who is a regular in the top ten, my team mate commented on how much quicker the series had become. I still wondered whether it was legal to strangle the Silverstone commentator. Sometimes murder is legal. For instance, if you are reversing into a parking space, and someone nips in forwards.

All Change – The Present and the Future

There had been much change at *Auto Italia* as the editorial staff became the publishers. Freelancer Chris Rees became the editor. Original editor Phil Ward's new role is that of the events director. Photo editor and designer Michael Ward is now the managing director.

Just before the global pandemic, I tested a Ferrari 812 Superfast comparing it with a Lamborghini Aventador. The Ferrari made the Aventador feel old-fashioned. I also compared the Ferrari with an Aston Martin DB9 Superleggera that I tested in the Alps for another magazine. Both cars had c800hp and choosing a winner was not easy. The Ferrari was the better car. However, as a gift and for everyday real-world use, I would choose the DB9 Superleggera.

In 2021, *Auto Italia* asked me to track test George Osbourne's fabulously butch Alfa Romeo 75 racing car at Silverstone. Next another *Targa Florio Storica,* this time in a Ferrari 812 Superfast. Another opportunity to enjoy the glorious chaos that is Sicily, but not at 211mph. In the UK, I get my southern Italian fix by binge-watching TV's *Inspector Montalbano*, which is filmed on Sicily. The Mediterranean's largest island is 5,700sqkm and bigger than Wales.

Turning a negative into a positive is normal strategy for sports psychology. This is something that works in all walks of life. If one activity decreases, it means another can flourish. For 2022/23, my motor racing and race coaching continues. After pre-season testing at Guadix in Spain, I am experiencing international races in some amazing cars. I am also racing my own early-specification Jaguar E-Type. Activity exercises the mind and the body. A healthy lifestyle should be regarded as an additional occupation. I am fortunate in that my wife thinks likewise.

For the opportunities given to me by *Auto Italia* and many others, as well as the great people that let me test or race their cars, I am eternally grateful. Thanks also to Chris Rea for his encouragement. I am halfway through a family history book (1911–1948), which shares my family's remarkable escapades in two World Wars. It is a story that would make a fine screenplay. As I was captivated by my grandfather's published wartime stories, perhaps my grandchildren Isabella and Leo will one day find the family history book of interest. To finish on a positive note is difficult, because as I write these words, I wonder if World War Three has already started. Instead, let us focus on the good things in life, like the roof over your head, your friends and your family. Consider the words from Joni Mitchell's song, *Big Yellow Taxi*, "You don't know what you've got 'til it's gone." Look after yourselves and thank you for reading this book.

1: *2022 GRRC Goodwood sprint class winner with the Duke of Richmond.*
2: *Spa-24hr class winning Group 2 BMW 3.5 CSL 'Batmobile' and the ex-John Watson Jody Scheckter Chevron B26 in the Guadix Circuit pit garages.*
3: *Superbly prepared Alfa 75.*
4: *Aston Martin DBS Superleggera in the Alps.*

ACKNOWLEDGEMENTS

My eternal thanks to those who made the stories in this book possible. Acknowledging all of them is impossible. The list of names is impractically long. From the eminent and influential people who opened doors or provided priceless machines to the humble owner of a modest car – where do I begin?

In a random order, here are just a few: Phil and Michael Ward for *Auto Italia* magazine work, particularly Phil who gets the blame for persuading me to write this book. Zoe Merchant (marketing) and Susanne Lewis (proofreading). John Collins (Talacrest) for trusting me with millions of pounds worth of cars. Much gratitude to the late Peter Crutch, without whom I would not have made a name for myself in the Alfa Romeo Championship. Thanks also to the Duke of Richmond, (then Lord March) for countless days testing at Goodwood, plus invitations to race there ten times at the Revival and Members' Meetings. Thank you, Sir Drummond Bone (ex-master of Balliol), for reviewing an early draft of this book, also for one Mille Miglia and two Targa Florio escapades. Many thanks to Paul Osborn for squeezing me into my first Formula One car. *Grazie*, Augusto Donetti, for the Turin test track and for vital and countless Italian introductions. Thanks also to the late great Lorenzo Prandina for two F1 Ferrari drives, plus more useful introductions – Italy doesn't work without introductions. Thank you, ex-Maserati press officer Andrea Cittadini, for welcoming me into the Maserati fold and for many race drives in the Trofeo series. Thank you to Michael O'Shea for trusting me to race the beast: a five-litre Cooper-Maserati.

Thanks to Claudio Casali (Vernasca Silver Flag) and Toni Berni (Abarth guru). Many thanks to Valentino Balboni, Lamborghini's legendary test driver, who helped me in many ways. Where would I be without Pat Blakeney (chairman of ARDS) who launched my race coaching career? Many thanks to everyone involved with the outrageous Alfa GTA Turbo race car, like Lee Penn (engine management) and Dave Hood (suspension). Thanks also to eminent collector Carlos Monteverde for his historic racing Ferraris. More thanks go to Hartmut Ibing, without whom I would not have completed the maddest test ever: £75 million on ice at the Nürburgring Nordschleife. Sometimes, life is about what you don't know; so, a big thank you to Ron Simons for showing me how much I don't know the Nordschleife. Eternal thanks to Hans Reiter for countless test drives in Lamborghini GT race cars.

Cheese and Maseratis..., a combination that can only mean thank you to Matteo Panini. Thank you, Chris Rea, for trusting me with your new car and for encouraging me to write a forthcoming history book. Many thanks to photographers like Peter Collins, Jeff Bloxham, Stuart Adams, Gary Hawkins, Steve Jones, Beasy Media (Drift Images), Ross Gamble but particularly Andrew Brown who many years ago, when I was broke, found me some lucrative writing work with an American publisher. Plus, an extra thanks to Andrew for a great two-week test driver trip to South Africa. Thank you, Warwick Bergin and Judith Ellard, for a 500bhp motorcycle, but chiefly for mant trips on their luxury yacht Seafin, where I was introduced to my future wife. *Grazie mille* to collector and yacht broker Nuccio Magliocchetti, Geometra Mario Vasta and motorsport executive Claudio Berro, who welcomed me to Sanremo. A huge thank you to Simon Watts for letting me loose in his amazing collection of racing cars and to all at John Danby Racing for looking after them so professionally.

Finally, thank you to my sons Niki and Dino for succeeding so well with a less than flawless father. Thank you to my grandchildren Isabella and Leonardo for endless smiles and laughter. And where would I be without my wife Jane? She deserves more thanks than I could ever give.

Lastly, thank you to everyone who bought this book.